YES! Please enter a subscription to Volume 32-34, 19 ☞ (3 issues) of *Cultural Critique* at the following rate:

Individual Rate: ○ US$38/£25 (Europe)
2-year subscription (1996 and 1997) at 1996 prices:
○ US$76/£50 (Europe)

Payment may be made by check, credit card, or money order (made payable to Oxford University Press). ○ Please bill me.
○ Payment enclosed ○ Charge my Amex/MasterCard/Visa

Card no.

Signature   Exp. date

Name

Address

City/State/Zip

Country

S0-BOL-089

Card

CULTURAL CRITIQUE

If card address differs from delivery address, please send details.

Orders must be accompanied by payment. The price includes handling and postage (US only). Subscriptions are entered on a per-volume basis only, and dispatch will commence only after receipt of correct payment. Subscriptions in Canada are now subject to the GST. Please add 7% to quoted prices. Personal subscriptions are available to individuals paying by personal check or credit card, and must not be donated to a library.

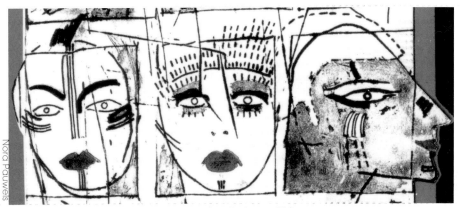

Nora Pauwels

1
8
0
0
8
5
2
7
3
2
3

Collections Department — Please enter a subscription to Volume 32-34, 1996 (3 issues) of *Cultural Critique*. It would be a valued and much used asset to our collection!

Does Your Library Subscribe?

Unfortunately, not all of the libraries that would benefit from a **Cultural Critique** subscription are currently receiving it!

You know how much you value your subscription; wouldn't your students and fellow collegues also benefit by having access to **Cultural Critique** in the library?

Help us reach those libraries who aren't currently subscribing by checking your institution's periodical list. If **Cultural Critique** is not currently included, please use this card to recommend a subscription.

Simply fill out this form and return to us. We'll send your recommendation along with a free sample issue to your library.

Name   Department

Signature

Annual Rate: ○ US$65/£44 (Europe)
2-year subscription (1996 and 1997) at 1996 prices:
○ US$130/£88 (Europe)

Library

Librarian

Address

City/State

Zip/Postcode   Country

Affix
Stamp
Here

Oxford University Press
Journals Marketing
2001 Evans Road
Cary, NC 27513
USA

Nora Pauwels

*Subscribe Now
to Cultural
Critique
for Two Years
at 1996 Prices!*
1-800-852-
7323 *or*
919-677-0977

Affix
Stamp
Here

Oxford University Press
Journals Marketing
2001 Evans Road
Cary, NC 27513
USA

Cultural Critique

34

Print and cover design: Nora Pauwels

Cultural Critique

Cultural Critique (ISSN 0882-4371) is published three times a year by Oxford University Press, 2001 Evans Road, Cary, NC 27513, in association with the Society for Cultural Critique, a nonprofit, educational organization.

Manuscript submissions. Contributors should submit three copies of their manuscripts to *Cultural Critique*, c/o African-American Studies, 480 SST, University of California, Irvine, Irvine, CA 92697–6850. Manuscripts should conform to the recommendations of *The MLA Style Manual;* authors should use parenthetical documentation with a list of works cited. Contact the editorial office at the address above for further instructions on style. Manuscripts will be returned if accompanied by a stamped, self-addressed envelope. Please allow a minimum of four months for editorial consideration.

Subscriptions. Subscriptions are available on a calendar-year basis. The annual rates (Issues 32–34, 1996) are £25 (UK & Europe), US$38 for individuals, and £44 (UK & Europe), US$65 for institutions. Single issues are available for £10 (UK & Europe), US$15 (USA and elsewhere) for individuals, and £17 (UK & Europe), US$25 (USA and elsewhere) for institutions. All prices include postage.

Personal rates apply only when issues of the journal are sent to a private address and payment is made by personal check or credit card. All subscription, single issue, back issue, changes-of-address, and claims for missing issues should be sent to:

NORTH AMERICA: Oxford University Press, Journals Subscriptions Department, 2001 Evans Road, Cary, NC 27513, USA. Toll-free in the USA and Canada 1-800-852-7323 or 919-677-0977. Fax: 919-677-1714. E-mail: jnlorders@oup-usa.org.

ELSEWHERE: Oxford University Press, Journals Subscriptions Department, Great Clarendon St., Oxford OX2 6DP, UK. Tel: +44 1865 267907. Fax: +44 1865 267485. E-mail: jnl.orders@oup.co.uk.

Advertising. Jane Parker, Oxford University Press, Journals Advertising, Walton St., Oxford OX2 6DP, UK. Fax: +44 1865 267835.

Indexing/abstracting. *Cultural Critique* is indexed/abstracted in *The Left Index, Alternative Press Index, Sociological Abstracts (SA), Social Welfare, Social Planning/Policy and Social Development (SOPODA), International Political Science Abstracts, MLA Directory of Periodicals, MLA International Bibliography,* and *Periodica Islamica.*

Postmaster. Send address changes to Journals Subscriptions Department, Oxford University Press, 2001 Evans Road, Cary, NC 27513. Postage paid at Cary, NC, and additional post offices. *Cultural Critique* is distributed by M.A.I.L. America, 2323 Randolph Ave., Avenel, NJ 07001.

Permission requests and photocopies. All rights reserved; no part of this publication may be reproduced, stored in a retrieval system, or transmitted in any form or by any means, electronic, mechanical, photocopying, recording, or otherwise without either the prior written permission of the publisher (Oxford University Press, Permissions, Journals Subscriptions Department, Great Clarendon St., Oxford OX2 6DP, UK. Tel: +44 1865 267907. Fax: +44 1865 267773) or a license permitting restricted copying issued in the UK by the Copyright Licensing Agency Ltd., 90 Tottenham Court Road, London W1P 9HE, or in the USA by the Copyright Clearance Center, 222 Rosewood Drive, Danvers, MA 01923. Fax: 508-750-4744.

⊗ The journal is printed on acid-free paper that meets the minimum requirements of ANSI Standard Z39.48-1984 (Permanence of Paper), beginning with Number 1.

Copyright. It is a condition of publication in the Journal that authors assign copyright to Oxford University Press. This ensures that requests from third parties to reproduce articles are handled efficiently and consistently and will also allow the article to be as widely disseminated as possible. In assigning copyright, authors may use their own material in other publications provided that the journal is acknowledged as the original place of publication and Oxford University Press is notified in writing and in advance.
Copyright © 1996 by *Cultural Critique.* All rights reserved.

Race Talk and *The Bell Curve* Debate: The Crisis of Democratic Vision

Henry A. Giroux and Susan Searls

Introduction

> Ever since the birth of our nation, white America has had a
> schizophrenic personality on the question of race. She has
> been torn between selves—a self in which she proudly pro-
> fessed the great principles of democracy and a self in which
> she sadly practiced the antithesis of democracy. . . . The white
> backlash of today is rooted in the same problem that has char-
> acterized America ever since the black man landed in chains
> on the shores of this nation. The white backlash is an expres-
> sion of the same vacillations, the same search for rationaliza-
> tions, the same lack of commitment that have always character-
> ized white America on the question of race.
>
> —King (68)

Writing a year before he was assassinated, Martin Luther King
Jr. was keenly aware that the reality of racism was at odds
with the principles of democracy. He recognized that the most explosive issue facing white America was its refusal to address its role

© 1996 by *Cultural Critique*. Fall 1996. 0882-4371/96/$5.00.

in a history steeped in racial oppression—a history of the Middle
Passage, slavery, Southern Reconstruction, segregation, and urban
ghettoization—that has crippled the nation since its inception.
Bearing witness to centuries of oppression, King consistently
sought to make visible the ways in which racism was invariably reproduced through a crisis of leadership in which white America
could neither confront the legacy of its white supremacist doctrines
nor, when individual conscience burned, take a firm and unequivo-
cal moral stand against racial injustice. Sustained by a moral vision
of a world without racism, King articulated a notion of politics that
might challenge and overcome injustices themselves. We want to
argue with John Brenkman and others that since Martin Luther
King, the moral dimension of the public sphere has been neglected
by critics and intellectuals, "especially the absence of racial justice
in the national political discourse" (Brenkman 11–12). As a result,
the language of public criticism and protest, of politics and public
life, have all been transformed by a shift in discourse about racial
justice to what Toni Morrison has described as "race talk." According to Morrison, race talk is "the explicit insertion into everyday life of racial signs and symbols that have no meaning other
than pressing African Americans to the lowest level of the racial
hierarchy. In race talk the move into mainstream America always
means buying into the notion of American blacks as the real
aliens. . . . Stability is white. Disorder is black" (57).

As the United States moves toward the close of the century, its
citizens have experienced the further erosion of democracy—and
the possibilities for democratization—that have resulted from the
unchecked reign of the market. Cornel West succinctly sums up
the contemporary cultural and economic scene: "Deindustrializa-
tion and deregulation have resulted in relative economic decline;
downward mobility for the majority of Americans, cultural decay,
unregulated markets now create market cultures, market moralities, market mentalities, shattering community, eroding civil society, undermining the nurturing system for children" (42). All of
this reinforces the breakdown of democratic public life and the
fragmentation of communities. Of course, race remains one of the
most explosive issues. The increasing visibility of whiteness as a
racial category and subject of scrutiny, coupled with the successful
attempts of people of color to write themselves into the history of

the United States, has generated a conservative backlash among many whites who define themselves as under siege as public discourse and space become more pluralized and racially diverse. In light of what we see as a current crisis of leadership and democracy, Martin Luther King's insights about racism take on a new urgency as race becomes one of the defining principles of a new conservative backlash that has emerged in the 1990s.

While the old racism unabashedly employed racist arguments in its endless quest for rationalizations and scapegoats, the new racism offers a two-pronged argumentation that, on the one hand, refuses to acknowledge that the issue of race is at the heart of its policymaking (as in welfare cutbacks, tougher crime bills, and anti-immigration legislation) and, on the other hand, offers rationales for policy changes that claim to be color blind (as in the call to end affirmative action and racial gerrymandering). In the first instance, the new racism articulates and legitimates a range of ideologies and practices that deeply affect both the privileges at the heart of the construction of whiteness and the racist practices that bear down heavily on the lives of people of color—while denying that race matters. For instance, Newt Gingrich denies that race has anything to do with the slash-and-cut polices at the heart of his *Contract with America,* and yet the policies produced by such legislation effect most drastically poor blacks and the urban poor. Similarly, in his defense of *The Bell Curve,* Charles Murray has consistently denied that the book is primarily about race since only one of its twenty-one chapters centers on arguments about black intellectual inferiority. However, *The Bell Curve* restricts the eight chapters of part II to a discussion of whites alone, demonstrating that over half the book is organized around questions of race—unless one is willing to make the argument that whiteness is not a racial category. Further, the denial that race is central to *The Bell Curve* is contradictory coming from an author who has legitimated his work by arguing that it provides a language for "a huge number of well-meaning whites [who] fear that they are closest racists . . . [and] tells them they are not. [This book] is going to make them feel better about things they already think but do not know how to say" (Murray in DeParle 50). Clearly, Murray's defense of white America is an argument for privileging whiteness as a racial construction. The authors of *The Bell Curve* make no apologies for arguing "that society is and must be stratified by intelligence, which is distributed unequally among individuals and racial groups and cannot be changed in either" (Reed Jr. 660).

In the second instance, national leaders propose changes in public policy that disproportionately affect African Americans and other minority groups in efforts to end the alleged reign of special interest groups and reverse discrimination. As critics have argued, social policies that have a far greater negative impact on the lives of blacks than whites cannot be seen as "race transcending" (Brenkman 19). Such gross distortions reveal not only the failure of conservatives and liberals alike to recognize that there are fundamental institutional obstacles to racial integration in contemporary American society but also the disappearance of racial justice and equality from public discourse. According to Newt Gingrich, criticisms of societal injustices such as racism, which he calls "our newfound sense of entitlement and victimization," are "exactly wrong and so corrosive to the American spirit" ("Renewing" 26). Appealing to a racially coded sense of nationalism and patriotism, he offers this pedagogical lesson from his new book, *To Renew America:* "But when confronted with a problem, a true American doesn't ask 'Who can I blame this on?' A true American asks, 'What can I do about it today?'" (39). For Gingrich, civic leadership has nothing to do with social responsibility and social justice since these demand some notion of social criticism and ongoing struggle. Actually, social criticism for him represents a whining and pessimism that "celebrates soreheads and losers jealous of others' successes" (*To Renew America* 33). Of course, the soreheads are feminists, critical multiculturalists, environmentalists, civil rights activists, critical educators, and all others who believe that dissent is central to any reputable notion of citizenship. Bob Dole appeals to a similar kind of numbing logic when he attacks affirmative action. Dole argues that "[t]he race counting game has gone too far" and that it is time for the federal government to "get out of the race-preference business" (Jackson 15). Nor, it appears, can President Bill Clinton support the conditions that foster equality and fair treatment. Ignoring the glass ceiling report issued by the United States Labor Department in 1994, in which massive racial and gender disparities were found in the workplace, Clinton panders to the right: "First of all, our administration is against quotas and guaranteed results" (Jackson 15).

As we will demonstrate, the new racism works through the power of the judicial and legislative processes, legitimating and rationalizing its policies through the use of public intellectuals who make racism respectable in their talk radio programs and through the wide circulation of magazines, national newspapers, television, and other forms of media. Housed and financed in right-wing foundations, the new conservative public intellectuals are enormously skillful in mobilizing racial fears and class resentment, and in undermining the basic principles of democracy and equality.

We want to argue that any analysis of *The Bell Curve* by Richard J. Herrnstein and Charles Murray has to be addressed within the crisis in democratic vision, ethical leadership, and moral conviction that has been spawned by the rise of the new racism and its growing defense by a number of conservative public intellectuals. In part, the popularity of *The Bell Curve* and the debate it has engendered need to be placed within a context that signals its continuity with a line of pseudoscientific reasoning, ahistorical confirmation, and quasi-scholarly documentation that has typified white America's response to race. Such appeals to natural "law" and empirical "truth" reflect the need to alleviate moral ambivalence by negating the possibility of social justice.

Racist Science and the Denial of History

That Richard J. Herrnstein and Charles Murray have acute political timing is evinced by the ocean of publicity spurred by the publication of *The Bell Curve* in the fall of 1994. Capitalizing on the resurgence of racism and racist exclusions in contemporary U.S. culture at the same time it flames racist expression and provides scientific and philosophic justification for it, *The Bell Curve* was heralded an "important" and "brave" book. Indeed, *The Bell Curve* and its pseudoscientific claims set the agenda for discussions on welfare, crime, affirmative action, and civil rights on public affairs programs such as *Larry King Live, Nightline*, the *MacNeil/Lehrer News Hour*, the *McLaughlin Group, Charlie Rose, Think Tank, Primetime Live*, and *All Things Considered* (Naureckas 12). The "controversy" made the covers of *Newsweek* and the *New York Times Magazine* and was reviewed in such prominent and respectful newspapers as the *Wall Street Journal,* the *New York Review of Books,* and the *New York Times Book Review.* In addition, journals such as the *New Republic* and *Discover* devoted almost entire issues to the debate.

The publication of *The Bell Curve* and the wide-ranging publicity it has received in the dominant media raise questions about the range of cultural, pedagogical, and social conditions that contributed to the book's widespread success and its relevance in the current political conjuncture. Of course, the diverse set of factors contributing to the book's success cannot be abstracted from the particular ideological interests that it legitimates. A few brave reviewers of *The Bell Curve* have exposed the contorted statistics, contradictory data buried in appendices, unsupported and illogical claims, research funding by a neo-Nazi organization, and "scholarly sources" including eugenicists, racists, and advocates of far right agendas. In spite of the evidence mounting against *The Bell Curve,* the alleged "fact" of genetically encoded racial differences and their correlation with large "behavioral" disparities between black and white in the areas of crime, welfare dependency, and teenage pregnancy undergird the call for social change.[1]

Bearing these exceptional critiques in mind, we want to examine the popular reception of *The Bell Curve* in order to understand how racist culture is both produced and legitimated by public intellectuals in the United States. Against the popularity of *The Bell Curve,* it seems reasonable to ask how mainstream commentators would have treated a book that relied upon statistics drawn from neo-Nazi sources to support the claim that the Holocaust never happened. In fact, when such books do get published, they are often denounced as anti-Semitic and dangerous in their whitewashing of the genocidal crimes of the Nazis. Yet, when *The Bell Curve* appeared in 1994, few reviewers in the mainstream media denounced the text as a racist tract or, for that matter, even questioned its basic propositions regarding the measurability of intelligence, the causal relationship between intellectual ability and race, or the hereditarian justification of inequality. Pseudoscientific babble as an apology for black intellectual inferiority, along with the advocacy of policies designed to justify the existence of an "inferior" black underclass, seemed to warrant little, if any, critical attention as an attack on the very nature of democracy itself. It is clear that Herrnstein and Murray anticipated an outcry against their antidemocratic rhetoric by providing a lengthy discussion of the limits, indeed the dangers, of egalitarianism in their concluding chapters. While their book provides an opportunity for educators and others to debate pedagogically and politically how racist cultural divisions are being legitimated through this book and its widespread popular support, this provides neither a rationale for the publication of the book by the Free Press nor an explanation for the fact that the book has sold over 400,000 copies. *The Bell Curve* is a popular expression of "race talk," and it resonates powerfully with a broader public discourse that increasingly finds expression on talk radio, film, theater, television, advertising, the press, and other channels of mass culture. We believe that underlying *The Bell Curve* is a racist agenda that is fundamentally at odds with any viable notion of democracy and demands that educators need to respond to it by engaging its implications for political and ethical leadership. We are not arguing that the book be censored; we are suggesting that educators and other cultural workers attempt to understand and confront the economic, political, and social conditions that provide the pedagogical and political contexts for the book's success.

In many ways, *The Bell Curve* not only suggests what Edward S. Herman has called "the renewed acceptability and/or tolerance of straightforward racist doctrine" (14), but also points to the refusal of the dominant liberal and conservative press, the White House, and numerous academics and public intellectuals to denounce the ever-increasing popularity of racist discourse as dangerous to the very precepts and principles of democracy in the United States. This is not to say that *The Bell Curve* has not been denounced by many critical commentators. On the contrary, the book has been treated as a racist tract by many reviewers in the academic press. But very few commentators have gone further and linked the racist assumptions that fuel the book as an attack on the most fundamental principles of democratic public life. In this instance, racist ideology can be denounced while supporting policy recommendations that are equally undemocratic but do not employ the discourse of race to legitimate themselves. Conservative and liberal commentators such as Mickey Kaus, Rush Limbaugh, and Nathan Glazer separate themselves from the racism of *The Bell Curve,* but support policies that are similar in their effects on the black underclass and urban poor.

The editors of the *New Republic* announced unapologetically in an issue devoted entirely to discussing *The Bell Curve* that the "notion that there might be resilient ethnic differences in intelligence is not, we believe, an inherently racist belief" (*New Republic* 31 Oct. 1994: 9). The *New York Times Magazine* ran a review of *The Bell Curve* and two other books on heredity and race in which the author, Malcolm Browne, argued that Herrnstein and Murray's basic premises were really important to society, especially to a democratic society. With no wrong intended, Browne argued that the authors under review, all of whom offered a hereditarian justification for racial inequality, were actually exercising a healthy form of truth-seeking in their plea for "freedom of debate and an end to the shroud of censorship imposed upon scientists and scholars by pressure groups and an acquiescing society" (Browne 45). The liberal-oriented *Chronicle of Higher Education* gave Charles Murray major coverage as a reputable scholar and argued that whatever evidence exists on race and intelligence "is open to widely varying interpretation, and how researchers read the data often suggest as much about their politics as anything" (Coughlin A12). In spite of the falsifications and misrepresentations of scholarship, the use of neo-Nazi research, and the racist implications of his writings, the liberal establishment praises Murray as a serious, albeit conservative, scholar rather than denouncing him for reproducing a legacy of racist science that supports a racially anti-egalitarian society. Herrnstein and Murray helped make racism respectable and even chic, and paved the way for the popular reception of *The End of Racism* by Dinesh D'Souza, another Free Press book full of racial invective and packed with over 150 pages of endnotes as verification for its "rigorous and scientific" scholarship. Intellectual respectability for "race talk" sells, and "today a racist tract, if impressively footnoted and aggressively marketed, can launch its author into the heady world of flashy cover stories, obsequious television interviews, and lucrative lectures" (Barnes 55).

The popularity of *The Bell Curve* points in part to a number of important considerations at work in American society that must be acknowledged by critical educators who wish to fight against the perpetuation of a racist culture and its deeply antidemocratic practices. First, it must be recognized that *The Bell Curve* represents a significant manifesto in what appears to be a developing and dangerous antidemocratic movement that uses pseudoscience and racial fear as a rationalization for white supremacy. Critical agency is reserved for those who are white and privileged and the "valued places" of mindless work, dead-end jobs, and grueling labor are allotted for those who happen to be black and of less intelligence. Low IQ in this scenario is linked causally with social pathology, suggesting that societal intervention is unproductive because inherited intelligence fixes one's level of accomplishment and agency. Hence, the new counterculture rationalizes racist thought and practice without having to evoke the critical language of ethics, democracy, or justice. In fact, these categories are irrelevant in the new beehive state imagined by Herrnstein and Murray. The force of such an argument and its interconnecting links to elitism, the market economy, and the emerging discourses of mean-spiritedness are well captured by Lee Siegel.

> Murray and Herrnstein's fantasy of a beehive society, in which mobility is frozen and stations assured, crops up across the political spectrum. So does their notion of aristocracy. At a time of collapsing boundaries—social, cultural, psychological—accompanied by new fragmentations, a pseudo-aristocracy based on genetic transmission simulates a sense of real aristocratic birthright and stability. And a pseudo-science nicely fits the modern, rationalist habit of mind, while also answering the need for comfort beyond reason's sterile categories. At the same time, the genetic "edge," the Darwinian struggle to survive, and the fiction of biologically inevitable social strata all mesh neatly with the dominant market ethos of untrammeled competition, no less than they did in Dickens's day. (28)

Second, the massive public attention that conferred upon *The Bell Curve* a halo of academic respectability suggests a crisis of moral leadership within American society that is as pedagogical as it is political. Civic leadership appears to have lost its ethical referents for sustaining, defending, and struggling over the principles of social justice, equality, and freedom. It comes as a surprise to no one to acknowledge that American political opinion has shifted to the right since the Reagan-Bush era. But what has been undertheorized is the retreat from racial justice that has accompanied the republican revolution. As John Brenkman insightfully observes:

> What has been insufficiently observed and what is perhaps crucial to understanding the dynamics of this moment in American political history is how Reaganism succeeded in dislocating a value painstakingly established in the years following the Second World War. Reaganism excised racial justice from public discourse, transforming this powerful, tenuously shared expression of a common good into a tabooed slogan. (4)

In the current seats of power, in both the nation's capital and the major cultural apparatuses of our society, intellectuals casually reject democracy as unworkable and embrace the laws of the marketplace as the most relevant principles driving society. Within such a context, there is no language to reinvigorate a sense of community, strengthen the bonds between various progressive movements, articulate a broader vision of power and passion, or educate the young in the discourse and practice of critical citizenship. Against the democratic imperative that grounds citizenship in social responsibility, the new conservative public intellectuals speak in a language that shuns human compassion, legitimates excessive individualism and greed, and encourages racial conflict. We can see echoes of such a discourse in the attack on welfare mothers, anti-immigration legislation, calls to dismantle public schooling, and Herrnstein and Murray's claim that "there is nothing [people with low cognitive ability] can learn that will repay the cost of teaching" (520). This is more than self-serving cynicism, it is an emerging worldview that considers mass democracy dangerous and racism acceptable.

Third, the popularity of *The Bell Curve* signals the rewriting of history through an omission of the legacy of slavery and racism in the United States. In this case, the history of the eugenics movement and its disparaging attempts to fashion a theory of scientific racism appears to have been lost in the mainstream discussions of *The Bell Curve*. The discredited research of Arthur Jensen and Cyril

Burt has not been called into question in popular discussions of *The Bell Curve*. With the exception of mostly academic reviews of the book, few theorists have revealed the bogus research relied upon by Herrnstein and Murray in their claims. Although much of their research was provided by the Pioneer Fund, described by the London *Sunday Telegraph* as a "neo-Nazi organization closely integrated with the far right in American politics," Herrnstein and Murray were consistently labeled as "serious scholars" by the American press (Naureckas 13). Richard Lynn, heavily quoted in *The Bell Curve*, has been less than subtle about his own scientific insights on race. In a 1991 article, "Race Differences in Intelligence: A Global Perspective," he concluded, forsaking all scholarly integrity, "Who can doubt that Caucasoids and the Mongoloids are the only two races that have made any significant contribution to civilization" (Rosen and Lane 14). Another pillar of research for Herrnstein and Murray's hereditarian defense of inequality and racism can be found in the work of J. Philippe Rushton. Rushton, whom many liberals have defended as a worthy scholar, was censured by his university for conducting a survey in a local mall in which he used Pioneer Fund money to sponsor a research project involving 150 participants—a third were black, a third were white, a third were Asian. Rushton asked the participants questions regarding penis size and how far they could ejaculate. But Rushton has done more than try to correlate the size and use of sex organs with racial groups; he also has suggested that "'Negroids' are genetically programmed for sexual behavior that spreads the deadly AIDS virus" (Miller 169).

Racist and bogus research aside, Charles Murray is a fellow at the American Enterprise Institute; he exemplifies the rise of a new breed of conservative intellectuals in this country who are heavily financed and educated within public spheres that are aggressively ideological, right-wing, and primed to develop and shape public policy in the United States. However, as we have suggested, it would be disingenuous to view the attack on the democratic principles of egalitarianism and social justice in *The Bell Curve* as an isolated event on the American landscape or a brief lapse of consciousness in a nation that has consistently fought for racial justice. Neither is the case. In what follows we would like to explore the current social and political contexts that have created the conditions for a favorable reception of *The Bell Curve* as an accurate depiction of the phenomenon of intelligence and legitimate commentary on race relations in America.

America's Turn to the Right

The November 1994 elections that ushered in Republican majority rule in Congress do not represent the beginning of a political and cultural revolution as much as they signal that one has already taken place. The shift to the ideological right and the circulation and affirmation of its particular constructions of (racialized) Otherness are everywhere apparent on the national landscape. Rising conservatism is visible not only in the nation's capital, but on the airwaves, in the media, in the judicial system, in education, in the workplace, and in the home. Moreover, the Right has won new allegiances among youth and minority communities.

One of the most disturbing signs of the times is the entrenched nature of right-wing talk radio across the country. Rush Limbaugh is estimated to reach twenty million people a week for a daily monologue of welfare trashing punctuated by the angry cry of the white male. Hosting New York City's WABC Radio Network is Bob Grant, a racist who has nonetheless emerged as an important figure in regional politics. According to Jim Naureckas, a reporter for *Extra! Magazine,* Grant repeatedly describes African Americans as "savages," arguing that the United States has "millions of sub-humanoids, savages, who really would feel more at home careening along the sands of the Kalahari or the dry deserts of eastern Kenya—people who, for whatever reason, have not become civilized" (25). His solution to the problem, frequently promoted on air, is the "Bob Grant Mandatory Sterilization Program." Yet Grant receives call-ins on his program from Senator Alfonse D'Amato, New Jersey Governor Christine Todd Whitman, New York City Mayor Rudolph Giuliani, and New York Governor-elect George Pataki to thank him for his support in their elections. WABC, where Grant and Limbaugh go back to back, claims to be the most successful radio station in America.

In San Francisco the former liberal talk radio station KSFO went conservative virtually overnight. The station's hosts and callers have described themselves as "beleaguered revolutionaries" in the new right-wing countercultural movement (Tierney A10). Jack Swanson, the operations director at KSFO, compares the station's new format to the first "Gay Talk" show fifteen years before: "We're letting the last group [i.e., conservatives] out of the closet" (Tierney A10). Attesting to the increasing influence of talk radio, Jonathan Freedland reports that according to one poll "44 per cent of Americans regard talk radio as their prime source of political information" (T2). Further, polls indicate that audiences are not drawn to talk radio because it shocks; on the contrary, "attitude surveys suggest that the firebreathers of AM radio are merely saying what everyone else already think[s]" (T2).

The national proliferation of overtly racist sentiment is repeated by "reputable scholars" such as Herrnstein and Murray, who quip that the white elite's "fear of the black underclass has been softened by the complicated mixture of white guilt and paternalism that has often led white elites to excuse behavior in blacks that they would not excuse in whites" (521). Herrnstein and Murray make good on their media reputation as "serious scholars" producing scientific truths by reassuring the white underclass in the next breath that "[t]his does not mean that white elites will abandon the white underclass, but it does suggest that the means of dealing with their needs are likely to be brusque" (521). It appears that promoting racial fears and divisiveness in *The Bell Curve* can be overlooked as long as it rests on a claim to scientific "truth."

On issues related to criminal justice, politicians meet the public outcry to "get tough on crime" with such policies as the "Three Strikes and You're Out!" that demands life imprisonment for the three-time offending criminal. Some politicians are backing a two strikes policy while others are willing to throw away the key with one violent felony conviction (Freedland T2). Doing his share, Newt Gingrich promises 10 billion dollars to construct new prisons in his *Contract with America*. Meanwhile, the media relentlessly hammered away on the O. J. Simpson murder trial, bent on forging the link between black men and criminality (Giroux, "Playing the Race Card").

One of the most important issues of the 1994 political campaign concerned immigration and how America's changing racial and ethnic demography affected the "core values of the country"

(Chideya). In efforts to exclude the racial Other, the passing of California's Proposition 187 effectively barred illegal immigrants from going to public school and prevented them from receiving nonemergency care in hospitals. And California's governor, Pete Wilson, effectively outlawed positive discrimination policies at the state level; likewise, President Clinton agreed to review affirmative action policies to see if they in fact work. More recently, the Supreme Court has declared that certain affirmative action programs are unconstitutional.

The Supreme Court considered right-wing allegations that enough is enough when it comes to forcing schools to desegregate. Supreme Court Justice Scalia argued that "societal discrimination" is discrimination that courts have no power to remedy. He insisted that it is not fair "to impose on a school district the obligation to remedy discrimination not of its own making" (Cole 43). Demonstrating not only its refusal to "remedy" discrimination but its capacity to perpetuate its legacy, the Court moved to invalidate a black-majority congressional district in Georgia, a decision the *Boston Globe* termed "a landmark ruling that could slash the number of minorities in Congress and local governments" (Puga and Kranish 1). Other rulings include a decision to allow the Ku Klux Klan to erect a wooden cross in a public square in front of the state capital in Columbus, Ohio, on the grounds that the display constituted private religious speech fully protected by the First Amendment.

Public schools have also come under fire in the Republican-controlled Congress. The GOP budget proposal not only would eliminate funding for President Clinton's Goals 2000 education program, but also would reduce or eliminate federal monies for more politically popular programs. Federal programs facing the chopping block include Head Start, a program designed to prepare young children, predominantly poor and non-white, for school; low-income college preparatory programs such as Upward Bound; and Pell Grants, which help low-income families pay for college tuition. Such cuts, disproportionately affecting the poor and children of color, not only reflect a complicity with the racist logic of social scientists such as Herrnstein and Murray, who make similar proposals on the grounds that federal aid can do little to help the cognitively disenfranchised (who also happen to be poor and often black), but also demonstrate how the logic of the market overwhelms the imperatives of a democratic society. Other issues facing the nation's educational system concern prayer in schools and the relative "waste" of the school lunch program. Advocates of school "choice" also see victory on the horizon in their quest to turn public schools over to the free market, encouraging parents to become consumers of education. Absent from national agendas are concerns with improving the conditions or quality of education per se.

The conservative backlash is also visible at the cultural level. Increasingly, there is a growing culture of violence in the United States that exhibits an indiscriminate rage, if not outright violence, against those deemed the racial Other, especially African Americans. This is obvious not only in the rise of police brutality against urban black youth, the high levels of incarceration among young black men, or the violent attacks on black college students across the United States, but also in the popular reception of racist films such as *Pulp Fiction,* hate talk radio programs, and the demonization of black youth in media culture (Giroux, *Fugitive Cultures*). The culture of racist violence is also evident in the discourse of right-wing public intellectuals, who have become apologists for a form of racism that parades as a legitimate voice for a universal white culture that defines itself as both under siege and willing to fight back in defense of its power and privileges.

Needless to say, Herrnstein and Murray's *The Bell Curve* fits well with current political agendas. Worried about the "cognitive capital" of the country, they suggest that Latino and black immigrants are putting downward pressure on the distribution of intelligence, effectively demonstrating a need to rethink current immigration policy. Abstracting equity and issues of racial justice from the discourse of educational excellence, Herrnstein and Murray further argue against funding for educational programs such as Head Start since it is alleged that special programs to improve intelligence have had negligible and short-lived effects. Of course, the positive effects of Head Start have been far from negligible, especially for poor and working-class children of color—an irrelevant concern for Herrnstein and Murray. In the name of excellence they argue that public schools simply waste their resources on those subordinate groups, especially blacks, who are too dumb to be educated when, in reality, they can be expected to perform only simple tasks. In this scenario, public schools become training centers warehousing poor and black urban youth while voucher programs funded by the federal government offer besieged whites a range of choices that will enable "all parents, not just affluent ones" to choose the school that their children attend. Thus free market choice becomes an attribute of inherited intellectual capital and provides an opportunity for intelligence to work in the service of quality education. Not only does choice form an unholy alliance with racial injustice in this discourse, it also serves as an ideological marker for ignoring how choice becomes a luxury for the rich in the face of massive economic, racial, and social inequality. Of course, since civil rights laws limit the rights of citizens regarding whom they can hire, who can run cultural institutions, who can administer the state, and who gets public assistance, Herrnstein and Murray argue against affirmative action and for draconian cuts in public assistance programs. Ironically, while arguing for in-tellectual inequality on genetic terms, they set out to disprove the underlying assumption of affirmative action—that ethnic groups do not differ in abilities that contribute to their success academi-cally or professionally—as a fundamental principle of political equality.

While few politicians and pundits sought to embrace Herrnstein and Murray's genetic determinism, many found the concluding chapters of *The Bell Curve* useful in justifying newly proposed cutbacks to federal programs. Patrick Buchanan, of course, did not miss a beat: "I think a lot of data are indisput-able. . . . It does shoot a hole straight through the heart of egalitar-ian socialism which tried to create equality of result by coercive government programs" (Naureckas 15). Indeed, Herrnstein and Murray not only offer a "compelling" social theory to legitimate the pursuits of the state, but also provide a potent, if skewed, cri-tique of egalitarianism in order to redefine state interests.

While Herrnstein and Murray support the notion that people are equal in terms of the rights afforded them, they contend that people are different in all other aspects. For them, the egalitarian ideal of contemporary political theory "underestimates the impor-tance of differences that separate human beings" as it simultane-ously "overestimates the ability of political interventions to shape human character and capacities" (532). According to their logic, the discourse of egalitarianism is at odds with the discourse of rights that grants people the freedom to "behave differently," which would necessarily lead to social and economic inequalities— inequalities that egalitarianism in turn attempts to suppress. What lies ahead of the nation if it continues to accept the main tenets of the welfare state? In short, the "coming of the custodial state." Murray and Herrnstein explain: ". . . by *custodial* state, we have in mind a high-tech and more lavish version of the Indian reservation for some substantial minority of the nation's population, while the rest of America tries to go about its business" (526). Such insipid rationalizations and fear mongering recall Jean Toomer's assertion: "white minds, with indolent assumptions, juggle justice and a nigger" (163).

Offered as a form of resistance to the uniformity that the state imposes in the interests of so-called social justice, Herrnstein and Murray condemn "egalitarian tyrannies" on the charge that they are "worse than inhumane. They are inhuman" (533). Their solution to this social democratic nightmare is a society in which all members occupy "a valued place"—whether IQ has destined them to manage a UniMart or head a multinational corporation—and presumably in which they know their place and stay there. The rigidity of the proposed castelike system in many ways masks as it reconfigures the centuries-old dream of much of white America for a racially homogenous society. And of course, members of such a society would not be expected to value other members' positions in quite the same way; that wouldn't be *discriminatory*, "a once useful word with a praiseworthy meaning" (533). The irony of Herrnstein and Murray's modest proposal, as David Theo Goldberg insightfully argues, is that people "assume value . . . only in so far as they are bearers of rights, and they are properly vested with rights only in so far as they are imbued with value" (37).

It would seem logical to assume that the resurgence of racism at a time when conservatives and liberals alike have insisted upon the urgency of moral reform and the return of "values" would appear deeply contradictory and troubling to most minds. Herrnstein and Murray, however, have a different worry, one that pits the principles of equality and social justice against the discourse of "truth."

The ideology of equality has stunted the range of moral dialogue to triviality. In daily life—conversation, the lessons
taught in public schools, the kinds of screenplays or newspaper feature stories that people choose to write—the moral
ascendancy of equality has made it difficult to use concepts
such as virtue, excellence, beauty, and—above all—truth.
(534)

The Crisis of Moral Leadership and Democracy

The rhetoric for truth and value were the mainstays of Nathan Glazer's commentary on *The Bell Curve*. As a prominent neo-
conservative, Glazer questions whether we should be talking about
a book that claims to prove the genetically encoded intellectual inferiority of black people at all (15–16). In light of the ocean of publicity it has received, he acknowledges that of course "we must"
and so ponders the question of the viability of racial improvement.
Glazer notes that Herrnstein and Murray do not specifically argue
against efforts to improve the education of blacks; however, in his
view, closing the gap between blacks and whites remains a vexed
possibility:

In a few cases, in our large cities in particular, greater resources are put into the education of blacks than whites. But
the kind of difference that might help close the gap is hardly
imaginable. And politically, it would be impossible. How could
one argue that the holding back of improvement of white intelligence so that blacks could catch up is morally legitimate, or
would improve society? (16)

Read as a kind of zero-sum game, Glazer invokes rights discourse to argue that black improvement necessarily impinges on
the possibility of white improvement insofar as disparities in intelligence foster unequal allocation of resources in education. (We are
left to imagine which inner cities provide greater resources for
black youth.) For Glazer, the scientific weight of Herrnstein and
Murray's analysis, coupled with the moral imperatives of truth and
the political philosophy of rights, sanctions a departure from the

principle of equal division and social justice. The necessary end of egalitarianism, as morally and rationally as it has been argued, is nonetheless a bittersweet moment for this alleged lover of the truth and the common good: "Our society, our polity, our elites, according to Herrnstein and Murray, live with an untruth: that there is no good reason for this inequality, and therefore society is at fault and we must try harder. I ask myself whether the untruth is not better for American society than the truth" (16).

There is more at stake here than Glazer's efforts to ground his racist and antidemocratic arguments in the acceptable sociopolitical discourses of science and philosophy; there are also a failure of moral leadership and an arrogance characteristic of a new breed of right-wing public intellectuals, who turn their backs on the poor and offer no language for challenging racism, discrimination, and social injustice.

As we have argued, the lack of vision and the mean-spiritedness that inform the conservative notion of leadership are not limited to *The Bell Curve* and its defenders but can be found among those who occupy honored positions in government, higher education, and other important public spheres. In a 1995 essay in *Newsweek,* Newt Gingrich argued that the most important elements of being an American are to be found in personal responsibility and individual ability. But these are not merely elements in a larger ethic of responsibility, they are the only elements and as such are transfigured into a notion of citizenship that eschews a moral focus on suffering, and abstracts individual agency from social responsibility. What is one to make of Gingrich's claims that entitlement is just another form of victimization, that social criticism is an escape from personal responsibility, and that "Captain John Smith's 1607 statement 'If you don't work you won't eat' [serves as] a guiding principle of social life" ("Renewing" 26, 27)? In Gingrich's model of leadership, nonmarket values such as community, generosity, and trust get sacrificed in the name of entrepreneurial spirit. Conservatives such as Gingrich seem unable to comprehend that it is "precisely unfettered markets which are now most responsible for the breakdown of community and traditional values. Walmart, not big government, is responsible for the demise of Main Street across America" (Michael Sandel qtd. in Friedman E9). Similar political ignorance and moral indifference fuel the conservative's assumption that school reform offers an opportunity to "comb through our educational system and laws to clean out the barriers to starting businesses and creating new wealth" (Gingrich, "Renewing" 27). The notion that community, generosity, and trust might be effectively employed to check market culture and immorality or that schools might be important in creating a critical citizenry rather than merely a work force for the global economy is lost in this model of leadership.

From Martin Luther King Jr. to Vaclav Havel we have alternative models of leadership that embrace the necessity for substantive democracy. King and Havel, living in different times, point to a notion of leadership and responsibility for public intellectuals that allows them to "identify with humanity, its dignity, and its prospects" (Havel 37). For Havel, public intellectuals represent the conscience of society and in doing so, they

> build people-to-people solidarity. They foster tolerance, struggle against evil and violence, promote human rights, and argue for their indivisibility. . . . They care about the fate of virgin forests in faraway places, about whether or not humankind will soon destroy all its nonrenewable resources, or whether a global dictatorship of advertisement, consumerism, and blood-and-thunder stories on TV will ultimately lead the human race to a state of complete idiocy. (37)

We began this essay with an allusion to the legacy of Martin Luther King Jr. and we want to conclude with his passionate reminder that "[w]e are now faced with the fact that tomorrow is today. We are confronted with the fierce urgency of *now*" (King 191). This urgency is signaled in the current threat to democracy posed by the rise of racist discourse, the attacks on equality and social justice, and the growing indifference to human suffering and misery. *The Bell Curve* is not *the* problem, it is symptomatic of a larger and more dangerous crisis of democracy in the United States—a crisis made increasingly visible as the intellectual storm troopers spread their messages of hate, greed, and racism through the airwaves, newspapers, halls of government, and other public forums across the nation.

Note

1. For a superb analysis of the shoddy scholarship and neo-Nazi sources of scholarship used in *The Bell Curve*, see specific articles in Jacoby and Glauberman, secs. I and II, especially Kamin; Miller; and Sedgwick. Also see Rosen and Lane 14–15; Lind 24–26. For a superb blasting of the basic assumptions underlying Herrnstein and Murray's scientific views on measuring and quantifying intelligence, see Gould 139–49.

Works Cited

Barnes, Joseph. "The Right and Racist Chic." *Z Magazine* Dec. 1995: 54–58.

Brenkman, John. "Race Publics: Civic Illiberalism, or Race After Reagan." *Transition* 5.2 (1995): 4–36.

Browne, Malcolm W. "What Is Intelligence and Who Has It?" *New York Times Book Review* 16 Oct. 1994: 3–4, 45.

Chideya, Farai. Letter. *New York Times Book Review* 13 Nov. 1995: 75.

Cole, David. "Hoop-Dreams and Colorblindness." *Legal Times* 23 Jan. 1995: 43.

Coughlin, Ellen K. "Class, IQ, and Heredity." *Chronicle of Higher Education* 26 Oct. 1994: A12+.

DeParle, Jason. "Daring Research or 'Social Science Pornography'?" *New York Times Magazine* 9 Oct. 1994: 48+.

Freedland, Jonathan. "The Right Stuff." *Guardian.* Jan. 1995: T2.

Friedman, Thomas L. "Buchanan for President." *New York Times* 24 Nov. 1995: E9.

Gingrich, Newt. "Renewing America." *Newsweek* 10 July 1995: 26–27.

———. *To Renew America.* New York: HarperCollins, 1995.

Giroux, Henry A. *Fugitive Cultures: Race, Violence, and Youth.* New York: Routledge, 1996.

———. "Playing the Race Card: Media Politics and the O. J. Simpson Verdict." *Art Papers* November/December 1995: 14–19.

Glazer, Nathan. "The Lying Game." *New Republic* 31 Oct. 1994: 15–16.

Goldberg, David Theo. *Racist Culture: Philosophy and the Politics of Meaning.* Cambridge: Blackwell, 1993.

Gould, Steven Jay. "Curveball." *New Yorker* 28 Nov. 1994: 139–49.

Havel, Vaclav. "The Responsibility of Intellectuals." *New York Review of Books* 22 Jan. 1995: 36–37.

Herman, Edward S. "The New Racist Onslaught." *Z Magazine* December 1994: 24–26.

Herrnstein, Richard, and Charles Murray. *The Bell Curve: Intelligence and Class Structure in American Life.* New York: Free, 1994.

Jackson, Derrick Z. "The Rhetoric of Job Freeze Out." *Boston Globe* 7 July 1995: 15.

Jacoby, Russell, and Naomi Glauberman, eds. *The Bell Curve Debate: History, Documents, and Opinions.* New York: Times, 1995.

Kamin, Leon J. "Lies, Damned Lies, and Statistics." Jacoby and Glauberman 81–105.

King, Martin Luther, Jr. "Racism and the White Backlash." *Where Do We Go from Here: Chaos or Community?* Boston: Beacon, 1968. 67–101.

Lind, Michael. "Brave New Right: Conservativism's Lunge into Its Darker Past." *New Republic* 31 Oct. 1994: 24–26.

Lynn, Richard. "Race Differences in Intelligence: A Global Perspective." *Mankind Quarterly* 31.3 (Spring 1991): 254–296.

Miller, Adam. "Professors of Hate." Jacoby and Glauberman 162–178.

Morrison, Toni. "On the Backs of Blacks." *Time* Fall 1993: 57.

Naureckas, Jim. "Racism Resurgent: How Media Let *The Bell Curve*'s Pseudo-Science Define the Agenda on Race." *Extra!* January/February 1995: 12–15.

Puga, Ana, and Michael Kranish. "Supreme Court Rejects Black Majority District." *Boston Globe* 30 June 1995: 1.

Reed, Adolph, Jr. "Looking Backward." *Nation* 28 Nov. 1994: 654–62.

Rosen, Jeffrey, and Charles Lane. "Neo-Nazis! Scouring *The Bell Curve*'s Footnotes." *New Republic* 31 Oct. 1994: 14–15.

Sedgwick, John. "Inside the Pioneer Fund." Jacoby and Glauberman 144–161.

Siegel, Lee. "For Whom the Bell Curves," *Tikkun* 10.1 (1994): 27+.

Tierney, John. "A San Francisco Talk Show Takes Right-Wing Radio to a New Dimension." *New York Times* 14 Feb. 1995: A10.

Toomer, Jean. *Cane.* New York: Perennial, 1969.

West, Cornel. "America's Three-Fold Crisis," *Tikkun* 9.2 (1994): 41–44.

Three Theories of the Race of W. E. B. Du Bois

Kenneth Mostern

> It is generally recognized today that no scientific definition of
> race is possible. . . . Race would seem to be a dynamic and not
> a static conception, and the typical races are continually
> changing and developing, amalgamating and differentiating.
> —W. E. B. Du Bois, *Black Folk* (1)

> The only possible objective definition of consciousness is a so-
> ciological one.
> —V. N. Volosinov, *Marxism and the Philosophy of Language* (13)

> Autobiographies do not form indisputable authorities. They
> are always incomplete, and often unreliable. Eager as I am to
> put down the truth, there are difficulties; memory fails espe-
> cially in small details, so that it becomes finally but a theory of
> my life, with much forgotten and misconceived, with valuable
> testimony but often less than absolutely true, despite my inten-
> tion to be fair and frank.
> —W. E. B. Du Bois, *Autobiography* (12)

© 1996 by *Cultural Critique*. Fall 1996. 0882-4371/96/$5.00.

Introduction

A t the opening of *Dusk of Dawn: An Essay Toward an Autobiography of a Race Concept* (1940), W. E. B. Du Bois places an "Apology" that serves to excuse his vacillation on the question of the generic status of the text: autobiography or sociology? He tells us that this book was initially intended as a third "set of thought centering around the hurts and hesitancies that hem the black man in America" (xxix), following the extremely popular *The Souls of Black Folk* (1903) and its less successful sequel, *Darkwater: Voices from Within the Veil* (1920). But, he explains, the celebration of his seventieth birthday provided him with the opportunity to compose an autobiographical speech, which he then decided could be used as a frame narrative for a book of general essays.[1] This narrative would not constitute the whole book, however, since

> In my own experience, autobiographies have had little lure; repeatedly they assume too much or too little: too much in dreaming that one's own life has greatly influenced the world; too little in the reticences, repressions and distortions which come because men do not dare to be absolutely frank. (*Dusk* xxix)

If reading about a life as self-representation is not interesting, nevertheless composing such a text may be forgiven if the author acknowledges at the start its partiality, specifically through the choice of a theme other than the "self" but of which the "self" provides some sort of reflection:

> My life has had its significance and its only deep significance because it was part of a Problem; but that problem was, as I continue to think, the central problem of the greatest of the world's democracies and so the problem of the future world. . . . I seem to see a way of elucidating the inner meaning and significance of that problem by explaining it in terms of the one human life that I know best. (*Dusk* xxix–xxx)

In introducing the text this way Du Bois recognizes that if his reader has read one of his other books, it is *The Souls of Black Folk*, written thirty-seven years earlier, which opens with the question,

"How does it feel to be a Problem?"[2] and goes on to assert, in prescient terms, "the problem of the twentieth century is the problem of the color line."[3] It is in this context, Du Bois asserts, that his life may been seen as a privileged representation of racial themes; and this representativeness explains the form of his narrative, which moves repeatedly between the "concept" of race and the "personal interest" in his life story (cf. *Dusk* 97). This movement between self and history provides the basic structure of the book. Thus, it can hardly surprise us that when we turn to "The Plot," as chapter 1 is called, we learn immediately that 1868–1940 are "incidentally the years of my own life but more especially years . . . that rush from the American Civil War to the reign of the second Roosevelt" and then encounter a list of historical events encompassing Europe, Asia, and Africa (*Dusk* 3). If this *is* autobiography, it is surely not the story of individuality that invites the identification of the reader with the narrator, as described in Georges Gusdorf's famous analysis of the genre (1980), nor, alternatively, is it the African American testimonial with its ironizing of the dominant "I was born" narrative (cf. Andrews ch. 1) and its reliance on a distancing between reader and narrator (cf. Sommer). Rather, it is structured as a dialectical account that presumes to locate the individual in a world history, and a specifically anticolonial account that, unlike those by European theorists of the period, is able to locate the colonial world as part of this history.[4]

The structure of the text—in which events of his life are followed by local events, which are, in turn, followed by international events, which then always circle back to describe their local meanings—reflects Du Bois's understanding of the ambiguous position of being inside and outside the dominant progressive narrative of world history, as taught in his Harvard Ph.D. program at the end of the nineteenth century, in ways that determine the existential fact of being within race: "in the folds of this European civilization I was born and shall die, imprisoned, conditioned, depressed, exalted and inspired" (*Dusk* 3). This doubleness, it is important to remember, emerges in Du Bois's account not merely as a defining force on his subjectivity but as already an objective given: a problem he "did little to create" but "did exemplify" (4).[5] Thus, to say that Du Bois "has" a race, acts in a raced manner, is to conceive of race primarily in terms of the existence of different levels of social existence, in which race is formed socially as a sort of common-sense explanation of skin color, which, as an autobiographical matter, has placed Du Bois in certain social positions and not others. In this narrative, race obtains its historical necessity on the economic level—that is, in the formation of a particular labor force for the purpose of capital accumulation—and is fetishized through racist "scientific" and ideological practice, which takes existing assumptions about the existence of race and literally makes them true. By the time Du Bois is able to write a book about race, it is already a fully internalized psychic structure,[6] an agency quite apart from its now scientifically understood nonexistence. Reflecting on this, Du Bois then writes his autobiography *as a Negro man*—and scare quotes would be particularly inappropriate around this phrase.[7] This complex autobiography of the racial concept, then, demands that political action regarding race always operate simultaneously at the levels of economy, culture, and psychology. Textually, *Dusk of Dawn* itself aims to provide a model for the exploration of "the interaction of this stream . . . on my work and in relation to what has been going on in the world since my birth" (7).

Thus, that *Dusk of Dawn* is a book about racial politics written in the form of an autobiography is the first concern of this essay. Throughout his career, Du Bois wrote argumentative texts in the form of autobiography or autobiographical essay, a strikingly common choice among African American intellectuals then and now. African American intellectual culture, initiated in and by the slave narratives, is one in which "the presentation of a public persona [is] a founding motif" (Gilroy, *Black Atlantic* 69) for those who would be "public intellectuals" (cf. hooks and West). Du Bois, then, follows an already established lineage when he proposes to place literally his body within the argumentative structure of his text and within his political practice. If Du Bois claims to find "little lure" in autobiography in general, he remains within a specifically racialized tradition that assumes that the interest of autobiography will lie in its narrative apparatus, examining the complex relationship between experiential truth and political-theoretical truth. In this light, no account of the seventy-year-old Du Bois's autobiography can ignore that it is but one of Du Bois's numerous autobiographical texts that, by his own account at age ninety-one, contain at least three distinct "theories" of his life (*Autobiography* 12). Each theory relies on a strikingly different apparatus of self-representation, corresponding on the formal and argumentative levels to three specific political formations common to twentieth-century African American intellectual history—liberalism, Pan-Africanist Marxism, and orthodox communism. The divergence in form and content of these multiple autobiographical accounts, none of which is *just* an autobiography, leads me to reflect on the meaning of autobiography in this essay.

Next, as the peculiar subtitle of *Dusk of Dawn* states, the text serves not merely as the "autobiography" of a "self" but also as a representation of the "concept" of the category "race"—which is distinct from the claim that he "is representative of the black race." Indeed, Du Bois's various autobiographical representations cannot be understood without further analysis of the meaning of "race," since that is precisely what he suggests that his life best represents: thus, the second concern of this essay. Given the recent attacks by several theoretical camps on the implementation of the concept of race as an analytical tool, it is necessary for me to explain and specifically to defend Du Bois's careful use of the word, in contemporary terminology, as a "social construction"; and, *having long been constructed,* race exists and assumes a significant presence in the social landscape. I will argue that race according to Du Bois is best understood as a particular formation of "social marginality" (Harper), one with a logic that consistently cuts through other social formations in the United States (Omi and Winant).[8]

Thus, the issues that drive my analysis of *Dusk of Dawn,* as well as the two other autobiographical texts discussed to a lesser extent, collectively and implicitly pose the questions "what is an autobiography?" and "what is a race?" When considered together, these two questions effectively raise the more general question of "identity politics," which I will argue should be understood neither as a solution nor as a problem, but rather as a fact; identity politics is a practice of politics in the United States that continues to be determined systematically in and by the social field. While one cannot, therefore, oppose identity politics (as though it could be replaced by something else), the limitations of Du Bois's understanding of autobiographical identity will appear interestingly as the result of his failure to address gender's part in the formation of race in *Dusk of Dawn.* Sex—not gender—is, however, a concern of Du Bois in the *Autobiography,* where it becomes divorced from race as a form of social determination, and thus separated from consciousness as Du Bois understands it. While Du Bois's practice of autobiography remains suggestive for contemporary leftist political analysis, it is clear to me that his practice is best exemplified and extended in the current period by those writers who further address the gendered component of autobiography, most notably bell hooks (cf. *Talking Back, Black Looks*).

The Three Theories

Darkwater: *The Individualist Theory of the Veil and Identity Politics*

If, as I will demonstrate, *Dusk of Dawn* provides a theory of identity politics dependent on the notion that collective political action always supposes a relationship of identification, and that in the United States all identification is funneled first through racial identification, then the best way to make this argument in terms of Du Bois's life will not be to analyze the argument of *Dusk,* but rather to recount the politics of Du Bois's most successful form of self-representation, the one that led, however unintentionally, to his political "leadership" of his race. The concept of racial identity during his liberal period—stretching from before *The Souls of Black Folk,* through the early autobiographical account that opens *Darkwater,* until the 1930s when he entered his period of serious engagement with Marxism—can be understood as a version of existential and intellectual individualism, appropriately articulated in Emersonian rhetoric, that is, in terms of the striving individual within a capitalized "Nature." Within African American history, this version differs sharply from Frederick Douglass' artisan, class-based commercial individualism. Further, its popularity suggests that what attracted so much of the black professional class to Du Bois's ideas in the beginning was not the account of racial identity *per se,* but the representation of individual heroism in its American form *as* Negro.

Darkwater's autobiography starts with a line Du Bois liked so much he repeats it in each later autobiography: "I was born by a golden river and in the shadow of two great hills five years after the Emancipation Proclamation" (5). The line remains conspicuous in its slightly anachronistic attempt at elegiac significance, a characteristic seen in Du Bois' writing far into the twentieth century. It becomes even more conspicuous given the explanation of why, exactly, the river was golden, which appears pages later: "That river of my birth was golden because of the woolen and paper waste that soiled it. The gold was theirs, not ours; but the gleam and glint was for all" (11). If the negative truth of pollution and economic domination helps to explain his politics later in the essay, the gold color is positioned rhetorically to afford Du Bois's birth, and perhaps his light brown skin color as well, significance. This rhetoric, often visual, always attesting to the personal or clan-based worth of the people in Du Bois's family tree, consistently emerges in the introduction of every new thought for several pages: "My own people were part of a great clan" (5); "Mother was dark shining bronze" (6); Alfred, my father[,] must have seemed a splendid vision" (7); "Long years before [my father was born] Louis XIV drove two Huguenots, Jacques and Louis Du Bois, into wild Ulster County, New York" (7). The reader here is asked to revel in the aristocratic beauty and character of these people who are of African descent, though race is not stressed in particular, inasmuch as the rhetoric is retained to describe white ancestors in the last example. The family's poverty is not entirely absent in this account (nor, of course, are the origins of poverty necessarily an embarrassment in Americanist narrative), but much of what one notices is that the narrator expresses amazement that he could have been impoverished, as is illustrated by the peculiar use of exclamation points: "I never remember being cold or hungry, but I do remember that shoes and coal, and sometimes flour, caused mother moments of anxious thought in winter, and a new suit was an event!" (6).

Over a third of this rather short narrative focuses on his background, almost pleading against itself that it is "respectable."[9] When he finally does turn our attention to his own abilities, he positions himself as very much "one of the boys" (*Darkwater* 11) and at the same time magically better:

Very gradually I found myself assuming quite placidly that I was different from other children. At first I think I connected the difference with a manifest ability to get my lessons rather better than most and to recite with a certain happy, almost taunting, glibness, which brought frowns here and there. Then, slowly, I realized that some folks, a few, even several, actually considered my brown skin a misfortune; once or twice I became painfully aware that some human beings thought it a crime. I was not for a moment daunted,—although, of course, there were some days of secret tears—rather I was spurred to tireless effort. If they beat me at anything, I was grimly determined to make them sweat for it! . . .

As time flew I felt not so much disowned and rejected as rather drawn into higher spaces and made part of a mightier mission. (11–12)

Interest in Du Bois's person, in this passage, does not derive from an interest in race; here, instead, the reader is positioned as someone who should be interested in the race problem primarily because it has intersected, arbitrarily, with Du Bois, whose extraordinariness does not depend foundationally on any sort of racial consciousness. While Du Bois's later autobiographies do suggest that his individual achievement is significant, they do not maintain this narrative of the extraordinary, instead referring far more to a narrative of luck (compare *Dusk* 15, where he reports that his high school principal, not mentioned in *Darkwater,* was a major figure in his getting an academic education, and that another principal could just as easily have encouraged Du Bois to pursue a trade). Here, though, he barely acknowledges anything but exceptional accomplishment: "I suspect that beneath all my seeming triumphs there were many failures and disappointments, but the realities loomed so large that they swept away even the memory of other dreams and wishes. . . . [On the other hand], I *willed* to do. It was done. I *wished*! The wish came true" (*Darkwater* 14, emphasis in original). The adult life has been divided into four conspicuously capitalized parts—"the Age of Miracles, the Days of Disillusion, the Discipline of Work and Play, and the Second Miracle Age" (14)—and even the Days of Disillusion, the period early in his professional career before he lands the job at Atlanta University, turns out to be "not disappointing enough to discourage me" (16).

In 1920, when editor of *Crisis* and the best-known Negro official of the integrationist, still white-led NAACP, Du Bois provides an *Americanist* myth that contains within it a large constituency of people who will be race-assertive precisely because the content given blackness in the psyche is portrayed as indistinguishable from any other form of human existence. It is especially indistinguishable with regard to gender. For instance, in these twenty pages of *Darkwater* Nina Gomer Du Bois appears in a manner that one associates with masculine narratives of success: "in 1896, I married—a slip of a girl, beautifully dark-eyed and thorough and good as a German housewife" (19).[10] Du Bois, like Douglass before him, was a liberal feminist whose life as an agitator frequently involved close collaboration with white women; indeed, later in the text of *Darkwater,* there is a chapter on the importance of women's issues to Negro politics. Yet it will take Du Bois until the *Autobiography,* after Nina's death and his remarriage, for a public accounting of his sexual identity and its connection to autobiographical representation.

Finally, what differentiates the *Darkwater* account from Du Bois's later narratives is that it contains no "apology"—no explanation of the reason for his own self- representation, no suggestion that people should read about him for any other reason than admiration of him as an individual. Autobiography in American ideology has never needed any apology because writing the exemplary self has been a moral imperative of individualism since the Puritans (cf. Bercovitch). Arnold Rampersad in *The Art and Imagination of W. E. B. Du Bois* claims that this moral sense—the idea that through work and politics he would be setting an example—was the driving force through Du Bois's life, through all his changes in organizational and political affiliation. On the other hand, I would suggest that since Du Bois's relatively consistent and compelling imagery of race was generated by the social space, which became the explicit form of his political subjectivity and with which his audience necessarily identified, *Darkwater*'s moral vision, disconnected from race, is appropriately described as an "uncompleted argument," in the sense Anthony Appiah regards *Dusk of Dawn.* The individualist and liberal narrative of *Darkwater* is the one Du Bois tries repeatedly to escape through claims to collective subjectivities he can exemplify, but never fully represent, later in life.

Dusk of Dawn: *Race and/as the Autobiographical*

What Is a Race?

In contrast to *Darkwater*, in *Dusk* Du Bois insists that his "auto-biography is a digressive illustration and exemplification of what race has meant" (221), that is, a sociology of race. More strikingly, he argues that the content of his intellectual thinking itself remains tied to, or determined by, his skin color: that intellectual thought is, among other things, a function of race. We are now used to calling this position "essentialist." Yet Du Bois knows that skin color itself is a thoroughly arbitrary sign, with no *natural* relationship to the ability of any individual to understand or accept the content of the arguments he makes. Race, for Du Bois in this narrative, is a social *construction* in the strictest sense of the term possible. Biological or scientific race does not exist, nor can race be given any global sense at all, since its psychic meaning is always defined in a specific local and intersubjective context in which one person is, as it were, "behind a barrier" (Baber 340). Constructed systematically in the widest variety of localities, this barrier's psychological form determines all who live inside it, even when they experience its meaning in different specific ways.[11] In such circumstances, because the racial barrier is already formed, black scholars (as one example) live their race in such a way that it causes them to make conscious and unconscious decisions *separately* from those defined outside their group, thus creating actual racial formations with, over time, distinct cultural and political manifestations. Thus, while there is no reason to believe that, for example, any given black person will become a socialist, or that a black American will always care more about Africa than a white American, one nevertheless cannot describe the path by which Du Bois adopts socialism or African solidarity in any terms other than as a result of various psychic events in which felt racial difference led to a choice in a particular direction. It is then precisely because the "scientific definition of race is impossible" (*Dusk* 127) that the concept of race, in the sense of the determined adoption of what Omi and Winant call "racial projects" (55–56), is called by Du Bois the "greatest thing in my life and absolutely determine[s] it" (*Dusk* 136).[12]

Du Bois had the most distinguished education available to any American in the late nineteenth century, including a Ph.D.

from Harvard—the first granted to an African American—two years at the University of Berlin, and three years at Fisk University in Tennessee. Du Bois's reflections on the climate of this intellectual milieu where "above all science was becoming a religion" (*Dusk* 26) suggests, at the outset, the workings of race:

> When I was a young man, so far as I was concerned, the foundations of present culture were laid, the way was charted, the progress toward certain great goals was undoubted and inevitable. There was room for argument concerning details and methods and possible detours in the onsweep of civilization; but the fundamental facts were clear . . .
> . . . Apparently one consideration alone saved me from complete conformity with the thoughts and confusions of then current social trends; and that was the problems of racial and cultural contacts. (25–26)

It is important to emphasize that this discussion views the process of the acquisition of knowledge to be identical among humans at the outset. Du Bois, a New England boy from a town with few African Americans, who has personal values that continue to seem conservative long after he has become a radical intellectual, makes it clear that race has not prevented him from initially accepting the premises of his education. The very fact that he is successful in the New England educational setting, where he knows no other black high school students, demonstrates his basic conformity. However, a social fact—the problem of racial and cultural *contacts*—requires him to examine the way that the social system is constructed. Thus, the racial barrier becomes sufficient cause for a preliminary investigation of the assumptions of his education.

In the previous chapter, Du Bois has already taken pains to demonstrate that he is first a New England child, and not a black child; we learn that for him there was simply no racial we-subject with which he could identify as there might have been had he been born in the South. For example, in describing his youth, Du Bois's first conception of the "problem of inheritance" is neither biological nor racial but rather economic and regional: a local fortune of a family for whom Du Bois worked, "the Hopkins millions," passed into the "foreign hands" of a scheming English architect, thus removing capital from the local Great Barrington economy (*Dusk*

22). The use of "inheritance" here is worth noting because social scientific testimony about race would take this word as its key category; Du Bois is suggesting that race is precisely that which he does *not* "inherit" as a child. In his childhood, "the color line was manifest and yet not absolutely drawn" (10), and to the extent it is defined, "the racial angle was more clearly defined against the Irish" than against him (14). His culture, then, is absolutely indistinguishable from that of white New England, his views of property are vague and conventionally American (17–18), and whatever manifest attitude he had toward race was one of "exaltation and high disdain" (14) for the white kids for being less smart than he was.

In retrospect, he reports, race manifested itself in small ways, through a certain implicit awareness that he should avoid situations where he would not be wanted. Only when he reached high school graduation and faced the problem of college—ironically, he claims that he was able to go to college only *because* he was black, since a smart white boy without money most likely would have apprenticed for positions in the local business class rather than go to college—was race made explicit in the efforts of local philanthropists to raise the funds necessary to send Du Bois south to "meet colored people of [his] own age and . . . ambitions" (*Dusk* 23). As a result of such cultural contact, Du Bois first hears the southern black music that he would become famous writing about, music in which he "*seemed to* recognize something inherently and deeply my own" (23, my emphasis).

This last sentence is ambiguous, but I believe that the emphasis must be placed on the word "seemed." The context of the quote reads as follows:

> I became aware, once a chance to go to [Fisk] was opened up for me, of the spiritual isolation in which I was living. I heard too in these days for the first time the Negro folk songs. A Hampton Quartet had sung them in the Congregational Church. I was thrilled and moved to tears and seemed to recognize something inherently and deeply my own. I was glad to go to Fisk. (23)

The process of psychic racial formation in Du Bois's youth, then, is as follows: there is no manifest content to blackness, just a minor, but socially enforced, sense of not being like others, a sense with consequences so great that at a certain point it begins to control the entire set of possible life choices. *Once this process is recognized,* Du Bois as the racialized subject unconsciously fills up the outward sign of this difference, skin color, with apparently arbitrary signs, cultural manifestations he does not necessarily possess, "seeming to recognize" them as "my own." This structure of argument is repeated several times in *Dusk of Dawn,* especially with regard to African identification, as I will demonstrate.[13] What will become most significant for understanding the way that "blackness" ultimately becomes socially constructed on a global scale is that, having had this sensation, this "seeming to recognize," Du Bois becomes an agent of its reproduction. Since this process is being multiplied throughout the United States, "a" race is formed and indeed reformed, since, in the twentieth century, it has been long-since formed. It should not, then, surprise us when the initially arbitrary formation "Negro identity" comes to develop cultural, political, and economic significance in the overtly political argument later in the text.[14]

The generation of this racial feeling or persona in turn leads Du Bois to make shifts in political/ideological allegiance, based on specific events that are coded in various ways as racial; the history of his racial formation leads to the particular theorizing in which he engages. This relationship is best illustrated by the three major changes in his intellectual position, in which he moved away from "complete conformity" with the ideas of his age and developed a highly original third worldist perspective that would in fact become common among Pan-Africanist intellectuals in the 1950s, though he started to conceive of it in the decade 1910–19. These shifts involved a redefinition of and move away from the notion of progress through scientific practice, the development of an interest in Pan-African studies, and his ultimate analysis of racial imperialism as an element of (though not specifically derived from) capitalism.[15]

In the case of the redefinition and move away from progress via scientific practice, Du Bois asserts that long before he began to develop the social analysis of race, he wanted to study, and indeed to help invent, the discipline of sociology due to his "firm belief in a changing racial group," which allowed him to "easily grasp[] the idea of a changing developing society rather than a fixed social structure" (*Dusk* 51). Social science would, in turn, serve as the hegemonic tool by which he could fight racism. But being a Negro sociologist at the turn of the century was essentially impossible for one structural reason—all funding of research or education for Negroes flowed from Booker T. Washington's Tuskegee machine and from the white philanthropists responsible for Washington's power. Unlike Du Bois, Washington opposed Negroes engaging in scholarly research, preferring "industrial education" and the concentration of efforts on expanding the race's economic resources. In this context, Du Bois found financial resources for research more and more constricted by Washington's machine and necessarily found himself, in spite of specific intentions to the contrary, engaged in the sort of racial politics which he felt had nothing to do with his work as a scientist—however much his subject matter was already the result of race. Du Bois ended up being the accidental leader of a black community faction in opposition to Washington.

His conflict with Washington's approach does not alone change his views of the effectiveness of science in fighting racism. Rather, in his estimation,

> Two considerations . . . broke in upon my work and eventually disrupted it: first, one could not be a calm, cool, and detached scientist while Negroes were lynched, murdered and starved; and secondly, there was no such definite demand for scientific work of the sort that I was doing. (*Dusk* 67)

The first consideration, evident in the phrase "one could not," is an ironic invocation of race; obviously "one" could engage in a variety of strategies, but Du Bois could not as he was literally the *one* trained Negro social scientist in the country positioned to do, and experienced in doing, social science during the decade 1900–10. And the second depends concretely on the approval of Washington's funders. As a result of these mechanisms, which effect only dark-skinned people, and only because they are dark-skinned, developing a forum for agitation or abandoning all intellectual interests can be the only *racially* possible alternatives.

In the second case, the construction of a Pan-African discourse, we must consider the significant discussion of Countee Cullen's famous question, "What is Africa to me?" in its context in *Dusk*.[16] In the thirteen pages that follow this question, Du Bois outlines his first point: what he has learned in his several trips to Africa (117–30). In short, he does not suggest racial identification between himself and residents of West Africa, except in a quotation from a speech given sixteen years earlier, in 1924. Even so, this quotation is itself not about Africans at all, but about Negro American "pride in their race and lineage"; the peculiar American subjectivity is again under discussion here. In a move that I find particularly objectionable, Du Bois invents the "primitive" African with whom he does *not* share an identity.[17] The concluding sentence of this section, "Now to return to the American concept of race" (130), in essence says that the discussion of Africa is *not* to be confused with the discussion of race in the United States. So what is this description of Pan-African ideology doing in the middle of a chapter called "The Concept of Race"? Primarily, it is describing how, as a young African-American intellectual, Du Bois developed a psychic imagination of Africa, an affective kinship which leads him to perceive and learn particular things from his connection to Africa and its intellectuals through the Pan-American movement that is particular to an American racialized self.

This is not to say that earlier in his life Du Bois never believed that he shared a "race" with Africans. In *Dusk* he specifically acknowledges his argument for this commonality in earlier writing, as in "The Conservation of Races" (1897), in order to disavow it. What remains for *autobiographical* exploration is precisely how the earlier belief in a shared race constitutes a moment of his blackness which can ultimately be described in terms of the "*American* concept of race." Having made *this* distinction, Du Bois writes that the African descendants of his distant African relatives do, however, share *something* with him:

> [They] have suffered a common disaster and have one long memory. . . . The physical bond is least and the badge of color relatively unimportant save as a badge; the real essence of this kinship is its social heritage of slavery the discrimination and

insult; and this heritage binds together not simply the children of Africa, but extends through yellow Asia and into the South Seas. It is this unity that draws me to Africa. (*Dusk* 117)

It is easy to see the problems in the idea of "one racial memory," though there are certainly benefits to this concept as well.[18] I find it more compelling, given the context, to notice the stress on power relations and social marginality uniting African Americans and Africans in addition to other "colored" peoples of the world. During the entire period of his editorship between 1910 and 1934, *Crisis* distinguished itself as one of the better popular sources for information on Asia.

How Do You Know a Race When You See It?

Du Bois, then, has not been trying to show that Africans and African Americans are members of "a" common race (though under some specific social circumstances it may be strategic to articulate them as such) but rather to show the "full psychological meaning of caste segregation" (*Dusk* 13). This segregation, in turn, makes the invention of the Negro race necessary and useful for the African Americans who invoke it (quite regardless of the racial projects of white people), and sustains this racial formation without reference to biology. "Negro" may not be a race in any coherent sense, but the psychic implication of the veil, which causes people to live "as Negroes," itself serves as a unifying characteristic. I am aware of the tautology; it is unavoidable. Du Bois, abandoning both "autobiography" and "science," attempts to provide a generalizing metaphor:

> It is difficult to let others see the full psychological meaning of caste segregation. It is as though one, looking out from a dark cave in a side of an impending mountain, sees the world passing and speaks to it; speaks courteously and persuasively, showing them how these entombed souls are hindered in their natural movements, expression, and development; and how their loosening from prison would be a matter not simply of courtesy, . . . but aid to the world. . . . It gradually penetrates the minds of the prisoners that the people passing do not hear; that some thick sheet of invisible but horribly tangible plate glass is between them and the world. They get excited; they

talk louder; they gesticulate. . . . Then the people within may
become hysterical. They may scream and hurl themselves
against the barriers, hardly realizing in their bewilderment
that they are screaming in a vacuum unheard and that their
antics may actually seem funny to those outside looking in. . . .
All my life I have had continually to haul my soul back and say,
"All white folk are not scoundrels nor murderers. They are,
even as I am, painfully human." (*Dusk* 130–32)

The positive characteristics given here to "Negroness," which does
not define a "culture" as such,[19] all emerge out of this negativity,
the normative condition of being beneath, behind, under. A race
is invented because such invention is the only means of articulation, of proceeding positively:

Perhaps it is wrong to speak of it at all as "a concept" rather
than as a group of contradictory forces, facts, and tendencies. . . . It was for me as I have written first a matter of dawn-
ing realization, then of study and science; then a matter of
inquiry into the diverse strands of my own family; and finally
consideration of my connection, physical and spiritual, with
Africa and the Negro race in its homeland" (133).

I cannot trace the argument of the next chapter, "The White
World," with the same detail with which I have approached the
previous one, since it covers a great deal of the same ground by
way of a humorous description of two fictional "friends," both
white, both of whom consider themselves not racist, or at least not
unusually so. What makes this chapter significant to the overall
argument of the text is its explanation of how race works as a psychic *differential* in conversations between Negroes and whites regardless of the fact that in the sample conversations, the black
voice, which is Du Bois's, primarily argues that race does not exist—or more precisely, that he himself is actually a white man and
thus fully complicit in the culture and ideas of the dominant majority, according to the white man's own definition.

bell hooks has recently remarked that white people are generally amazed that black people look at us with an ethnographic eye,
themselves scrutinizing our whiteness (*Black Looks* 167). Du Bois's
procedure here attempts to scrutinize by inhabiting the position of

whiteness, therein ironizing the white race, to the horror of his (fictional) white interlocutor. For example, at the end of a long exchange, the white man asks in exasperation (I have heard this question in the 1990s, and probably you have too): "Why don't you leave [us], then? Get out, go to Africa or the North Pole?" Du Bois responds:

> I am as bad as [you] are. In fact, I am related to [you]. . . .
> "By blood?"
> By Blood.
> "Then you are railing at yourself. You are not black, you are no Negro."
> And you? Yellow blood and black has deluged Europe. . . .
> "What then becomes of all your argument, if there are no races and we are all so horribly mixed as you maliciously charge?"
> Oh, my friend, can you not see that I am laughing at you? . . . Human beings are infinite in variety, and when they are agglutinated in groups, great and small, the groups differ as though they, too, had integrating souls. But they do not. . . . Race is a cultural, sometimes a historical fact. . . .
> "But what is this group; and how do you differentiate it; and how can you call it 'black' when you admit it is not black?"
> I recognize it quite easily and with full legal sanction; the black man is a person who must ride "Jim Crow" in Georgia. (*Dusk* 152–53)

The social irony inhabiting race in *Dusk* pervades all racial interaction for the late Du Bois. You cannot make sense of this passage without understanding that, in any biological sense of the word, racially the white and black participants are the same; simultaneously their inability to understand one another, even to agree to a discursive framework, results from occupying different racial spaces. Because this phenomenon is the *normal* form of interaction between educated, liberal, black and white Americans, teaching people the biological meaninglessness of race is largely irrelevant to political strategy. It does not matter whether "race" is scientific in most contexts. Politics in the United States is *necessarily* built around racial identity precisely because such identity is first of all defined and enforced by such politically charged interactions.

The Negro Political Subject in Dusk of Dawn

At the time *Dusk* was written, Du Bois had recently completed, in collaboration with a few students at Atlanta University, a lengthy and elaborate political platform called the "Basic American Negro Creed" (republished in *Dusk* 319–22), which attempted to create a black political subject. From an ideological standpoint, it is the most elaborate attempt to combine the assumptions of three major tendencies in Afro-American political thought of the time: liberalism, "nationalist" self-segregation,[20] and socialist economic planning. Du Bois's plan for action assumes that what African Americans want, in the abstract, is political rights, economic growth and full equality, and participation in public culture. These things, however, are not specific to race or claimed as somehow being "black." But because of the "fact" of blackness as determined by the existence of segregation, the path to achieve these things must also be specifically black and draw specifically on the cultural and political icons of black and African history. Precisely at this point in the presentation of a complete political program, Du Bois's reliance on autobiographical method fails him, for he knows that he speaks for no one except perhaps a few intellectuals (so few that he will be chased from Atlanta University, as he was from the NAACP, because of his growing engagement with socialist and antiwar politics in the next few years). The objective structure of blackness with its tremendous subjective impact on his life and his theorizing has placed him, at age seventy, in a profoundly different position than many other blacks, whose self-accounts typically articulate any one of the three positions he is attempting to combine, but not all three together.

As he has for most of his life, Du Bois speaks of racial uplift first as a member of the black professional class (he has dropped the term "talented tenth" and the commonly used "bourgeoisie" was never appropriate from a Marxist point of view), a category that corresponds specifically to the liberal tendency of his thinking. However, contrary to his self-account in *Darkwater,* he here no longer identifies with this class, which, he argues, (*Dusk* 179) is essentially self-hating, sharing the suspicions of whites about the inadequacies of the race. Du Bois argues, for example, that this self-hatred spurs "younger educated Negroes" to diverse action, leading them to widely divergent personal strategies:

One avoids every appearance of segregation. . . . He will take every opportunity to join in the political and cultural life of the whites. But he pays for this and pays dearly. He so often meets actual insult . . . that he becomes nervous and truculent through expectations of dislike. And on the other hand, Negroes . . . suspect that he is "ashamed of his race".

Another sort of young educated Negro forms and joins Negro organizations; prides himself on living with "his people"; withdraws from contact with whites, unless there is no obvious alternative. . . . Between these two extremes range all sorts of interracial patterns, and all of them theoretically follow the idea that Negroes must only submit to segregation "when forced." In practically all cases the net result is a more or less clear and definite crystallization of the culture elements among colored people into their own groups for social and cultural contact. (*Dusk* 186–87)

Just as race has produced him, it has spontaneously produced a segregated black group with an autonomous culture formed not in spite of but because individuals are split by ideology and class in much the same ways they are in other recognizable social groups. At the same time, a partially segregated black economy already exists, due to the capital furnished by churches, segregated schools, professional services, and a variety of in-community businesses that always offer the best opportunity for black investment in a racist society (197). Thus, he proposes, in place of the political movement with which he has so long been identified (that is, the NAACP), an argument that would not become influential until at least the mid-1960s under the auspices of Black Power: "Instead of letting this segregation remain largely a matter of chance and unplanned development, and allowing its objects and results to rest in the hands of the white majority or in the accidents of the situation, it would make the segregation a matter of careful thought and intelligent planning on the part of Negroes" (199–200). Such an economy is plausible precisely because the professional group has a nationalist motivation—their own psychic self-hatred and white-enforced embarrassment about being identified with an oppressed race. Rejecting this particular identification and its negative repercussions depends on an alternate identification by the whole group, on developing a racial consciousness.

What such a proposal does not address, however, is how an

identifiable group, even a group with which people explicitly identify, will successfully drop the various incoherent strategies that
have led to its formation and adopt Du Bois's strategy in 1940.
Having developed an elaborate dialectical argument connecting
his own autobiography to race and then to a particular analysis of
political economy and practice, Du Bois is faced with the reality
that he speaks for *absolutely no one.* In contrast to his cofounding of
the NAACP, when he represented a definable segment of the black
American population, Du Bois is not able to demonstrate in 1940
that in *exemplifying* a race, he also *represents* it politically. It is only
at this stage of the argument that he finds himself moving, arbitrarily, back to Africa, pleading for a sort of ethical racial identification that he knows perfectly well is not generalizable to the black
American group:

> In the African communal group, ties of family and blood, of
> mother and child, of group relationship, made the group lead-
> ership strong. . . . In the case of the more artificial group
> among American Negroes, there are sources of strength in
> common memories of suffering in the past; in present threats
> of degradation and extinction; in common ambitions and
> ideals; in emulation and the determination to prove ability and
> desert. Here in subtle ways the communalism of the African
> clan can be transferred to the Negro American group. . . . We
> have a chance here to teach industrial and cultural democracy
> to a world that bitterly needs it. (*Dusk* 219)

It is impossible to read this regression without sensing that Du Bois
is grasping at straws. He knows that race is not culture, but spatial
delimitation, and that while autobiography explains the existence
of the racial formation, it does not unify it politically.[21] Although
engagement with this particular form of identity politics may, in
fact, be a viable proposal, Du Bois the scientist fails to provide a
detailed analysis of the formation of political blocs and social
movements that might indicate the conditions under which his
proposal could be effectively realized.

Last Words on the Argument of Dusk of Dawn
   The first three chapters of *Dusk of Dawn* narrate the life of
W. E. B. Du Bois to exemplify the formation of racial conscious-
ness; the second three chapters engage humorous anecdotes, fic-

tional encounters, and family genealogies to define the political meaning, in the United States, of this personal story; and the last two chapters complete the dialectical structure by returning to Du Bois's life story of the years 1920–40, amid a now global analysis. The portion of his life he now narrates involves his study of economics and his Marxist analysis of the colonization of the third world. Black American subjectivity, with its centrally important political component, nevertheless must be contextualized as one part of a larger struggle against the cultural and economic subordination of peoples of color internationally. Although the political analysis is useful, the contradictions in the structure of autobiographical representation come clearly into focus; as the subject matter becomes that of global capitalism, the autobiographical narrative becomes far more individualized than in the first two thirds of the text, since it is the narrative of the scholar who *knows*. While the objective argument becomes clear, subjectivity becomes less and less a framework for understanding social formations and more an account of his fights within and outside of his political organization. It is not just that his political analysis becomes framed in objective terms for the first time in the text; it is that the rejection of his political analysis, the failure of the Basic American Negro Creed to generate an audience, is also faceless and nameless: "This creed proved unacceptable both to the Adult Education Association and to its colored affiliates. Consequently when I returned from abroad the manuscript, although ordered and already paid for, was returned to me as rejected for publication. Just who pronounced the veto I don't know" (*Dusk* 322).

Autobiography: *The Communist Theory and the End of Identity Politics*

The Autobiography of W. E. B. Du Bois (1968) provides a radically new frame for Du Bois's life, despite the fact that about 200 pages are taken nearly word for word from the two previous autobiographical texts. About half of the *Autobiography*'s 423 pages are new, addressing material not published in either previous text; a structure of nearly two hundred pages, which addresses almost exclusively the changes in his theory of self-representation during his last twenty years of life, has been added. Thus, the new account's construction maximizes attention to the new view of politics, race, and the historical significance of his life—the particular ways it differs from earlier accounts. The new material, in effect, folds the theory of race, which provides *Dusk*'s largest framework, into the narrative of working-class revolution that he has adopted; he argues that the earlier notion is simply subjective and of no "historical" significance, while his participation in communist politics at the end of his life is the only politically viable framework for the social deconstruction of race. In making this claim for the first time in his autobiographical work, he attempts to analyze his own psychological motivation in a fascinating chapter called "My Character," which is stuck, apparently arbitrarily, amid the narrative of his life at age seventy, which is to say, the point where *Dusk of Dawn* leaves off. This chapter, it seems, provides the outline of an answer to the question of what autobiographical issues exist outside *Dusk*'s narrative of racial identity.

The communist superstructure imposed to explain the life differs radically in style from that of the racial nationalist superstructure in *Dusk* because this time Du Bois does not claim that his life in particular allows for privileged access to the narrative of revolutionary social change. He is a member of a coherent but small segment of the international division of classes, in which no special place is provided for American Negroes, and his joining of the international movement is non-identitarian, if not quite a "choice." In the first paragraph he is literally escaping from the United States:

> August 8 was a day of warm and beautiful sunshine, and many friends with flowers and wine were at the dock to bid me and my wife goodbye. For the 15th time I was going abroad. I felt like a released prisoner, because since 1951, I had been refused a passport by my government, on the excuse that it was not considered to be "to the best interests of the United States" that I go abroad. It assumed that if I did, I would probably criticize the United States for its attitude toward American Negroes. This was certainly true. (*Autobiography* 11)

While he was one of many leftists denied passports during this period, ostensibly for being Communist party members, in fact Du Bois officially joined the party only in 1959, after leaving the country. His opposition to the United States as an imperialist power appeared in the anticolonial texts dating back to the 1910–19 decade and was quite distinct from any interest in the political program of the Comintern.[22] Though my argument differs from that made by Gerald Horne in *Black and Red*—that Du Bois's decision to join the party was not an aberration but a logical consequence of the political position he outlined in the early 1930s—it is clear that the Cold War forced a sharp split between Du Boisian socialism (which was acceptable, if eccentric, within the pre-Depression NAACP) and Du Boisian liberalism, a split between the black middle class, with whom he was affiliated for so long, and the predominantly white left, who would provide his only community now. The textual strategy of this later work effectively marginalizes the narrative of personal identity, privileging instead a narrative of international travel, in which Du Bois looks at the rest of the world as an outsider, a privileged observer. The first five chapters of the *Autobiography*—entitled "My 15th Trip Abroad," "Europe," "The Pawned Peoples [of Eastern Europe]," "The Soviet Union," and "China"—textually decenter the story of Du Bois' identity within a global narrative.

Despite the promise of the opening chapter titles, they do not provide much description of his travels. Rather, we are given a fairly straightforward account of twentieth-century history in each of these places that, while often merely accurate ("There is no European labor party ready to help emancipate the workers of Asia and Africa" (*Autobiography* 21), engages an immensely predictable rhetoric, effectively eliding the complications and contradictions of *Dusk*'s investigation of subjectivity ("In the Soviet Union the overwhelming power of the working class as representing the nation is always decisive" (*Dusk* 36). These chapters, in turn, lead comfortably into what can only be termed religious conversion. "Interlude: Communism" replaces the complicated and local engagement with the political economy of black America in the earlier autobiography with a statement of "belief" so abstract and unargued as to erase subjectivity (to say nothing of race) as an element of dialectical narrative:

> I have studied socialism and communism long and carefully in lands where they are practiced and in conversation with their adherents, and with wide reading. I now state my

conclusion frankly and clearly: I believe in communism. . . . I shall therefore hereafter help the triumph of communism in every honest way that I can: without deceit or hurt; and in any way possible, without war; and with goodwill to all men of all colors, classes and creeds. If, because of this belief and such action, I become the victim of attack and calumny, I will react in the way that seems to me best for the world in which I live and which I have tried earnestly to serve. (*Autobiography* 57–58; entire passage italicized in original)

It is impossible to overlook in these passages a Christianity that Du Bois claimed to abandon as a youth for something he called "science."[23] One of the results of this move to a Christian doctrine of conversion and proselytization is that *Dusk of Dawn's* "Apology" (cited above), phrased as a doctrine of autobiography as sociological representation, is now rephrased as enlightenment narrative:

Who now am I to have come to these conclusions? And of what if any significance are my deductions? . . . The final answer to these questions, time and posterity must make. But perhaps it is my duty to contribute whatever enlightenment I can. This is the excuse for this writing which I call a soliloquy. (*Autobiography* 58; entire passage italicized in original)

In contrast to Du Bois's earlier argument that the black self is in some way always constructed by the social institution of the racial veil—an idea that appears in some manner at every point of Du Bois's career after 1897 (whether the veil is described as less or more important to individual agency)—here he claims that in the movement of world history such social construction of the subject is of no account. If Du Bois has arrived at such an argument, having asked certain questions and come to certain conclusions, we are not to attribute it to his racial experience, as he previously claimed, but to his enlightenment.[24] On the other hand, self-representation does not disappear altogether from the scientist's text; rather, it returns in its most traditional form in the question asked by "that older generation which formed my youth" (277)—the question of "character"—about which Du Bois provides the most interesting new material in the book.

For as little as Du Bois actually relies on anything we would understand as Freudian theory, he does mention Freud by name in *Dusk of Dawn* as having influenced his claims of what might be understood as a racial unconscious. In light of this allusion, his rejection of such an unconscious in the *Autobiography* becomes especially significant:

> When I was a young man, we talked much of character. . . . It is typical of our time that insistence on character today in the country has almost entirely ceased. Freud and others have stressed the unconscious factors of our personality so that today we do not advise youth about their development of character; we watch and count their actions with almost helpless disassociation from thought of advice.
>
> Nevertheless, from that older generation which formed my youth I still retain an interest in what men are rather than what they do. (277)

This distinction between "are" and "do" simply does not appear in *Dusk* or in *Darkwater* and is, in fact, impossible if our investigation intends to discover the subject as racialized. Here, the list of characteristics that Du Bois can be said to be proud of includes honesty, unwillingness to go into debt, unwillingness to make money on immoral businesses even given the specific opportunity—all fairly predictable. What appears next, and strikes me as particularly important for the ways it retrospectively reflects on Du Bois's understanding of blackness, leaves the reader quite unprepared: the "one aspect of my life I look back upon with mixed feelings [is] on matters of friendship and sex" (279). Du Bois, an outspoken advocate of gender equality all his life, here, in the midst of a discussion of what he "is" rather than what he "did," explicitly discusses his own *sex*, which he is not prepared to address in sociological terms.

Du Bois explains that his coupling of "friendship" and "sex" in the passage just quoted is sensible because he has "always had more friends among women than among men" (*Autobiography* 279). While this statement is perhaps true, one would not arrive at this conclusion from reading the autobiographies, which indeed mention little about friends, especially in the early part of his life. Certainly in the peace movement of the 1940s and 1950s, which forms the context of *Autobiography*, this statement about female friends is true; but the need to make it a general statement about his life should be greeted with suspicion. Continuing this self-analysis, Du Bois states, "This began with the close companionship I had with my mother. Friends used to praise me for my attention to my mother; we always went out together arm in arm and had our few indoor amusements together. This seemed quite normal to me; my mother was lame, why should I not guide her steps?" (279). The analytical mode quickly disappears, however, with no attempt by Du Bois to explain these "indoor amusements" nor to connect the relationship with his mother to later friendships: "Later in my life among my own colored people the women began to have more education, while the men imitated an American culture which I did not share" (279). Quickly changing the subject again, Du Bois moves on to his early sexual experience:

> Indeed the chief blame which I lay on my New England schooling was the inexcusable ignorance of sex which I had when I went south to Fisk at 17. I was precipitated into a region with loose sex morals among black and white, while I actually did not know the physical difference between men and women. . . . This built for me inexcusable and startling temptations. It began to turn one of the most beautiful of earth's experiences into a thing of temptation and horror. (279–80)

Finally, Du Bois relates these disclosures to his marriage:

> I married at 29 and we lived together for 53 years. It was not an absolutely ideal union, but it was happier than most, so far as I could perceive. It suffered from the fundamental drawback of modern American marriages: a difference in aim and function between its partners; my wife and children were incidents of my main life work. (280–81)

In light of the absence of gender in previous accounts of his life, it is clear that "character" and "sex" have not been coded as aspects of "racial" life at any point in the three theories. (From a strictly political point of view, one wishes to know if the reason the mainstream antilynching campaign, as represented, for example, by Du Bois's *Crisis* writings, consistently attempted to sidestep its most talented and persistent writer, Ida Wells Barnett, was her insistence on talking about sexuality along the racial border.)[25] Accordingly, one can see the theory of race in *Dusk* as necessarily masculine, because race, unlike other psychic issues, is uniquely sociological, while "character" and "sex" can apparently not be analyzed the same way.[26]

To make this statement is not merely to state the obvious; rather, it is to say something about the structure of representation in autobiography which, though Du Bois tries to overcome it through a dialectical sociology, continues to plague his narrative. He works particularly hard, in the manner of the best contemporary theory, to account for the conditions that produce him as autobiographer within *Dusk of Dawn*. Yet the category of subject production continues according to masculinist notions of production through the maintenance of the public/private split,[27] a split that itself corresponds to Doris Sommer's distinction between metaphoric (representation as replacement) and metonymic (representation as membership) representations in autobiography, as outlined in "Not Just a Personal Story." Only through the ironically "old-fashioned" category of character does Du Bois make small analytical insights about this separation and then state that he wishes he had married someone as politically involved as himself.[28]

Conclusion

The three theories of race of W. E. B. Du Bois follow this pattern: race as peculiar shading, or veil, on the achievements of the great individual; race as the determining feature of the subject; race as of some importance in a person's life, but of no particular importance to the narrative of history, which is toward the elimination of race. This summary permits me to suggest tentative but specific answers to my original questions, "what is a race?" and "what is an autobiography?" in the context of African American identity politics in the twentieth century.

What is a race? It seems to me that the methodology of *Dusk of Dawn*, really inaugurated in 1897 with the question "How does it feel to be a Problem?" but elaborated with the greatest sophistication only in 1940, provides a useful starting point for addressing the social construction of race, the most plausible means for avoiding the notion that "racial consciousness" of the sort Du Bois's life enacts is somehow dirty, and for understanding its workings. Specifically, because *Dusk* goes back and forth between the historical and personal events and rules that enforce racial distinctions, and demonstrates the ways in which the actions of individually raced people act as agents on behalf of these events and rules, it provides a dialectical vision of race without imagining that there is some moment of transcendence at which point we all—those of us who are white definitely included—stop being raced. Dialectics, thus, do not obligate the social analyst to predict moments of transcendence. Race is in this sense a habitus, and antiracism—which is never color-blind—can only proceed through the continual working within it. The United States today is as segregated as it was in 1940 (Massey and Denton), and there is no more room for pretense in our political proposals today than there was then.

Because of this fact, I take the particularly unpopular position that identity politics is not something that "we" can somehow "go beyond," as nearly all liberal, Marxist, and poststructuralist arguments within the theory-driven academy have claimed recently. *Dusk of Dawn* illustrates that the case for black nationalist (as an example of identity) politics has never depended on so-called essentialism; numerous other examples of this can be found. But *Dusk of Dawn* is significantly less helpful in getting us to the point where we can understand the workings of bloc formation that identity politics depends on than it is in helping us understand the meaning of racial identity. The same argument in which Du Bois demonstrates that there are grounds for the coherence and mutual trust of the black middle class as a class, and additionally ties its interests to the improvement of conditions for all black people, also depends on an assumed diversity of this class's political activities. Du Bois is able to show that people may act as they do by working through a fully reified—indeed, *centered*—racial identity and their actions can only be interpreted on that basis; but this in no way implies that they will act collectively or in the same ways. Put differently, the black person who refuses to be segregated and the black person who self-segregates are both acting *racially* and, thus, will experience the results racially (i.e., through the experience of racial subordination within a white supremacist system). Social movements will necessarily be intersected by such relations of identification; as a result the formation of cross-identity movements depends on the conscious promulgation of a form of volunteerism, which in contemporary terms is best understood as "coalition" (cf. essays by Reagon and B. Smith in Smith).

For liberals, nationalists, and communists of the first half of this century, including those who are explicitly (in whatever sense) feminist, race is generally not a category that is gendered. That gender is untheorized in *Dusk of Dawn* does not, of course, mean that it doesn't appear, and another account of the book might stress a great deal more its presence as an absence. It has become typical to note the relationship of certain notions of blackness popularized in the 1960s to masculinism, but what I want to emphasize here is that gender exclusiveness in Du Bois's case seems tied not to his protonationalism but rather, ironically, to the gender-blind version of feminism to which Du Bois adhered. Thus, the women who appear as named activists in his texts have no existence as women, in much the same way that black communists have no existence as blacks. Nina Gomer Du Bois is not named in *Dusk's* world history. Du Bois' onetime mistress, Jessie Fauset, is entirely absent from the discussion "My Character." What all this means, finally, is not that the methodology of autobiography around which Du Bois constructs his analysis of race is untenable, but that any future feminist project would necessarily consider "black male" as a raced-gender category[29] and would insist that all future Du Boisian racial practice center gendered experience. bell hooks' account of race in *Black Looks* strikes me as a good example of such an autobiographical procedure.

What is an autobiography? After abandoning liberalism, Du Bois practices autobiography as the dialectical representation of the self's habitus in a multiply determined social space. "Black" appended to the category "self" is the central category through which, on a conscious level, he experienced himself in the United States in the twentieth century. Marxist political economy is used, first as background, later as foreground, to link this level of consciousness to a global totality. An autobiography becomes that text in which the determinate recall of self and the determinate recall of history are consequences of one another; this should be true even in a text, like *Darkwater*, where the author is unconscious of the fact: which is precisely why ideology can be read in any given autobiography.[30] In this context, consciousness of race in self-representation, for "colorless" white people as well as already racialized people of color, is required for political effectiveness; this is the reality of racial identity politics. Yet, when an autobiography is written with no other intention than to theorize this point, the self's resistance to nonracial psychic determinations provides the specific limitations of racial identity politics.

Notes

1. The original speech is available as "A Pageant in Seven Decades," in *W. E. B. Du Bois Speaks*, 21–72.

2. It is in many ways instructive to compare this question to its more directly Hegelian (in the sense of a social dialectic built on recognition) corollary, the statement "Look, a Negro," often cited as the childhood basis of the psychological understanding of race in Frantz Fanon's *Black Skin, White Masks* (109). Du Bois's question addresses not the general problematic of the Negro child but rather a very specific social location, that of the adult black intellectual who inhabits the social position of being a "problem." I would claim that this formulation and the theory of double consciousness that follows from it originate the discourse of postcolonialism as it is presently understood, fifty years earlier than most of the texts cited as originary.

3. If the reader doesn't agree that this statement has been true, there is no way of my arguing the point.

4. I discuss dialectical autobiography in some detail in the context of Carlos Bulosan's *America Is in the Heart* in my essay "Why Is America in the Heart?" See also Barbara Foley's *Radical Representations,* for an evaluation of autobiographical writing that uses similar structures, and Frederic Jameson, *Marxism and Form,* for the general discussion of the attempt to write narrative which shares the form of its theoretical claims.

It is interesting to note, in this context, scholars who have read *Dusk* have disagreed on whether it is best understood as a collectivist or an individualist text, with Albert Stone (171) taking the position that it is the exemplary collectivist text in recent African-American writing, and Stephen Butterfield (106) arguing that Du Bois's account ultimately centers his specificity as an intellectual separate from the collectivity. Arnold Rampersad implicitly agrees with Butterfield, arguing that the subject of *Dusk* is ultimately the same ethical subject which has appeared in the writings of his life (241–44). My assessment of the conclusion of *Dusk* will be relatively consistent with the latter two critics; what differs in my analysis is that I presume, at the start, that Du Bois is engaged in an explicit attempt to conarrate, in a dialectical manner, individual and collective subject positions (I- and we-subjects, in the Sartrean terminology I will periodically employ).

5. Double consciousness is, thus, a *fact* of black intellectual life, before it is a *value;* it would be inappropriate to read doubleness then as some sort of privileged "third space" of mediation or brokerage between otherwise undoubled

spaces. Gilroy articulates the continuing significance of Du Bois's concept of double consciousness (127ff.).

6. Though it is clear that he did not understand Freud in any depth, Du Bois does suggest the usefulness of psychoanalytic theory to his conception of a racial unconscious. I suspect that, had he theorized it explicitly, he would have moved in the direction of marxists like Althusser, Jameson (*The Political Unconscious*), and Eagleton, all of whom in different ways see the description of the unconscious as being appropriate to a theory of ideology. Volosinov (*Marxism and the Philosophy of Language; Freudianism*), as my epigraph suggests, is the sociolinguist who grounds the connections between consciousness (i.e., social class, ideology, language) and the unconscious as I understand them in this paper.

7. It is important, however, that "Negro" and not "black" or "African American" be used to describe the specific racial agency which appears in Du Bois's narrative. My own commentary in this paper uses African American and black interchangeably.

8. Such a defense will make clear why, contrary to much current practice, I do not place the word "race" within scare quotes except for occasional and specific reasons. In making this choice, I follow Du Bois's practice.

9. It wasn't, particularly. Du Bois's mother had had an affair with her cousin, resulting in an illegitimate half-brother that Du Bois never met; his father left when he was an infant because the "great clan" didn't like him. Lewis suggests that long after Du Bois's stated political positions became pro-sex and pro-working class he continued to be personally embarrassed by these facts (21–22).

10. Mrs. Du Bois seems to be the obvious reference in this passage from *Dusk*, already cited above: "autobiography . . . assumes . . . too little in the reticences, repressions, and distortions which come because men do not dare to be absolutely frank" (xxix).

11. The verb "determine" here, the use of which should not imply *determinism*, derives from Raymond Williams: specifically "the setting of limits" on the possible, and the "exertion of pressures" on the probable (87). Like commodities in marxist analysis, race appears as a kind of fetish, and, thus, Eagleton's analysis of commodity fetishism applies: human subjects' socially constructed conditions of existence are "now inherent in social reality itself. It is not simply a question of the distorted perception of human beings, who invent the real world in their consciousness and this imagine that commodities control their lives. Marx is not claiming that under capitalism commodities *appear* to exercise a tyrannical sway over social relations; he is arguing that they actually do" (Eagleton 85).

12. It should be clear from this that I consider Anthony Appiah's argument in the well-known essay "The Uncompleted Argument" to be quite wrong both in terms of his reading of *Dusk of Dawn* and the contemporary meanings of race. Appiah argues that the account of race in *Dusk of Dawn* is "incomplete" because it never comes to an acknowledgment that race is a scientifically unsound concept, though it makes several moves in that direction. I analyze Appiah's text, and the responses it drew from Houston Baker and Joyce Joyce, in great detail in the longer version of this essay, which appears as chapter 3 of my dissertation, "*Autobiography and Identity Politics.*" In brief, it is possible to show that for Appiah a sharp differentiation is drawn between scientific truth and unscientific happenstance opinion, and that any usage of race which does not meet scientific rigor is simply "wrong." As such, Appiah's argument is anything but attentive to concepts as socially constructed, which I argue ultimately is in particular a *sociological* concern.

In this way, my own links to Omi and Winant, and theirs to the tradition which Du Bois started, become clear. For further arguments that Du Bois strives from early in his career for a sociological and socially constructed definition of race, regarding texts other than the autobiographies, see the excellent essays by Holt and Lott.

13. Race as a fetish, then, in the sense I pointed out in note 11, can be given a history by articulating Du Bois's explanations of the genesis of racial feeling and self-identity the category of "habitus," as described by Pierre Bourdieu in *Outline of a Theory of Practice*. I have replaced "the habitus" with "race" in this quote to elaborate Du Bois's position:

> As an acquired system of generative schemes objectively adjusted to the particular conditions in which it is constituted, [race] engenders all the thoughts, all the perceptions, and all the actions consistent with those conditions, and not others. The paradoxical product is difficult to conceive, even inconceivable, only so long as one remains locked in the dilemma of determinism and freedom, conditioning and creativity. . . . Because [race] has an endless capacity to engender products—thought, perceptions, expressions, actions—whose limits are set by the historically and socially situated conditions of its production, the conditioned and conditional freedom it secures is as remote from a creation of unpredictable novelty as it is from a simple mechanical reproduction of initial conditionings. (95)

Omi and Winant's theory of "racial formation" works well within the Marxian-Bourdieuian epistemology I am proposing. Gilroy (*There Ain't No Black*) also proposed a similarly existential framework for race-as-habitus in 1987.

14. There are, of course, also cultural inheritances that many black and non-black Americans take from Africa. The point of emphasizing this particular genesis of twentieth-century black identity is to indicate that, however much of an African cultural legacy is maintained, its particular coding as "black" and "racial" is the legacy of the veil.

15. Lewis (503–04) notes than the economic argument of Lenin's 1917 *Imperialism* pamphlet was anticipated in articles Du Bois wrote for the *Crisis* in 1914–15, and in his book *The Negro* (1915).

16. Anthony Appiah's argument against Du Bois' racial narrative, described in note 12, is based largely on this passage, so it deserves particular attention.

17. Of course, simultaneously he rejects the idea of the primitive as a temporal designation: "primitive men are not following us afar, frantically waving and seeking our goals; primitive men are not behind us in some swift footrace. Primitive men have already arrived" (127). What is striking is that this passage is not dated as a result of its false notion of racial identity, but rather because his otherwise contemporary sounding critique of civilization-as-teleology nevertheless retains the ideologically loaded binary primitive/civilized.

18. The problem of memory in Toni Morrison's novels is a much noted place to begin thinking about this issue. For example, both Satya Mohanty and Barbara Christian address the memory of Africa in their accounts of *Beloved;* see also Gilroy, *The Black Atlantic* ch. 6, whose extended treatment of the memory of slavery takes Morrison's "not a story to pass on" as his chapter title.

19. In this article, which is not about "culture," I certainly accept the necessity of distinguishing the cultural from the racial. Within the U.S. cultural matrix,

which must in its abstraction be conceived as a whole, race identifies difference; as a result, subcultures *tend* to form racially, with, however, mixed racial exceptions everywhere you look. Thus, the (true) statement that African-American culture is a hybrid multiculture, just like all others, does not mean that one must refuse the charge (made in different contexts by Toni Morrison, Houston Baker, and Barbara Smith, among many others) to define what distinguishes this (sub)culture from the dominant white (sub)culture, or even how the circumstances of race-as-differential continue to enforce cultural distinctions even while significant numbers of individuals cross racial lines through their participation in normal cultural processes. (Relatively mixed racial groupings, like that of "cultural studies scholars", are themselves subcultures, and cannot to be taken as anything other than exceptional.)

20. Many of his proposals are those later articulated as "nationalist," but Du Bois himself rejects the term as senseless (possibly in reaction against the CPUSA description of the Black Belt as a "nation"). Further, since he never recommends that black people already intertwined with white economics or politics disentwine (any more than he argues that he is not implicated in the work of white intellectuals), his plan can't really be called "segregation" either—making coherent use of already existing segregation is the most accurate description of his recommendations.

21. I have already mentioned that Rampersad (241–44) reads *Dusk* as more or less a repetitive plea for an ethical community, and not as adding anything in particular to Du Bois's corpus of ideas. While I obviously disagree with this general assessment of the book, it is at this moment—the pleas for certain humanist ethical ideals as seen through the metaphor of African tribal community—that Rampersad's reading seems most compelling.

22. Space prevents me from discussing the long section on the Soviet Union in *Dusk of Dawn;* in short, in 1940 he considered the Soviet Union an inspiring example that it was possible to organize a society with the express intent of eliminating poverty, and says that his trip there in 1926 convinced him that the revolution was first of all a good thing. He also criticizes Stalin's purges and most importantly, indicates that so-called international communism doesn't know the first thing about conditions in the United States and provides no program relevant to black Americans.

23. Because I take seriously the notion of Marxist social science, to which Du Bois contributes during the 1930s and 1940s, I note the following: the socialist political argument in *Dusk* is sociological; the communist political argument in the *Autobiography* is theological.

24. In this sense, *contra* Appiah, Du Bois did in fact "complete" the "scientific" argument about race, through the anti-social construction frame of Marxist-Leninist science. Appiah's essay strategically ignores Du Bois's writing after *Dusk of Dawn,* perhaps because to include it would necessitate Appiah admitting that his position with regard to race, and that of the Communist party in the 1950s, is the same.

25. Wells Barnett is addressed in "Racial and Cultural 'Depth': The Genders of Liberal Anti-Lynching Politics," ch. 4 of Mostern [*Autobiography and Identity Politics*]

26. Even among the most important black feminists of the first half of the twentieth century, only Pauline Hopkins and Ida Wells Barnett had much to say about the *sexualized* (as opposed to *gendered*) construction of race. Du Bois's position on women is best seen as rather similar to that of Anna Julia Cooper, in *A Voice from the South* (1892); meanwhile, for Zora Neale Hurston racial meaning is entirely

abandoned (in the sense Appiah currently endorses) for the description of southern black *culture*, through a lens that I continue, unpopularly, to see as conditioned as much by Boasian anthropology as her own "roots". For a fair, and not very sympathetic view of Du Bois' intellectual work on woman, see Morton (ch. 4).

27. bell hooks's *Talking Back* is particularly helpful on elaborating the significance of the public/private distinction in this analysis; she appears to derive her position from that of 1970s socialist feminism rather than feminist deconstruction.

28. The seriousness of this wish is, of course, borne out by his affair with Jessie Fauset, toward whom, there is every reason to believe, he acted significantly less superior.

29. I am aware of two arguments that articulate the necessity of raced-gender as an ongoing analytical category: Spillers (1987) and Ferguson (1990). I believe that consistently making use of such a category would help us to articulate a range of phenomena at the intersection of race and gender determinations—for example, the analysis of the specifically *gendered* criminalization of black men (which is not inconsistent with the analysis of misogyny by black men), and the particular sexist metaphorics of the Moynihan report (which is Spillers's example)—without falling into a theory of radical indeterminacy, as though no patterns of race and gender subjectivity recur.

30. The absence of a concept of historicization or dialectics in a given autobiography is actually of no consequence here. One learns the ideological backdrop of the narrative as much by the absence or implicitness of the parallel narratives of history as by their explicit presentation. What I have said about gender in this analysis is a small example of the reading of such an absence.

Works Cited

Althusser, Louis. *Lenin and Philosophy*. New York: Monthly Review P, 1971.

Andrews, William. *To Tell a Free Story: The First Century of Afro-American Autobiography, 1760–1865*. Urbana: U of Illinois P, 1986.

Appiah, Kwame Anthony. "The Uncompleted Argument: Du Bois and the Illusion of Race." *"Race", Writing, and Difference*. Ed. Henry Louis Gates, Jr. Chicago: U of Chicago P, 1986. 21–37.

Baber, Willie L. "Capitalism and Racism." *Critique of Anthropology* 12:3 (1992): 339–64.

Bercovitch, Sacvan. *The Puritan Origins of the American Self*. New Haven: Yale UP, 1974.

Bourdieu, Pierre. *Outline of A Theory of Practice*. 1972. Trans. R. Nice. New York: Cambridge UP, 1977.

Butterfield, Stephen. *Black Autobiography in America*. Amherst: U of Massachusetts P, 1974.

Christian, Barbara. "Fixing Methodologies: *Beloved*." *Cultural Critique* 24 (1993): 5–15.

Cooper, Anna Julia. *A Voice from the South*. 1892. New York: Oxford UP, 1988.

Du Bois, W. E. B. *The Autobiography of W. E. B. Du Bois*. New York: International, 1968.

———. *Black Folk Then And Now*. New York: Holt, 1939.

———. *Darkwater: Voices from Within the Veil.* 1920. New York: Schocken Books, 1969.

———. *Dusk of Dawn: An Essay Toward an Autobiography of a Race Concept.* 1940. New Brunswick: Transaction, 1984.

———. *The Souls of Black Folk.* 1903. New York: Signet, 1969.

———. *W. E. B. Du Bois Speaks: Speeches and Addresses 1890–1919.* Ed. P. Foner. New York: Pathfinder, 1970.

Eagleton, Terry. *Ideology: An Introduction.* New York: Verso, 1991.

Fanon, Frantz. *Black Skin, White Masks.* 1952. Trans. Charles Lam Markhamm. New York: Grove P, 1967.

Ferguson, Ann. "The Intersection of Race, Gender and Class in the United States Today." *Rethinking Marxism* 3.3–4 (1990): 45–64.

Foley, Barbara. *Radical Representations: Politics and Form in U.S. Proletariat Fiction, 1929–1941.* Durham: Duke UP, 1993.

Gilroy, Paul. *The Black Atlantic: Modernity and Double Consciousness.* New York: Oxford UP, 1993.

———. *There Ain't No Black in the Union Jack: The Cultural Politics of Race and Nation.* Chicago: U of Chicago P, 1987.

Gusdorf, Georges. "Conditions and Limits of Autobiography." 1956. *Autobiography: Essays Theoretical and Critical.* Ed. J. Olney. Princeton, NJ: Princeton UP, 1980. 28–48.

Harper, Phillip Bryan. *Framing the Margins: On the Social Logic of Postmodern Culture.* New York: Oxford UP, 1994.

Holt, Thomas C. "The Political Uses of Alienation: W. E. B. Du Bois on Politics, Race, and Culture, 1903–40." *American Quarterly* 42.2 (1990): 301–23.

hooks, bell. *Black Looks: Race and Representation.* Boston: South End, 1992.

———. *Talking Back: Thinking Feminist, Thinking Black.* Boston: South End, 1989.

hooks, bell, and Cornel West. *Breaking Bread: Insurgent Black Intellectual Life.* Boston: South End, 1991.

Horne, Gerald. *Black and Red: W. E. B. Du Bois and the Afro-American Response to the Cold War.* Albany: SUNY P, 1986.

Jameson, Frederic. *Marxism and Form.* Princeton, NJ: Princeton UP, 1973.

———. *The Political Unconscious.* Ithaca: Cornell UP, 1981.

Lewis, David Levering. *W. E. B. Du Bois: Biography of A Race. 1868–1919.* New York: Holt, 1993.

Lott, Tommy L. "Du Bois on the Invention of Race." *Philosophical Forum* 24.1–3 (1992–93): 166–87.

Massey, Douglas, and Nancy Denton. *American Apartheid: Segregation and the Making of the Underclass.* Cambridge: Harvard UP, 1993.

Mohanty, Satya. "The Epistemic Status of Cultural Identity: On *Beloved* and the Postcolonial Condition." *Cultural Critique* 24 (1993): 41–80.

Morton, Patricia. *Disfigured Images: The Historical Assault on Afro-American Women.* New York: Praeger, 1990.

Mostern, Kenneth. "Why Is America in the Heart?" *Critical Mass: A Journal of Asian-American Cultural Studies* 2.2 (Spring 1995): 35–65.

———. "Autobiography and Identity Politics: The Narrative Politics of Race-ness in Twentieth Century African American Intellectual Thought." Ph.D. diss., University of California at Berkeley, 1995.

Omi, Michael, and Howard Winant. *Racial Formation in the United States from the 1960s to the 1990s.* 2nd ed. New York: Routledge, 1994.

Rampersad, Arnold. *The Art and Imagination of W. E. B. Du Bois.* New York: Schocken, 1976.

Smith, Barbara, ed. *Home Girls: A Black Feminist Anthology.* New York: Kitchen Table/Women of Color, 1983.

Sommer, Doris. "'Not Just a Personal Story': Women's *Testimonios* and the Plural Self." *Life/Lines: Theorizing Women's Autobiography.* Ed. B. Brodski and C. Schenck. Ithaca: Cornell UP, 1988.

Spillers, Hortense. "Mama's Baby, Papa's Maybe: An American Grammar Book." *Diacritics* 17.2 (1987): 65–81.

Stone, Albert. "After Black Boy and Dusk of Dawn: Patterns in Recent Black Autobiography." *African-American Autobiography: A Collection of Critical Essays.* Ed. W. Andrews. Engelwood Cliffs, NJ: Prentice Hall, 1993.

Volosinov, V. N. *Freudianism: A Critical Sketch.* 1920. Trans. and ed. I. R. Titunik and N. H. Bruss. Bloomington: Indiana UP, 1976.

———. *Marxism and the Philosophy of Language.* 1929. Cambridge: Harvard UP, 1973.

Wells Barnett, Ida B. *Selected Works of Ida B. Wells Barnett.* Comp. T. Harris. New York: Oxford UP, 1991.

Williams, Raymond. *Marxism and Literature.* New York: Oxford UP, 1981.

"Never shoulda been let out the penitentiary": Gangsta Rap and the Struggle over Racial Identity

Michael Quinn

In January 1994, a CNN/USA Today poll argued that the issue most troubling Americans was crime, an anxiety that has arisen despite the statistical decreases in violent crimes from 1973 to 1992. During this period, violent crime against white Americans dropped from 31.6 to 29.9 per 1,000 people. The statistics, however, show a different picture for blacks as the numbers rose in the same period from 41.7 to 50.4 crimes per 1,000 people. Homicide rates were even more alarming, almost doubling for black males under twenty-four, from 84 to 159 per 100,000 people between 1980 and 1991 (Morganthau 66). One of the culprits often singled out for the rise in black-on-black violence is black culture, and in particular, rap music. It has become standard practice for television news and other news sources to make a connection between rap and crime; for instance, *Newsweek* placed rappers on its cover twice in the last five years, both times in articles about rap and crime. The year 1994 also marked the beginning of congressional "exploratory hearings" about the dangers of rap in general and Gangsta Rap in particular. Although the mainstream media con-

© 1996 by *Cultural Critique*. Fall 1996. 0882-4371/96/$5.00.

tinues to criticize rap for its supposed glorification of gang culture and violence, other groups find rap offensive for different political reasons. Public Enemy has been accused of anti-Semitism, while rap's tendency to depict women as "bitches and hoes" (whores) has come under fire from feminists. And yet, this African American cultural form, linked so often to crime, sexism, and racism, has become a significant part of mainstream culture. Rap plays an increasingly important role in films (*CB4, Poetic Justice, Menace II Society*), television (*The Fresh Prince of Bel-Aire*), and advertising (with McDonald's, Burger King, and Nike, among many others, using rap as a major component of their commercials). MTV, which ten years ago was notorious for its exclusion of black artists (Marsh 202), now devotes much of its music video programming time, particularly in the afternoon, to rap. Even the most hardcore Gangsta Rap artists, limited until recently to a tape trading underground, can sell millions of copies to both urban blacks and white youth. Academics have also jumped on the bandwagon, seeing rap as occupying a crucial position within a relationship of politics, culture, and audiences; for some, rap suggests how audiences exist within a nexus of subjugation and resistance to the dominant political order.

As with any generic form, the boundaries of rap music are quite difficult to isolate in any systematic way. Rap's tendency to absorb other pop music genres has obscured the origins of rap in general and even individual rap elements. Despite the fact that many critics have traced rap to the seventies, with George Clinton, and even the sixties, with James Brown, the first rap hit is generally considered to be "Rapper's Delight" by the Sugarhill Gang in 1979. By this time, hip-hop had already become an entrenched underground form: it was a black person's street music, derived from the social realities of inner city ghettos, created by people who intimately knew of those realities, and listened to by those who lived them. As David Toop shows us in his hip-hop history *The Rap Attack*, the very first hip-hop artists literally made their music on the street, with two turntables, an amplifier, and speakers, drawing electricity from lampposts or other found sources. Hip-hop was also a force in New York dance clubs in the seventies, where disc jockeys began to use turntables not simply to play already produced records but to create new sounds by cutting between songs.

This technique kept the music going for long periods of time, ensuring a continuous danceable beat. Eventually, DJs brought their monologues to the music; bragging about their abilities and cutting down other DJs were prime topics for these raps, as were attempts to push dancers to new heights, to "rock the house." These dance club origins resonate in "Rapper's Delight," which is clearly in the tradition of a disco song; the video was filmed in a dance club, complete with a multiracial, jumpsuit-wearing crowd. Besides being the first rap song, "Rapper's Delight" also has the distinction of being the first rap song ripped off by white artists. The white rock group Queen, foreshadowing mainstream acceptance of rap, garnered a number one hit in "Another One Bites the Dust," a song entirely written around the bass line from "Rapper's Delight." Despite such early hits, rap's foray into the mainstream was limited until Run-D.M.C.'s cover of the Aerosmith song "Walk this Way." Aerosmith, a white heavy metal band from the seventies whose renewed success began with this collaboration, participated in both the new recording and the video, giving Run-D.M.C. access to (white) rock stations and then notoriously white MTV, in effect opening the doors, as well as the charts, to rap and hip-hop. Run-D.M.C.'s achievement was to crossover, appealing to both whites and blacks while not appearing to "sell out" by compromising rap to appeal to whites. Rap's other early success was the group Salt 'N Pepa, whose 1986 debut *Hot, Cool, and Vicious* sold over two million copies, becoming the first album by a female rap group to go platinum. However, the sales and air-play achievements of these groups pale in comparison to what happened in 1990. For the first time since the beginnings of rap, the first and second positions on the overall album sales charts belonged to two rap acts, Vanilla Ice and Hammer, who eventually sold five million and an incredible eight million albums, respectively; rap had become mainstream. In the nineties, a variety of bands have reached multiplatinum status; Public Enemy, N.W.A, Salt 'N Pepa, Ice Cube, Dr. Dre, Snoop Doggy Dogg, and Cypress Hill, among others, have all sold over one million copies of one of their albums. Public Enemy's *Fear of a Black Planet* and Snoop Doggy Dogg's debut *Doggystyle* both went platinum in their first week of release, garnering sales numbers usually limited to artists with a seemingly wider audience such as Madonna or Janet Jackson. The clearest indication of rap's move to the mainstream is its appearance in television commercials, particularly commercials aimed at black audiences or youth in general and marketing products such as sneakers, fast food, and soft drinks.

The success and overall mainstream acceptance attained by rap in a mere eleven years is quite surprising considering the political and economic climate of the eighties. In the music industry, the large corporations controlling the vast majority of popular music, which are, in turn, owned by even larger conglomerates such as Sony and Time Warner, are heavily biased in favor of conservative, already accepted musical groups and genres. The ability of Madonna or Janet Jackson to release seven or eight successful singles from an album is not only predicated on their fans' loyalty but also due to the expense of promoting and nurturing new acts; the risks of releasing the seventh Madonna single, not to mention the promotion costs, are far less than for songs by new groups. The growth of "classic rock" radio stations, which play primarily sixties and seventies (white) rock groups, are part of the reason for this stagnation, as are the various oldies-based adult contemporary formats. These radio formats, which play little new music, limit their playlists to a few hundred "oldies," which repeat day after day with little variation. While this trend does not suggest that the popular music charts have become totally immobile, it does imply the steadily increasing difficulty of getting new music played, except, of course, for new music that sounds like old music: witness the groundbreaking success in 1995 of Hootie and the Blowfish. When new music does appear, it often seems as if it has taken over the charts, for instance, the prevalence in 1993 of the Seattle sound personified by Nirvana and Pearl Jam; musical clones are, of course, much easier to promote than more original bands. Besides this music industry conservatism, there was the general political conservatism and racism fostered by the Reagan era. In such a racially hostile climate, rap's success would seem virtually impossible, particularly given its direct ties to inner-city blacks. And yet, rap entered the mainstream so quickly that its most commercially successful practitioners quickly lost credibility, becoming little more than joke fodder for late-night talk shows. The cries of "sell out" directed at Hammer, who proved more successful with whites than blacks,[1] and the general critical disdain of Vanilla Ice, who was brought up in an upper-middle-class suburb and yet claimed to be from the ghetto, suggest that something has been lost in the popular acceptance of rap music.

Not all rappers today are considered completely mainstream; in fact, several rap groups have engendered enormous controversy in not only the cultural arena but the political arena as well. The 2 Live Crew album *As Nasty as They Wanna Be,* with its explicit depiction of sexual acts and sadism, was banned in Gainesville, Florida, and the group was actually arrested, and later acquitted, for performing its songs in an adult nightclub. Groups like N.W.A (Niggers with Attitude) and the Geto Boyz remain within a rap subgenre called Gangsta Rap, a genre based on the construction of an urban mise-en-scène of drugs, rape, and murder. The parade of rappers in trouble continued in 1995: Gangsta Rapper Snoop Doggy Dog was recently acquitted of murder charges, as was rapper and film actor Tupac Shakur. However, Shakur remains dogged by allegations of abusive and violent behavior. Public Enemy, with its overtly political rap that ranges from theoretical discussions of essentialism in "Fear of a Black Planet" to more micro-level political interventions in its own backyard ("911 Is a Joke"), achieved enormous popularity among blacks and whites as well as critics, despite alliances with the Nation of Islam. These rap groups, along with the media and fan discourses surrounding them, raise many questions about the political efficacy of culture in the eighties and nineties. The controversies in which rap found itself embroiled, and the various responses that different socially situated listeners have to rap, reveal much about how popular culture can act as a force for social change. Rap also gives a number of examples of how artists and fans struggle with each other, as well as with the culture industry and political groups, over the meanings of the music. In particular, we find rap musicians as well as their audiences creating and responding to discourses around notions of black identity. Different forms of rap—from De La Soul's mellow sixties-inflected Afrocentrism to Dr. Dre's L. A. Gangsta rhymes—coexist in a dialogue over racial, cultural, and sexual identity, sustained through both lyrics and music. This dialogue does not exist only among rappers and listeners; the media engages in interpretive practices of its own around rap, attempting to enter and control the debate around black identity. Finally, rap exists within a culture industry and economic system that not only influences but often is deeply invested in these questions of identity and their political meanings.

The question of what constitutes a politically, as opposed to aesthetically, progressive or radical popular culture is perhaps the most crucial issue in cultural studies. An initial impetus of cultural studies was to question and overturn notions of subjugated and passive audiences, controlled by dominant ideology at every level of existence. This aim led cultural studies' practitioners to investigations of real audiences and their cultural practices, concentrating on subcultural groups and other disenfranchised peoples to discover how they resisted dominant ideology. More recently cultural studies has begun to go beyond what Laura Kipnis calls "the tendency to locate resistance, agency, and micro-political struggle just about everywhere in mass cultural reception" (374–375). It is no longer enough to show that dominant ideology, delivered in either cultural or more traditional political forms, is not blindly accepted by meek, subjugated audiences. Rap music is easily theorized in terms of resistance, for it is based on urban black culture and made for economically and politically marginalized groups. For instance, this tactic is taken in Ted Swedenburg's excellent article "Homies in the 'Hood" about the bias reflected in rock critics' creation of the canon of popular music to include Elvis, the English Invasion, punk, mid-eighties authenticity, and techno-dance music, a canon populated almost exclusively by white males. Swedenburg argues that rap artists, through their relationship to an "imagined but real" community of young urban blacks, "articulate an ethico-political agenda that . . . is both utopian and pragmatic" (57). While this statement might be true of overtly political acts such as Public Enemy and Queen Latifah, the issue becomes more problematic when dealing with the Gangsta Rap of N.W.A, Ice Cube, and Snoop Doggy Dogg. I would like to explore Gangsta Rap and its inscription of notions of racial and sexual identity, as well as how different artists and fans respond to and rework these notions. In the case of rap, simplistic oppositions of resistance and subjugation to ideology and racism are problematic: first because the struggle over identity has no easy answers and second because of the extent to which rap has become co-extensive with the culture industry itself.

Rap and Black Identity

With the recent "war on crime," the gains made by African Americans in the areas of civil rights and media representations are being washed away by a sea of racist rhetoric and "social reforms" aimed at curbing crime. Network news and news magazines depict urban settings as war zones, black gangs as armies outnumbering and outgunning the police, casually killing other people for wearing the wrong colors or walking down the wrong streets. An advertisement for the "reality TV" program *Cops* screams "The muggers are in your neighborhood; the drug pushers are on your street." Media panic over rap and crime hit its first peak in 1989, the year of the Central Park jogger rape, when a gang of black male youths raped a white female investment banker jogging through Central Park in New York (Baker 36–60). In the nineties, the connection between African American culture and crime has been mediated by Gangsta Rap, a genre favoring depictions of lawless black urban gangs. Rather than questioning or denying the veracity of mainstream representations of life in inner cities, Gangsta Rap accepts the gang member–drug seller role assigned to urban black youth by the media and then hyperbolizes these representations until the rappers become exactly what whites fear:

> Straight outta Compton
> Crazy motherfucker named Ice Cube
> From the gang called Niggers With Attitude
> When I'm called off, I got a sawed-off
> Squeeze the trigger and bodies are hauled off
> You too boyee if you fuck with me
> The police are gonna have to come get me.
> (N.W.A, "Straight Outta Compton").

By exploding the media's representation of young black males as gang members and pushers, N.W.A. inverts a power relation in which whites are on top and blacks on the bottom, the latter only able to succeed illegally. The result of this inversion is a terrifying mise-en-scène of gang rape and casual violence: "Just 'cause I'm from the C.P.T. / Punk police are afraid of me, / A young nigger on the warpath / And when I'm finished, there's gonna be a bloodbath" (N.W.A, "Straight Outta Compton").

It is quite possible to argue that Gangsta Rap is a form of resistance, however misguided one might believe it to be, to economic and cultural marginalization, empowering black youths by showing them other blacks who, as Ice-T puts it, "don't take no shit from nobody." This form of empowerment is certainly not new; crime has had a long, if marginalized, history of being considered transgressive, from writers such as the Marquis de Sade to Bataille and Genet. Swedenburg, however, does not adopt this view in "Homies in the 'Hood"; instead, by opposing Gangsta Rap to Public Enemy's overtly political rap, he argues that "occasionally the 'prophets of rage' . . . seem to be turning into the profits of rage, as some gangsta rhymers appear less concerned with fighting stereotypes than in selling them" (63). On the other hand, in his extremely incisive book *Black Studies, Rap, and the Academy,* Houston A. Baker Jr. argues that Gangsta Rap reveals "the inversive and brilliant powers of symbolic transformation possessed by African Americans. The 'X' of white-motivated legal erasure and "unnaming" is recuperated as black re-nominalization" (35). He also argues, as opposed to Swedenburg, that groups such as 2 Live Crew operate as independents within an otherwise Wall Street–controlled economic system, and part of the media furor surrounding Gangsta Rap is a result of young African American males' "success, inventiveness, and basic black entrepreneurship . . . that locates Tone-Loc and 2 Live Crew successfully outside the law, challenging Wall Street dominance and prime-time American media to a public showdown" (53). Although Baker does not posit a simple binary between Wall Street and rap—claiming that while Gangsta Rap's antagonistic success is remarkable, it may not be commendable—both his and Swedenburg's approaches leave many questions unanswered. What role does Gangsta Rap play in struggles over notions of black identity? What are the relationships between the culture industry and Gangsta Rap? Does Gangsta Rap play any function within the media's own attempt to hyperbolize fear about crime? And finally, what about the many white fans of Gangsta Rap; what is their investment in it? From what in this form do they derive pleasure?

The first question that must be answered, however, is what is at stake within Gangsta Rap's appropriation of the crime-gang discourse of the media and the Right. We can begin to answer this question by referring to Foucault's analysis of delinquency in *Discipline and Punish*. In his study of the genealogy of the prison, Foucault argues that the prison arose as a technique for the coercion of individuals, a way to produce habits and behaviors in the body itself. Foucault argues that prison is not intended to eliminate offenses but to distinguish them, to distribute them, to use them; it is not so much that prison renders docile those who transgress the law, but that it assimilates the transgression of the law in a general tactic of subjection. This distinction helps to explain why prisons are so singularly unsuccessful in their avowed purpose, for reform is not the point; prisoners exist to be appropriated within a technology of discipline in an effort to gain further control of society. Foucault argues that prisons exist, therefore, to foster delinquency, to create an underclass which then serves to deflect criticism from the illegalities of the dominant class. Delinquency is a localized criminality, centering around the lower classes, to help keep them in line. However, this strategic use of delinquency is not universally successful; it is a tactic, not a guaranteed formula, and it has been successfully resisted. Separating delinquency from the lower classes, from which delinquents arise, is vital if delinquency is to be used to divert attention away from the dominant classes. Delinquents must be constructed as both alien and omnipresent, "close by, everywhere present and everywhere to be feared" (286), a contradiction that sometimes breaks down, thereby locating delinquency not with criminals but with lower classes in general. For some groups, delinquents clearly are not a dangerous other, but are instead most demonstrably themselves, something demonstrated most clearly by the Rodney King–inspired riots in Los Angeles.

Foucault helps us see how Gangsta Rap "subverts the signification of difference through strategies that operate 'in and against' the same symbolic codes that had once circumscribed their subjection and oppression" (Mercer 430), a notion of appropriation so overt in Gangsta Rap that Ice Cube named his pre-N.W.A group CIA. Gangsta Rap appropriates a racist discourse—blacks are criminals—and re-articulates it as a local struggle for power, a struggle in which blacks' subjugation has placed them all the more in command, because they have so little to lose:

> Here's a little something 'bout a nigger like me
> Never shoulda been let out the penitentiary . . .
> . . . Since I was a youth, I smoked reed out
> Now I'm the motherfucker that you read about
> Taking a life or two that's what the hell I do
> You don't like how I'm livin' well fuck you.
> (N.W.A, "Gangsta, Gangsta")

Gangsta Rap appropriates notions of criminality and delinquency for black identity. Within Gangsta Rap, delinquency appears as a necessary and positive result of society; it is articulated not as a fantasy, but as a real response to a lack of power. And delinquency is all the more potent a metaphor for power because of the discursive reversibility within its construction; it is used both against and by oppressed groups. This potential for reversibility emerges not simply in the struggle over delinquency between the media and Gangsta Rap, but in Gangsta Rap itself, which talks far more about killing other blacks than "fighting the power." Gangsta Rap does what it says; it demands immediate gratification from all the politicians and lawmakers who seemingly never do what they say, or never give back to the community. In essence, it is about local struggles for power and validation in urban environments: avoiding, or killing, police and driving around looking for "bitches and hoes" are its main topics. Gangsta Rap is about "takin' what's yours" pure and simple, without regard for consequences, just for your own pleasure and feeling of empowerment.

However, this discourse of delinquency does not exist in a vacuum; it also exists within the culture industry as a whole, as well as within media and political discourses of race and criminality. First, delinquency is not an identity with which all African Americans wish to align themselves. One of the fascinating differences between the *Newsweek* cover stories of 1990 and 1993 is the comparatively "evenhandedness" of the latter. The racist comparison of Gangsta Rap to "sudden footsteps in the dark" and conservative columnist George Will's argument that high-minded, anticensorship liberals are being used by corporations with "the morals of the marketplace" (Adler 57) gave way to "No matter how successful they become, [rappers] feel justifiably threatened by the dangers of the poorest communities in Black America . . . the real problems are outside the music, not within" (Leland 64). This change may well be a result of certain African American leaders' attempts to engage with the discourses of criminality and their racist connotations. Jesse Jackson, for one, has taken an explicit stand against crime, calling it "the new frontier of the civil-rights struggle" (Morganthau 66). Academic writers have also taken this stance; for instance, both Swedenburg and Baker argue that criminality hurts the oppressed far more than the oppressor. Gangsta Rap's narratives of black-on-black crime are often used to support such an argument:

> AK 47 is the tool
> Don't make me act a motherfucking fool
> Me and you can go toe to toe no maybe
> I'm knocking niggers out the box daily
> Yo weekly, monthly and yearly
> Until those dumb motherfuckers see clearly
> That I'm down with a capital C.P.T.
> Boyee you can't fuck with me.
> (N.W.A, "Straight Outta Compton")

One could write about Gangsta Rap in terms of a local resistance informed by delinquency and pleasure, a notion of resistance that proves problematic for leaders such as Jackson who are thinking at a more macrolevel about racism and oppression. However, what we find in Gangsta Rap is a discourse fought within the African American community itself, a struggle occurring at several levels simultaneously over the meanings of rap and African American culture, and by extension, racial and sexual identities. I would like to take a look at two examples of this struggle in terms of first the political efficacy of Gangsta Rap and then the genre's avowed misogyny.

Interestingly, among the many groups vying to define Gangsta Rap are those who hold to a more assimilationist politics and those who are more radically against a white-controlled society. Gangsta Rap problematically speaks to both sides of the struggle for identity and political change and of the debate over what position African Americans should take against racism; it is not simply or easily aligned with one side or the other. For instance, Jesse Jackson derides it for promoting a gang culture of violence within black communities, while Eugenia Harris, a thirteen-year-old rap fan from Chicago's West Side, interprets Snoop Doggy Dogg's Gangsta Rap as follows: "He's saying you gotta take what's yours. If you want to get out of the projects, which always there are people trying to keep you in, he's saying you gotta take that chance" (qtd. in Leland 62). Both Jackson's and Harris' interpretations of Gangsta Rap acknowledge its ability to lead you out of the ghetto; they simply disagree about the end of such a journey—the morgue or the mansion on the hill—and, thus, about the need for radical positions to enact radical change. Harris implies that violence might be one way out of the ghetto, since it is a form of violence which keeps you there, an analysis Jackson would, of course, condemn.

This struggle over racial politics is played out among more overtly political rappers as well. For instance, some rappers have joined the Nation of Islam despite an uneasy relationship with the organization, particularly its anti-Semitic rhetoric. Public Enemy was widely accused of anti-Semitism after Nation of Islam and PE member Professor Griff said "Jews are responsible for the majority of wickedness around the world" (qtd. in Smith 102) in a newspaper interview. Public Enemy's song about the incident, "Welcome to the Terrordome," contained these often-quoted lines:

> Crucifixion ain't no fiction
> So-called chosen, frozen
> Apology made to whoever pleases
> Still they got me like Jesus.

These lyrics, clearly referring to the idea that Jews crucified Jesus, were quoted all over the media and used by religious groups to confirm Public Enemy leader Chuck D's anti-Semitism. However, the next lines are equally important for discussions of racism and anti-Semitism, even though they were ignored:

> I rather sing, bring, think, reminisce
> 'Bout a brother while I'm in sync
> Every brother ain't a brother cause a color
> Just as well could be undercover
> Backstabbed, grabbed a flag
> From the back of the lab

Told a Rab get off the rag
Sad to say I got sold down the river
Still some quiver when I deliver
("Welcome to the Terrordome")

In this context, the former lines become not quite as clear cut as
before. The "So-called chosen" becomes not just a reference to
Jews, although that element is certainly still there, but also to
blacks and the idea that an experience with racism automatically
leads to an effective politics, for "Every brother ain't a brother
cause a color." At moments like this, Public Enemy leaves essentialist notions of race behind (another example appears in the "Fear
of a Black Planet" lines "What is pure? Who is pure? / Is it European state of being, I'm not sure"), not to question the oppression
of blacks, but rather to point out that neither race nor oppression
automatically leads to a transparent identity with a self-evident
politics. Public Enemy is a case in point, as its apparent anti-
Semitism coexists with its criticisms of racism, prejudice, and essentialism. PE is the clearest, but far from the sole, example of how
rap engages with the struggle over notions of black identity and
political efficacy.

Valorizing Public Enemy is easy to do from the perspective
of leftist white male intellectuals, a group to which I belong. PE
makes so many of the right political moves—demanding that we
"Fight the Power," claiming, and coming close to proving, that its
revolutionary discourse is "Louder than a Bomb"—that it is perhaps too easy to overlook political views that may not be so constructive. Gangsta Rap, however, is a different matter because its
sexist, consumerist, and violent politics are difficult to defend.
Gangsta Rap—which, as a genre, garnered far more popular success than Public Enemy ever did—must be investigated as it inter-
sects and engages an entire series of discourses around race, ethnicity, gender, and sexuality; yet most discussions of Gangsta Rap
revolve around whether to defend or criticize its politics. While
this consideration remains vitally necessary, it is equally true that
cultural studies must avoid simplistic binary understandings of regressive vs. progressive or resistance vs. co-option in favor of a nu-
anced approach that analyzes all of the cultural and political aspects of the phenomena. Gangsta Rap exists within a capitalist,

racist society that condemns it for inciting other blacks to turn to crime and sexism but simultaneously promotes it as a successful money-producing musical genre and as a response to the society's racism. Simple notions of progressive or regressive thus become necessarily inflected and complex when investigating the case of Gangsta Rap.

Gangsta Rap has come under enormous criticism for its depiction and treatment of women, which is perhaps best exemplified by N.W.A's "Gangsta, Gangsta," in which at one point a large chorus of women yell, "We want to fuck you Eazy," and N.W.A member Eazy-E cries, "I want to fuck you too." Gangsta Rap's lyrics and videos are filled with images of women as bitches, hoes, and skeezers (golddiggers). Dr. Dre's recent hit "Let Me Ride" was on one level a song against black-on-black violence, in favor of "chillin' in L.A.;" yet on another level the video's representation of chillin' involved Dre driving around the city picking up and dumping several women as prostitutes.[2] Gangsta Rap artists are not the only rappers accused of sexism; 2 Live Crew, LL Cool J, Public Enemy, and many others have been labeled with the charge. In fact, rap is often viewed as a dominant force in the subordination of women; for instance, C. Delores Tucker, chair of the National Political Congress of Black Women, argues that most rap is misogynist and should therefore be given an "X" rating to prevent its sale to children under eighteen (George 76). Yet rap does at times question its often admittedly misogynist content. Many female rap artists address this issue in their own ways. As Tricia Rose argues in "Never Trust a Big Butt and a Smile," Salt 'N Pepa tries to pose an alternative to the "skeezer" stereotype through its representations of sexual but independent women (114). It sometimes even turns the tables on male rappers, as in the video for "Shoop" in which Salt, Pepa, and Spinderella lie on a beach watching scores of scantily clad men while discussing their bodies in detail. Some female rappers also deal overtly with male hegemony in the rap world; Queen Latifah's "U.N.I.T.Y." is an example:

> Instinct leads me to another flow
> Every time I hear a brother call a girl a bitch or a hoe
> Trying to make a sister feel low
> You know all of that's gotta go
> (Queen Latifah, "U.N.I.T.Y.")

Fans engage in this dialogue about gender identity as well. Sixteen-year-old rap fan Erica Brown maintains that "they [Gangsta Rappers] talk like that to look hard. They don't actually treat people that way. . . . Most girls won't let them" (qtd. in Adler 64). She views Gangsta Rap's representations of women as simply a way to gain the street credibility necessary to become a success. Even rap's evident heterosexism has, slowly, begun to be questioned: Ice-T has argued in "Straight Up Nigga" that queerness is a valid sexuality, while De La Soul and others have constructed queer or bisexual identities in their music. However, as filmmakers such as Marlon Riggs and Isaac Julien have shown, heterosexism remains prevalent among both blacks and whites, and is rampant within black culture in general; rap is no different, and its views on heterosexism seem too monolithic as yet to be characterized as a struggle.

The conflict over black identity is not limited to the lyrics and images of rap. In "Why is it? (Funk dat!)" rapper Sagat asks the question, "Why is it that when I walk into a bank, the tellers look at me like I'm the one that robbed them. . . . Funk dat!" Funk, as an oppositional cultural force, is taken as one answer to what bell hooks calls "the way in which whiteness acts to terrorize" through unspoken accusations (346). Hip-hop music itself is related to black identity and oppositional culture. The most overt example of this connection is rap's sampling of other songs. Sampling has its roots in the origins of hip-hop, as DJs moved with lightening speed from record to record, using bits and pieces of other music in assembling their own mix. Older forms of black music are, of course, a gold mine for this, as rap asserts the importance, if not the primacy, of the African American musical tradition. Two of the most frequently sampled artists are James Brown and George Clinton, both innovators often omitted from white histories of rock. In sampling such music, rap artists situate themselves within an often marginalized cultural history and, by valorizing that history, affirm notions of black identity as part of a cultural and historical continuum. One of the most recent phenomena in rap is the use of jazz by groups such as Us3; the mining of the black cultural heritage, the valorizing and updating of black cultural forms, are far from exhausted. Hip-hop also samples white artists, even those most associated with white rock, such as Led Zeppelin. Ted Swedenburg writes that "by placing instantly recognizable rock riffs in the context of black music, rap artists 'reinvest' them as black. They thereby assert African-Americans' familiarity with, and claim to, the segregated rock heritage, while proclaiming the largely unacknowledged debt of that heritage to the work of black musicians" (55). This use of sampling is sometimes ironic in its recontextualization of rock, but it can also be an appreciative melding of different forms, recycling the best riffs of rock for the benefit of both rock and rap.

Lyrics are not the only element of rap that takes part in the construction of identity. One of the standard elements of hip-hop is a deep, imposing, aggressive bass—a bass that can be heard in cars for blocks around. Hip-hop's extremely low and loud bass comes from its roots in dance music and reggae; however, the beat does not take on the same meaning in each of these genres. Although the "rap" might seem the most recognizable element of rap music, the bass is what turns your head when a car drives by; it is often used—and parodied in such films as *Do the Right Thing*—as an attention-getting device, drawing gazes, as well as more than one angry look, to the one who "brings the noise." The angry looks are, of course, part of the attraction of the rap aesthetic, working clearly to separate the listener from the aggrieved rap-hater. Additionally, hip-hop's immediately recognizable sound, a sound driven by the bass, works to reveal one's allegiance to a particular group, as well as, at some level, to rap and its notions of racial identity in general. The music therefore marks an assertion of individuality as well as group identity, becoming a way to deal with one's disenfranchised status on both a personal and political level. As hip-hop has developed, some artists have tried to make this relationship between music and identity explicit. We can see this effort most clearly in the use of digital technology to create increasingly dense musical textures. The most critically and commercially successful rap groups to emphasize the creation of a distinctive sound is Public Enemy, whose Bomb Squad production team uses digital technology to produce a musical landscape of panic and apocalypse. *It Takes a Nation of Millions to Hold Us Back* (1988) opens with siren sounds and a voice screaming over a loudspeaker, "The revolution is in effect"; this is merely the beginning of an incredibly complex montage of musical and nonmusical elements, which is explored further in *Fear of a Black Planet* (1990). Besides this use of music to create a "setting" or mise-en-scène, PE's mixing and recontextualization of quotes from both black leaders and racist whites throughout their music places the group in overt dialogue with African American history and identity. On the other hand, Gangsta Rap often tries to create an environment of street violence through its musical textures. N.W.A's *Straight Outta Compton* is a canonical instance of this, as sirens, gunfire, screams, and even little scenes of black-on-black, black-on-white, or police violence are added to the mix. Their "F... tha Police" (clearly articulated as fuck) contains mini-scenes of the group's different rappers (Ice Cube, Eazy-E) bragging about their badness, then getting arrested. Both Public Enemy and N.W.A's use of found quotes and sounds is a way to reinvest these forms with new meanings, what Tricia Rose calls the "art of signifying" (113), while still maintaining a link to black history, culture, and everyday life.

Rap and the Culture Industry

Rap and its fans, therefore, are engaged in a discursive struggle over competing notions of gender and racial identity; discursive, yet intimately related to real oppression. But how is the culture industry invested in this struggle? Why are multinational corporations involved in circulating these discourses, some of which are explicitly anti-white and pro-crime? The culture industry is just as committed to circulating these discourses and struggling over their meanings as are the artists and the fans. Again, the issue is not simply that the culture industry tries to seize and control the meanings of certain forms of rap (although this happens, for instance, in music magazines and mainstream news articles on music and violence). Nor is it simply the case with rap that audiences find it necessary to create their own meanings against those fostered by the culture industry (although again, it is clear that this happens, and research on rap fans would prove illuminating in this regard). What is intriguing about rap is that it is the culture industry's main strategy for bringing economically and culturally marginalized blacks into the consumer society. To this end, it is necessary that contemporary notions of black identity must be engaged by the culture industry itself. It's no longer enough to show George Jefferson livin' large uptown; what must be dealt with are issues important to black identity today, such as Afrocentrism, street culture, racism, drugs, black cultural history, and gender politics.

In terms of Gangsta Rap's status within the culture industry, we need to consider authenticity and black urban street culture, both of which are issues vital to rap as a whole and Gangsta Rap in particular. They are important, in fact, that Vanilla Ice had to create a street identity where he "claimed to have spent a great deal of time with 'brothers' in the 'hood, who taught him to rap"; interviews with Gangsta Rappers also commonly investigate the street credibility of the rapper (Swedenburg 61). There is perhaps no better example than Snoop Doggy Dogg's arraignment for murder in the same month (December 1993) that his debut record reached number one; this coincidence effectively demonstrates the idea that rap artists are living their music, a crucial factor in their commercial and critical appeal. Besides adding validity to their expressions of delinquency, street credibility also serves to sell rap and whatever else rap is used to sell. As I have noted, rap has become an almost ubiquitous cultural phenomenon, used in commercials for McDonald's, Burger King, beer, sneakers, N.B.A. basketball, and soft drinks (rap star Young M. C., author of "Wild Thing," was a pitchman for Pepsi). Sesame Street uses rap to teach the alphabet to its viewers. The rap magazine *The Source: The Magazine of Hip-Hop Music, Culture & Politics* screams "24 NEW SNEAKERS YOU MUST OWN" on its front cover. Rap, simply, is used to sell products, particularly to groups traditionally left out of, and thus seemingly immune to, capitalism: angry young dispossessed blacks. Of course, blacks are not the only group targeted; toughness, coolness, and authenticity sell with many youths. Brian Massumi puts it bluntly: "'Culture' . . . is a source of capital. Even those in the 'underclass' are 'productive workers' to the extent that they invent new styles that are commodified with lightning speed for 'cross-over' audiences" (16). Rap's existence within and use by the culture industry is not merely an example of microlevel, everyday resistance vs. macrolevel, societal subjection, nor a simple matter of co-option. Instead, rap's expressions of delinquency or Afrocentrism are coextensive with its consumerist use value, and Gangsta Rap, as the most credible, street-level form of rap, is the guarantor of rap's authenticity, and thus of its usefulness to the culture industry. Lawrence Grossberg has argued that rock music throughout its history has based itself on a binary between inauthentic, establishment culture, and authentic rock, which "depends on its ability to articulate private but common desires, feelings and experiences into a shared public language" (207). Gangsta Rap, its groups and listeners coming from what Reagan called "black 'holes' of urban blight" (Baker 89), exists at the moment as the ultimate expression of African American rage, a discourse that becomes a part of this shared public language, giving rap the authenticity needed for whatever purpose: speaking to and for marginalized groups, making money for talented artists and their record companies, and selling sneakers.

At an economic level, Gangsta Rap shows how pervasive the culture industry is today, how it works on a variety of levels. Public Enemy's brand of black power is released by Columbia records and owned by Sony. Until 1995, the Death Row/Interscope record label of Ice Cube, Dr. Dre, and Snoop Doggy Dogg was partly owned by Warner Brother records, a subsidiary of Time Warner. Ironically, Time Warner also releases *Time* magazine, which occasionally sells copies by feeding the United States' crime paranoia with stories on black violence and rap. In 1995, Time Warner gave up its stake in Death Row/Interscope because of political pressure from the Right, headed by Senate Majority Leader Bob Dole. Despite its apparent cave-in to political pressure, the multinational maintained a distribution deal with some of Interscope's more successful artists even after the two companies supposedly ended their relationship. Quite simply, the relationship between the culture industry and rap is not merely another example of an authentic culture co-opted by commerce. What is important about rap as a genre—its play with notions of black identity—is maintained within and by the culture industry. This is not to say that rap remains unchanged by its evolution from a street culture into a mainstream cultural force, yet the tie to street culture remains and is, in fact, crucial to the culture industry.

"All snakes ain't poisonous, but they all snakes": White Fans and Black Culture

If rap exists as part of a struggle over black identity, what is at stake for rap's many white fans? This is not purely an academic question; it is an issue for rappers themselves, particularly Gangsta Rappers. For instance, Ice Cube's *Lethal Injection* opens with "The Shot," a mini-narrative in which a white man waits in a hospital room for Dr. Cube, in the words of The Source, "much like the way eager white fans line up at the cash register to purchase their annual hit of Ice Cube's funk-laden Black anger" (Coker 62). Instead of the expected hypodermic needle, Ice Cube pulls out a gun, crying, "You want me to blow your head off you gullible muthafucka? / And you're actually gonna pay me for it? / Brace yo' self" (Ice Cube, "The Shot"). The appeal of Gangsta Rap to whites cannot be viewed as equivalent to other white appropriations of black cultural forms; jazz, funk, rhythm and blues, and gospel do not depict anything like the murderous mise-en-scène of Gangsta Rap, nor do they articulate a form of black rage in nearly as overt a manner. The question becomes not only, "What is it about whiteness that made them want to be black?" as Kobena Mercer puts it (432), but what is it about this extreme form of black cultural expression that is attractive for whites? The practitioners of Gangsta Rap all share some confusion about their white fans. Ice Cube, a Nation of Islam member, follows the group's ideology by claiming that white people are devils, yet cannot entirely mesh this ideology with his own experiences: "All snakes ain't poisonous, but they all snakes. . . . I don't think no white person is going to come to our side to fight their people . . . [yet] if you cool with me, Black or white, I'm cool with you" (qtd. in Coker 62). This confusion is not surprising given Gangsta Rap's aggressive stance toward whites, for it is not at all obvious why Ice Cube's white fans stand in line for his music. What do white fans derive from Gangsta Rap, and are there relations between whites' and blacks' understanding of the form?

As I have written, Gangsta Rap is a site of struggle for identity among blacks; although its violence toward other blacks is condemned by political leaders such as Jesse Jackson, and its misogyny condemned or even parodied by female rappers, many writers consider Gangsta Rap an authentic expression of black rage about limited opportunities and racism, topics often dealt with overtly in rap. White fans, then, for the most part, would seem to be outside of this struggle for black identity, so at least one side of Gangsta Rap must be lost on them. And yet I don't believe this conclusion is entirely the case; in fact, certain aspects of this identity discourse successfully transgress racial boundaries. White heavy metal fans, while not entirely embracing rap, do support the "toughness" and "authenticity" of Gangsta Rap; one is reminded of MTV's Beavis and Butthead, whose positive reviews are given only to thrash metal and grunge groups, until the (admittedly rare) rap video appears, to which white fans happily groove along. Post-punk rock and heavy metal, from White Zombie to Pearl Jam, bear some similarity to Gangsta Rap in the importance they place on authenticity. After Nirvana, authenticity now requires a representation of the various forms of teen and twenties angst, as well as—particularly for heavy metal—some reference to the increasingly limited opportunities offered to America's youth of whatever ethnicity. Of course, Gangsta Rap's authenticity is based to a much greater extent on racial and economic oppression. Interestingly, by identifying with this repression, white fans are attaching themselves to a more legitimized form of rage, which they also feel but cannot easily express, or rather, cannot legitimately express, for the Left has, in the explosion of identity politics, often left marginalized whites—such as teens and the working class—out of its discourse. Of course, another form of rage-expression, one appreciated by many marginal whites, is the Rush Limbaugh–style radical right attacks on the obviously "guilty" others; unfortunately, the Left in all its guises seems to be unable to articulate political concepts as attractive as Gangsta Rap or Limbaugh. Politically effective alternatives to such discourses, alternatives that take all excluded groups—of whatever color, class, gender, sexual preference, and national origin—seriously and yet remain "fun" (something that has been crucial in the recent victories of the Right) are becoming increasingly fewer. Given this context, Gangsta Rap should perhaps be considered a positive alternative to other discourses, for at least Gangsta Rap allies one with a historically and socially marginalized group instead of with white oppressors.

Also important for understanding white fans of rap is the notion of style. According to Simon Frith, "rap is part of a shared subculture of dressing up and strutting free, of house calls and designer charms. This is the performance of identity in which the face behind the mask (all those names) is just another mask." Style is vital because it is such a marker of rap: with Run-D.M.C, the black hats, black jeans, sneakers, and gold chains; with Gangsta Rap, hooded sweatshirts, baseball caps (usually of the L. A. Raiders, L. A. Clippers, or N. Y. Knicks—choices related to the East/ West Coast arguments among rappers) or wool hats, pro–marijuana legalization shirts, gold teeth, sometimes a pick, and of course a gun or an extra large beer bottle.[3] Within rap, style becomes a marker of visual power; not only the guns and bottles, but the "uniform" of rap becomes crucial for this visual power. If every homie invests in the same style, minorities turn into (local) majorities—witness the importance of gang colors. Style, therefore, becomes an empowering, yet completely non-essentialist marker of rap, a marker intimately related to consumerism—for example, the skyrocketing of sneaker prices. And of course, there is the questionably "empowering" rhetoric of Gangsta Rap—the "bitches and hoes," the "muthafuckers" and "niggers"—which also becomes an easily copied marker of style. "Nigger" has almost returned to the level of acceptable language, at least among the "alternative" crowd; Quentin Tarantino's *Reservoir Dogs* and *True Romance,* not to mention New Black Cinema films such as *Boyz N the 'Hood,* have at the very least returned the once-banished term to the movie screen. For the most part, at least for the moment, white fans who copy these styles are limited to big cities and the club scene, but since rap's move into the mainstream shows no sign of slowing, it is possible that in five years the news media will be fearfully reporting on white urban youths who have completely adopted a form of black identity for themselves. The 1995 film *Kids* gets some mileage out of this, as the white teens in the film not only engage in casual sex and violence but do so while wearing the latest urban black styles. Now I do not wish merely to produce the antiquated argument that white fans merely appropriate the style of a black cultural form without its content, depoliticizing it in the process. Although this might have some merit (as does the argument about the culture industry's commodification and evisceration of rap), it fails to answer the question: why rap? Why appropriate a black urban cultural form with explicit ties to notions of black identity and rage against subjection?

One possible way to answer these questions would be to look at the historical and cultural construction of white identity in the United States. bell hooks has argued that this project has yet to be undertaken because in the West "whiteness" has often been taken as the norm, as the basis of identity itself, whereas "blackness" has had a long history of being constructed as the "Other" and, therefore, a long history of struggle over such a construction. Since white is the unarticulated norm, perhaps it is more difficult to grapple with what "whiteness" itself means, with white identity. hooks's incisive argument can be used to suggest how racist attitudes and representations have changed over time, but her theory has other aspects as well. Because they are the "norm," whites who have a problem with this unilaterally imposed identity simply do not have a legitimized mode of struggle available to them. Latching onto the conflict over black identity gives white fans a way to combat their otherwise normative position in society. As the norm, whiteness has no identity, being "everywhere"; other colors, other races and ethnicities, can battle over an identity against or apart from whiteness, but whiteness itself stands outside the conflict. In battling against hegemony, one way for whites to escape is to relocate themselves in relationship to the center, to marginalize themselves.

What is crucial about this relocation is also crucial about rap in general, which has become one of the front lines in the struggle over racial and sexual identity. And it is a struggle where the answers are far from clear and determined. Should Gangsta Rap be valorized for bringing African American rage into the spotlight after the Reagan era or criticized for its glorification of violence and misogyny? Should neonationalist rappers Public Enemy be congratulated for bringing a variety of racial issues to the foreground or condemned as anti-Semitic? Is Queen Latifah's brand of feminist empowerment more effective than Salt 'N Pepa's brandishing of their sexuality? What, if anything, has rap lost (or gained) in its move into the cultural mainstream? While these questions are, of course, impossible to answer definitively, they should be fought over all the more, particularly since this fight is vital for understanding race, gender, and culture today. My article therefore argues that Gangsta Rap should be both valorized and criticized, Public Enemy congratulated and reproached. There are no easy answers when struggling over what position to take against racism and sexism, no easy way to determine if Queen Latifah or Salt 'N Pepa have the more effective political voices. What is vital, however, is engaging with the struggle itself. Even though recently cultural studies has moved away from simple notions of resistance or political effectivity, we must continue to problematize and maintain these terms in order to move toward a more complex analysis of culture and society.

Notes

1. Hammer did get support from some rappers, such as Chuck D of Public Enemy, who respected his attempt to maintain ties with urban blacks by giving free shows and making contacts with local black leaders when on tour. However, in early 1996 Hammer filed for bankruptcy, claiming over ten million dollars in debt; despite the removal of "M.C." from his name and the attempt to toughen his image, Hammer was unable to shake the cries of "sell-out" that followed his enormous early success.

2. Little distinction between these terms is made in Dre's lyrics or videos.

3. Style is such a clear marker within rap that Hammer has recently changed his look from baggy-pants dancer to scowling, goateed, wool-hat-wearing Gangsta. I would also like to note that my list is undoubtedly already out of date; new rappers are constantly developing new styles in both music and dress.

Works Cited

Adler, Jerry. "The Rap Attitude." *Newsweek* 19 March 1990: 56–59.

Baker, Houston A. *Black Studies, Rap, and the Academy.* Chicago: U of Chicago P, 1993.

Coker, Cheo H. "Down for Whatever." *The Source: The Magazine of Hip-Hop Music, Culture, & Politics* 53 (1994): 60–66.

Foucault, Michel. *Discipline and Punish.* New York: Vintage, 1977.

Frith, Simon. "Art of Poise." *Village Voice* 9 April 1991: 74.

Gates, David. "Decoding Rap Music." *Newsweek* 19 March 1990: 60–63.

George, Nelson. "Rockbeat." *Village Voice.* 22 February 1994: 76.

Grossberg, Lawrence. *We Gotta Get Out of this Place: Popular Conservatism and Postmodern Culture.* New York: Routledge, 1992.

———, Cary Nelson, and Paula Treichler, eds. *Cultural Studies.* New York: Routledge, 1992.

hooks, bell. "Representing Whiteness in the Black Imagination." Grossberg, Nelson, and Treichler. 338–46.

Ice Cube. "The Shot." *Lethal Injection.* Priority Records, 1993.

Kipnis, Laura. "(Male) Desire and (Female) Disgust: Reading Hustler." Grossberg, Nelson, and Treichler 373–89.

Leland, John. "The New Frontier for Civil Rights." *Newsweek* 29 November 1993: 60–64.

Marsh, Dave. *The First Rock and Roll Confidential Report.* New York: Pantheon, 1985.

Massumi, Brian. "Everywhere You Want to Be: Introduction to Fear." *The Politics of Everyday Fear.* Ed. Massumi. Minneapolis: U of Minnesota P, 1993. 3–37.

Mercer, Kobena. " '1968': Periodizing Politics and Identity." Grossberg, Nelson, and Treichler 424–38.

Morganthau, Ivan. "Criminal Records: Gangsta Rap and the Culture of Violence." *Newsweek* 29 November 1993: 65–66.

N.W.A. "Gangsta, Gangsta." *Straight Outta Compton.* Priority Records, 1988.

———. "Straight Outta Compton." *Straight Outta Compton.* Priority Records, 1988.

Public Enemy. "Fear of a Black Planet." *Fear of a Black Planet.* Def Jam, 1990.

———. "Welcome to the Terrordome." *Fear of a Black Planet.* Def Jam, 1990.

Queen Latifah. "U.N.I.T.Y." *Black Reign.* Motown Records, 1993.

Rose, Tricia. "Never Trust a Big Butt and a Smile." *Camera Obscura* 24 (1990): 105–20.

Smith, R. J. 'The Enemy Within," *Village Voice.* 20 June 1989, 102.

Swedenburg, Ted. "Homies in the 'Hood: Rap's Commodification of Insubordination." *New Formations* Winter 1992: 53–66.

Toop, David. *The Rap Attack: African Jive to New York Hip Hop.* London: South End, 1984.

"Uplift the Race!": *Coming to America, Do the Right Thing,* and the Poetics and Politics of "Othering"

Tejumola Olaniyan

> This is how scared white people have black people [sic]. I was sitting in my office with Mike Tyson and Don King—*my* office, at Eddie Murphy Productions. The only two people that work there that are white are my managers that work for me. And we got on the subject of white people, and the government, and shit like that, and what happened is, we started whispering, "The white man. . . ." They got you so scared you whisper in your own house about that motherfucker.
>
> Now that's a helluva thing. Me, Mike Tyson, and Don King, sitting in my own office whispering about the white man. I said, "Yo, man, they have done such a thing on us that we whispering and he ain't even here." And that's just something that's in you naturally—what the fuck is up?
>
> —Eddie Murphy ("Eddie!" 36)

The efficiency of power, its constraining force have, in a sense, passed over to the other side—to the side of its surface of application. He who is subjected to a field of visibility, and who knows it, assumes responsibility for the constraints of power; he makes them play spontaneously upon himself; he inscribes

© 1996 by *Cultural Critique*. Fall 1996. 0882-4371/96/$5.00.

in himself the power relation in which he simultaneously plays both roles; he becomes the principle of his own subjection. By this very fact, the external power may throw off its physical weight; it tends to the non-corporeal; and, the more it approaches this limit, the more constant, profound and permanent are its effects: it is a perpetual victory that avoids any physical confrontation and which is always decided in advance.
—Michel Foucault (*Discipline* 202–3)

The degree of reciprocal illumination in the two epigraphs above is so obvious as to need no explication. In fact, any further attempt to gloss over their similarity would suppress the graphic agon of their correspondence. The first, Eddie Murphy on the production of racialized black subjectivity, perilously approximates the second, Foucault on the classic stage of subjection-tranformed-into-absolute-self-subjection.[1] The major subtext of Murphy's "testimonial," which has had profound implications for black modes and foci of resistance to oppression, centers on the perception that class position has little or no effect on racial subjectification. If this realization explains in large measure the nearly exclusivist racial focus of the trope of "race uplift," the dominant African American response to racial subjection since the American "age of reaction" (Andrews vii–xx), it is mute on why such a mode, "race uplift," is favored in the first place. This silence calls for closer scrutiny, and I will return to it. The most active terrain of this mode remains the *cultural*, where it is manifested largely as a campaign against "negative" symbolic representations.

In his interview with Spike Lee, Eddie Murphy expresses amazement and frustration at the negative reviews of *Coming to America* (1988) on its release. He says it was his "best" film so far: "When I did *Coming to America* I felt that was a really good movie and it got bad criticism. It was like, Well what the fuck do they want me to do, you know?" ("Eddie!" 34). Perhaps Murphy has every reason to be shocked, for *Coming to America* appears to situate itself in firm opposition to the standardized images of poverty, decay, death, and devastation that have, in the American press and imagination, come to stand for "Motherland" Africa. The Africans of *Coming to America* are wealthy and live in great opulence. "I am very black and I have a very black consciousness" (36); thus, Mur-

phy avows his commitment to "uplifting the race" through en-
nobling representations. In the interview, Spike Lee claims a similar basic goal. The title of his "production diary" for *School Daze*, we
should note, is *Uplift the Race*. Further, his reputation as a politically
engaged "race man" was well established by *Do the Right Thing*
(1989).

I return, then, to the problematic mentioned above: why is
"race uplift," as the struggle over representations, privileged as a
response to the landscape of vastly *unequal power relations* vividly
sketched out by Murphy and Foucault? I proffer two tentative sug-
gestions.

First, there is the much talked about "power of representation." "Representations are social facts"; they do not simply "reflect" existent, given "realities" but are active participants in the
construction and understanding of such realities and the very category of "reality" itself (Rabinow 234–61). In effect, Rabinow implies that the individual is *not* central to the often elaborate processes of knowing; in addition, what he/she can know is shaped by
representation that provides positions and invites, "interpellates,"
the individual to locate him/herself in these as a subject capable of
cognition and of consciousness of distinctions—distinctions between the "self" and the "non-self," the "same" and the "different."[2] To be in control of (the means of) representation is, therefore, to be in a position of *power:*[3] that is, to be in control of the
production, promotion, and circulation of subjectivities.

Second, there is the relative overvaluation of resistance at the
level of "culture" by various dominated groups in varying degrees
of subordinate relations to the hegemonic group. According to this
approach, culture, as the context and constitutive force of representations, remains the last source of defense against the subjugated group's "social consent," in Gramsci's phrase, to the subject
positions offered by the dominant group. Perhaps Foucault is right
to argue that the dominant phenomenon of this century is the
struggle against subjection, against forms of subjectivity ("The
Subject" 212–13). I must add, however, that those groups who are
both "exploited" and "dominated" are forced to occupy the thickest
theaters of this struggle and so bear its most gaping wounds.[4] The
realm of subjection, where the formative power of representation
is best dramatized, remains important as a site of contestation be-

cause it is where "the identity of individuals and groups is at stake, and where order in its broadest meaning is taking form. This is the realm in which culture and power are most closely intertwined" (Rabinow 260).[5]

While Murphy's *Coming to America* and Lee's *Do the Right Thing* may have the same aim—to "uplift the race" as the slogan goes— popular opinion (rightly, I think) often contrasts their achievements.[6] My intervention in this debate will take the form of an investigation of the films' specific poetics of "othering": the models or fragments of models of "cultural identity" they offer us to identify with and yet wield as weapons to achieve their proclaimed arduous goal of racial uplifting." First, however, we need to find a *productive* way of entering the cinematic worlds presented.

To a certain extent, every film demands that it be viewed in some ways rather than in others. It does so by a calculated selection and deployment of stylistic or thematic conventions, which, thanks to the weight of cultural tradition (simultaneously a liability and an asset), activate appropriation along intimated lines, but only to a certain point, after which indeterminacy of appropriation rules. Conditions of reception are usually active and conflict-ridden, in spite of the famed immobilizing effects of the cinematographic apparatus (Baudry 299–318).

In brief, *Coming to America* tells the story of Prince Akeem, the son of an immeasurably rich king of the African country of Zamunda who rebels against his people's tradition of arranged marriages and travels to the United States of America to find a bride. *Do the Right Thing,* on the other hand, examines the manifest animosities of a racially explosive set-up, animosities the film presents as engendered by an unequal allocation of societal perks and preferments along racial lines. Given the social context in which these films were produced and consumed—patriarchal, capitalist, consumerist, racist—I think there is a strong bond that unites them: their promise of an extraordinary, even unusual *show*—a spectacle.[7] Wealth, fame, and aristocratic heterosexual romance are some of the indispensable elements of the dominant narrative of spectacle; in addition, *Coming to America* provides the extra satisfaction created by the exotic Other, locale, and perspective. In the case of Lee's movie, antagonistic racial or ethnic confrontation readily advertises itself as spectacle, a claim that hardly needs substantiation. I am, then, approaching the films as "spectacular" constructs.

The title *Coming to America* presents us with a degree of ambiguity. It sounds very much like one of those circus show ads, "Coming to Charlottesville"—a reading that is, indeed, relevant to my interest in both the title's exhibitionist form and promise of exhibition. However, the ambiguity is even more fundamental. If the title suggests a particular point of view, then this point of view has no space, no location in the film: an African prince from *Zamunda* travels to the United States in search of a bride, only to return later with her. Because the film generally assumes Akeem's point of view, his position could best be described as "Going to America." As long as the enunciative, inscribed space is extra-diegetic, it is a transcendental space, and the voice is that of the ruler of that space, God Himself. But to be extra-diegetic and transcendental is not to lack a specific, nameable space. After all, although Moses could not see or physically locate God while receiving the Decalogue, he knows His voice is located somewhere—heaven. "Coming to America," then, is inscribed from a position in America; that is, Akeem the rich African prince is coming *here to America* to find a bride. And as long as the film shows no one in America with any calculated investment in Akeem's coming, America becomes an *invisible* space, transcendental, the space of God. Perhaps the movie's transformation is accurate as the cliché in many parts of the world about America being "God's own country."

However, the ambiguity persists. As the movie begins and credits come up, we see a high-angled long shot moving over a dense jungle toward a breath taking white mansion—isolated deep in the forest—where we soon discover Akeem in all his spectacular, palatial splendor. Even as the screen says *COMING* TO AMERICA (my emphasis), the long shot is *going* deeper into the bush of Zamundan Africa. It is interesting that the shot capturing all this is a *long shot:* the authorita(rian)tive vision of the omniscient eye of Big Brother. Is it surprising, then, that the name for this kind of shot in filmmaking is the "establish(ment)ing" shot? But where is this shot coming from? From whose point of view? Whose gaze? The gaze, I have argued, is that of the United States. In view of what this gaze later performs, I suggest that we see the dominant gaze of *Coming to America* as the classical anthropological gaze par excellence.

And what does the classical anthropological gaze do? It appropriates and ahistorically *fixes* (photographers know this process best) the native Other, denies it "coevalness," and freezes it ready for exhibition "at home," in the Western metropole.[8] This process implies, although rarely acknowledges, the hierarchized power relations enabling its condition. *Difference* has its rough, untamable edges chiseled off and is thus modified to fit held opinions and "scientific" generalizations theorized a priori,[9] the scandal against which some self-conscious practitioners have proclaimed a "local knowledge," albeit with their own myopic results (Geertz, *Local* 243–76). The film *Coming to America* and what Jonathan Friedman describes as a central occupation of anthropology involve the ahistorical conception and "spectacularization" of Otherness (161–70). Interestingly, the movie performs these with equal vigor in both locales of the film, Zamunda and the United States. It succeeds in doing so through its strategic implementation of the Hollywood "star" system and subsequent problematizing of our understanding of the relationship between *fact* and *fiction*. As viewers, we know Eddie Murphy is an African American movie star playing an African prince, the native Other, with the weight of the Hollywood as an institution behind him. And when he becomes the fictive Akeem the African, who comes/goes to America, the film serves to privilege the vision of Eddie Murphy as Akeem. As a result, we see our country and its "natives"—black, white, and others—through the character's eyes, and for the most part the same mode of gazing occurs: ahistorical, shallow, exhibitionist. Critical scrutiny of a few sequences of the film bear this out.

Coming to America simply refuses to ascend beyond the level of inanity and cliché. According to Hollywood history, the opening of the film in deep and perhaps tropical jungle, complete with roaming elephants and zebras, signals a familiar theme of the threatening Other, usually the African (Shohat 41–70). We need only recall *Heart of Darkness, Tarzan of the Apes, King Solomon's Mines, Zulu, Out of Africa,* even *The Color Purple,* and so on. However, there is a significant difference; many of these films depict brute savages, primitives without "culture" who possess only "barbaric customs." In

Coming to America, though, the African natives have a "culture" that is highly "civilized," as defined by Hollywood's fantasy managers. The components of this "civilization" make a veritable paean to royalism: a mighty palace; a retinue of attendants, including musicians; a bevy of women to quench the most prurient royal thirst (Akeem in the bath pool with naked female attendants), to be used and discarded like undergarments (Akeem does not mind that a woman was trained all her life to be a subservient, self-effacing wife to him, he only minds that she is not assertive!); and the richly plastered walls of mirrors, which is indeed fitting, for the aristocratic occupants live largely in their own imaginations. In essence, the narcissistic notion of a "full" and "completely enjoyable" life that "... oney can buy" prevails. But is there any difference between the two "paradigmatic" representations—that of the uncultured primitive and that of the capitalistic savage? Are these not the familiar extremes framing the narrow space in which the native Other has long been cast, between the Hobbesian savage brute and the Rousseauian noble savage? The difference between the "bad" and "good" "nigger" is the difference between six and a half dozen, and the engine of their construction in discourse is fueled by equally ahistorical notions.

Significantly, what foments the crisis in the film involves the constructed oppositions of bad and good, tradition and change/modernity/Westernization. Akeem challenges a tradition of arranged marriages overdue for change, but since his culture appears incapable of autocritique or internally induced change and is sustained only by the spectacle of wealth and mindless ostentation, the challenge can only be realized through the omnipotent force of America. Excitedly, Akeem rhapsodizes on his arrival in Queens, New York: "Here is real life, a thing we've been denied for far too long!" There is a self-deprecating irony here that borrows from chauvinistic aspects of the discourse of American liberal democracy: the "free" ghetto, Queens, is more liberating than the opulent but "stifling" Zamunda palace.

Since Zamundan people are portrayed as prisoners of "tradition," of an organic, *Gemeinschaften* culture in the unyielding grip of a tyrannical and unquestionable *Wesenwille*, it is not surprising that they are all represented as puppets and obeying zombies, even those "lucky" to come/go to school in America. They live their lives as predictably and faithfully as the natives *captured* in the tomes of many of our famous and not-so-famous anthropologists do.

Perhaps this picture is too bleak. Let us concede that Zamundan African culture is really not that dead but can sometimes be self-critical. In such moments, however, there is usually a recuperation of the concession: the catalyst of the culture's self-critique, exemplified by Akeem and his "questioning" of tradition, routinely comes from the ruling class, the preferred "noble savages," the very retainers of the crippling tradition. Within the aristocratic world, which the film unconscionably celebrates, those men and women who do the real labor and (un)willingly finance royalty can only be invisible or figure as mindless servants, always complying.

In addition, women figure as something else: the indispensable pivot of the plot and the spectacular gaze. Akeem's "want [is] a woman who is going to arouse my intellect as well as my loins." As the film clearly shows, there are beautiful women in Zamunda who are willing to even "[b]ark like a dog" and scrub/bathe Akeem's "royal penis." But they apparently appeal only to the prince's loins. In the context of this "atrophied" culture, the "radicalism" of Akeem's request can only be grasped from Semmi's despairing question: "Where [on earth?] will you find such a woman [. . .] a woman with grace, elegance, taste, and culture?" Of course, nowhere near Zamundan Africa. The Zamundan women are merely bearers of a frozen culture locked in and unable to win the war between "The Indigenous Way of Life" (such as unquestioning obedience to elders or to tradition, implied by King Joffer's statement, "[We have gone to] a great deal of trouble to select for you a very fine wife. Since the day she was born, she was taught to walk and speak and think as a Queen"; and by Yemani the prospective bride, "Ever since I was born, I have been trained to serve you") and "The Spirit of the Age" (such as self-assertion, displayed by Akeem's questioning of tradition, "Why can a man not pick his own wife?").[10] Akeem finally finds a woman in America who satisfies both his intellect and his loins.[11] But there is no cause to congratulate American women, for though they may be smarter and more assertive than their docile Zamundan sisters, they, as women, serve the same function in Akeem's "bodyscape," operating between the two and a half feet between his head and his loins, where they can only play the determined role of objects of spectacle and erotic gratification. From Yemani the servile bride and the naked bath-room attendants in Zamunda, to the New York nightclub "show" of black women with a myriad of obsessions, and back to the wedding pageant in Zamunda at the end, what we have is not change but rather more of the same. In considering the issue of gender, I find Laura Mulvey's views on how the unconscious of patriarchal society structures the form of conventional film very relevant:

> In a world ordered by sexual imbalance, pleasure in looking has been split between active/male and passive/female. The determining male gaze projects its fantasy onto the female figure, which is styled accordingly. In their traditional exhibitionist role women are simultaneously looked at and displayed, with their appearance coded for strong visual and erotic impact so that they can be said to connote *to-be-looked at-ness*. Woman displayed as sexual object is the *leitmotif* of erotic spectacle: from pin-ups to strip-tease, from Ziegfeld to Busby Berkeley, she holds the look, and plays to and signifies male desire. Mainstream film neatly combined spectacle and narrative. (19)[12]

I am positioning Spike Lee's *Do the Right Thing* against *Coming to America*'s self-deprecating (to the extent that the "noble savage" theme it deploys against a pervasive representation of Africa as brutish and poverty-ridden is still a racist discourse), vulgarly sexist, and aristocratic deployment of spectacle. To be sure, the former does not abolish spectacle—this, in fact, is impossible, given the fact that art, as textualization, as representation, is inherently linked to the regime of the spectacle. Nor does it join the harmless, easily recuperable genre of the "spectacular critique of the spectacle" (Debord par. 196). What *Do the Right Thing* does is rethink the economy and constitute a new politics of the spectacle, somewhat akin to Bertolt Brecht's "non-illusionistic" theater, which, of course, does not abolish illusion but displaces and reconceptualizes it.

Coming to America, on the other hand, arrests its "subject"— Zamundan African culture—in a one-dimensional frame and lifts it out of its material and historical contexts of production and apprehension. The result is a neatly packaged product ready for consumption in the metropole.[13] Difference, which is at the center of the economy of the spectacle, is, in its dominant deployment, simply valorized and exhibited, relativized and ignored, or denied and repressed. Rarely is it conceived as a category to apprehend relationally *and* critically. The reason for this trend is that understanding difference relationally and critically could potentially turn a gaze back on itself, interrogating its position and history and relations with the object (Friedman 168). In *Coming to America*, difference is merely valorized and exhibited. In *Do the Right Thing*, on the other hand, a relational understanding of difference directs its bold and risky mode of deployment of spectacle.

Tina's dance sequence that opens Lee's film promises eroticism and entices the voyeur, but it is defamiliarized by being "distastefully" executed. The object of the gaze appears *too* "muscular" and aggressive (perhaps tolerable under certain sadomasochistic conditions), prancing agilely and energetically throwing professionally gloved punches that fiercely and unmistakably warn "back off!" For this brief sequence in the film, the soundtrack serves a complementary function, propelling the earnest, high-decibel, unnerving rhythm of Public Enemy's "Fight the Power" rap. The object simultaneously tantalizes and threatens, invites and repels, and therefore is of neither extreme.[14] As the identity of the object is problematized, the voyeuristic gaze is disoriented. The spectacle liberates itself precisely as spectacle, that is, as construction, neither natural nor inevitable. We could cite countless instances of this radical subversion of spectacle, for the film's basic mode of image production seems to be governed by a "scandalousness and obtrusive theatricality" (Mitchell, "Violence" 884) that continually slips its tether. Mother Sister swears enmity against Da Mayor, but this is precisely the closure of history against which the film is fighting. History constitutes not only a burdensome structure but also an open possibility. Mother Sister has clearly recognized this point before the end of the film, as her enmity turns to friendship. These two, the local drunk and self-proclaimed mayor, and the neighborhood termagant, grow morally throughout the film, thus shedding the restrictive labels slapped on them and disappointing the dominant racialized gaze.

Turning our attention to another seemingly peripheral character we should note that Smiley is a stammerer. In an immediate urban ghetto economy whose mode of exchange is rhetorical virtuosity, to be incoherent is to be damned and invisible; it is to lack the capacity for self-representation and, therefore, to lack power. Yet the very first shot of Smiley we see, a very low angle with a "cathedral" as background, gives him a larger-than-life solidity, undercuts our "obvious" interpretation of his affliction, and tells us in clear terms to keep our objectifying "do-good" sympathies to ourselves. And by the end, we cannot say we were not warned to take nothing for granted. The burning of Sal's Pizzeria, one of the most *discussed* scenes of the film, turns out to be the handiwork of the *stutterer* Smiley. The ghetto, according to the film, is a realm of flux, not of unchanging eternal truths. Even the taciturn Radio Raheem, friend of few and enemy of most, simultaneously a product and a critique of an unrelenting commodity culture,[15] reveals his proudly unapproachable self as a mask, one he deliberately dons in response to an exclusionary order that has shut the door firmly in his face. Witness his philosophy of the unceasing dialectic between love and hate and his hope that the tragically blind dialectic may be arrested more often within the topography of love.[16] Even the obdurate parochialism of Pino cannot be attributed to genetics. He is exasperated that he has to repeatedly defend his racially Manichaean logic against assaults even from those he expects to support his views, such as his brother, Vito. As Vito appropriately censures him, "You don't know anything. You think you know but you don't. . . ." In words that effectively exemplify an effect of this general subversion of spectacle, James Wall notes: "In Lee's hands, these characters emerge not as frightening stereotypes but as fully developed, ambiguous individuals, as prone to error and as capable of meritorious conduct as *anyone*" (740, my emphasis).

However, at moments, *Do the Right Thing* appears to forget the agenda it sets for itself. The amnesia is first signaled in Lee's insistence on a *The* with capital T in the film's title. Even if this is grammatically correct, philosophically it is no more than a desire for the absolute. For harassed culture in search of liberatory options, nothing could be more self-defeating. I have used a humble, unassuming small *t* throughout this essay as a cog in the wheel of Lee's costly positivism.

The film's main action is precipitated by the cultural nationalist, Buggin Out, who insists that Sal, the pizzeria owner, add some pictures of black heroes to those on his "Wall of Fame." If Buggin

Out is an unstoppable force, Sal is an immovable object. But the truly disturbing issue here is the hero-worship that unites the two "enemies." Smiley, we should remember, hawks pictures of Martin Luther King Jr. and Malcolm X throughout the film. "We want some brothers upon the wall," Buggin Out roars; "Malcolm X, Nelson Mandela, Michael Jordan," he continues. Sal, of course, wants no such people beside his own "American Italians": Frank Sinatra, Al Pacino, Liza Minelli, Robert De Niro, Sylvester Stallone, etc. In this conflict, history becomes one vast eerie grayness lit up occasionally only by the superhuman glows of great men. This ahistorical privileging of the hero is one of the main pillars of the conservative deployment of spectacle, with its implied aristocratic interpretation of honor, dignity, and performance. We need not give up our heroes, but we need to historicize them. Always.

There is, of course, no need to ask why men dominate the "halls of fame" of *both* Sal and Buggin Out. Women, "we all know," are hardly the stuff of which "famous persons" or "history makers" are made. The productively ambiguous image of Tina that opens the film is counterbalanced by her arrest later in the familiar conventional roles of lover and mother, growling interminably on the failure of Mookie to live up to his "responsibilities" as father and lover. The idea of interracial, intergender solidarity that the opening sequence of a mutually complementary relationship between the combative female body and the militant voices of male rappers suggests disintegrates to the sinister image of a female body as a marionette controlled by unseen male voices. The exclusivist racial politics of "Fight the Power" need to be exploded by gender politics; the voice that hollers "fight the power" itself needs to be fought.[17]

What I am emphasizing here is a degree of continuity of gender representation in both films, in spite of their opposed politics on other issues. The difference is that *Do the Right Thing*, even if not deliberately, figures gender relations as a *problem*, a problem that—unlike *Coming to America*—its nonmainstream Hollywood conventions fail to hide or recuperate. Michelle Wallace has argued persuasively that, except for the brief scene where Jade successfully resists her brother Mookie's attempts to force her away from the pizzeria because he believes Sal wants to seduce her, *Do the Right Thing* artificially purifies "'racism'" of gender difference. The film's failure to consider fully the intersections of race and gender, Wallace continues, shows its narrow conception of the "material reality of representations of 'race' in American culture, which has always been profoundly entangled with the issues of gender, sexuality, and the female body" (109). Evidently, Lee's film is not one of solutions but of explorations of the very conditions of possibility of solutions.[18] For another instance, Mookie is the "race-man" deeply angered by Radio Raheem's murder, but he is also the cold and calculating apprentice capitalist who remembers to return to Sal for his pay even before Raheem was safely "six feet" in the ground. How does the peculiarly American permutation of race and class intersect with "dignity" and "pride"? Mookie would probably respond by saying that African Americans cannot afford to dream with their eyes closed, as evidenced by Ellison's "invisible man."

As tendencies toward two recognizably different propositions of cultural identity are evident in the two films, I have borrowed from the vocabulary of religion to label these *sacred* and *secular.* The sacred or divine notion of cultural identity understands culture— the entire system of signifying practices whereby a people produce, reproduce, and conceptualize themselves, their world, and the relations among these; and relations between these practices and other peoples—as an unchanging essence. It is conceived as a totality that is complete, self-sufficient, and protected from other cultures by an impenetrable curtain. As an organic entity whose constitutive elements appear glued together by *necessary* laws, culture becomes essentially univocal and homogeneous. Identity is sacred and inviolable, a "boundary to be maintained [rather than a] nexus of relations and transactions actively engaging a subject" (Clifford and Marcus 344). This superstitious model of cultural identity and difference denies culture any autosuggestion or self-critique: hegemony is umbral, and change can only occur with outside influence. Tradition is not an invention, a process of selection and rejection (Hobsbawm and Ranger), but an essence that is transhistorical.

The secular or profane model, on the other hand, insists on the historicity, that is, the "made-ness" in time and space, of culture and therefore the invented character of every identity. Far from being a given, seamless totality, culture is perceived as a complex strategic articulation of most often mutually contradictory elements.[19] These elements are necessarily negotiable because they are governed by a relation of articulation (a *historical* process of examination, discrimination, and selection from disparate choices to mold a temporally distinct identity) rather than one of inviolable organicity. Thus, neither the articulated identity nor its elements possess a natural or unchanging character. The only essence culture has is its permanent openness, in a sense, a "negative essence." Cultural identity can, thus, not be closed and positive but always fragile, vulnerable, and constituted as transition, relation, difference, contingence, dispersion. It is a *process* rather than a *product*, a "complex historical process [. . .] of appropriation, compromise, subversion, masking, invention, and revival" (Clifford and Marcus 338). Cultural identity, in this secular conception, refuses to be a stable otherness.[20]

However, in spite of the pervasive privileging of dispersion and contingence, the secular identity subjects itself to its very own logic by secularizing itself, that is, by admitting "necessity" or privileged elements. It does this, however, only situationally. It holds as essentialist illusion absolute sacredness or absolute secularity and, therefore, eschews both. Both erase the very notion of identity through their erasure of the categories of relation and imbrication with other identities. Hence, true to its character, the secular model accepts "honorary" sacredness, or *partial fixations*. This sacredness, because it is within the secular, loses its divine, ahistorical character and becomes an identifiable, historically expedient rallying point, or as Laclau and Mouffe would have it, a nodal point (112). Since the nodal point is historical and within a general regime of the contingent, it stands little risk of petrifying into an absolute. This nodal point or "necessity"—Derrida calls such structure a "necessary evil" (88)—articulates, or gives the contingent elements, a "focus" while the same elements constantly challenge and scrutinize the credentials of "necessity" to occupy the privileged nodal point.

Coming to America, in its packaging of the Other—woman, native, the lowly on the rungs of the social ladder—as passive objects of spectacle, its presentation of an Other culture as doxic and fixed, and its unabashed celebration of a patriarchal and aristocratic male gaze, largely suggests the sacred conception of cultural identity. Its sumptuous use of the long shot, designed to achieve expansive communicativeness and denotative clarity, proposes a foreclosure of thinking by urging the spectator to construct a totally univocal and coherent world of the story.[21] Its deployment of the ideologically dominant "Harlequinade" plot locates it firmly in the long tradition of the "well-made play" and popular romance—the "And They Lived Happily Ever After" world of Serenity-Disturbance-Struggle-Resolution-Serenity. The constitutive assumptions of this circularity include the necessary fixedness of identity and the unnecessariness, even impossibility, of any fundamental change. The circularity privileges the ruling norms against contestation.

There is something else to the circularity of *Coming to America*'s plot. The film's narrative is rigorously *motivated and reactive:* one action necessarily follows another; a glance is followed by a reciprocal one, as evidenced in the scene in which the king and Akeem dance a choreographed sequence prior to the entry of the Zamundan bride. Further, even while in America the Zamunda theme music soundtrack—introduced from the very opening scene—unfailingly follows the Zamunda royal crowd, the film's focus on royalty "justifies" so much pomp and pageantry. And so on. Tidy. Neat. Everything in its place. Kristin Thompson has adroitly revealed the politics of this rigorous motivation as the absorption of the viewer in a completely naturalized narrative structure, thereby identifying the narrative, a told story, not as arbitrary—which it really is since a told story could always be told differently—but as inevitable. Thus, criticism or revisioning is thereby precluded (130–42), effectively resulting in the process Carter G. Woodson once called "mis-education."

Do the Right Thing, on the other hand, proposes the secular identity. It presents itself largely as a construction, a stringing together of loosely connected *episodes,* none of which appears necessary or inevitable. This effect is achieved largely through its heightened technical devices: predominantly mobile shots, the low angles, the thinly motivated shots (even entire sequences), the Brechtian intrusive interventions of Dee Jay Love Daddy, the simmering tension generated not only by the heat—the waves of which we can literally see—but also by the *unpredictability* of events and characters. The culture here is besieged but alive. Identity is a process, constantly transforming itself. Only Italian-Americans qualify for the Wall of Fame of Sal but the film has already subverted him and his parochialism: he is neither *Italian* nor *American* but Italian-American. The space of the hyphen is not of identity but of its interrogation *of context,* of all American hyphenated identities and their relations: for Sal's socioeconomic existence is inextricably bound to the fortunes of the black community in which he has been making his livelihood for over twenty years.

Buggin Out, sharing Sal's essentialist notion of identity, hollers what the hell a *white* Clifton is doing in "*my* block, *my* neighborhood . . . *black* neighborhood." Clifton must be a pure Other, an outsider from a "white" place. Still fuming in righteous anger over his soiled sneakers, Buggin Out confidently takes solace in his fantasies and asks when Clifton would disappear back to his "Massachusetts." He is thoroughly deflated when Clifton coolly announces he was born in Brooklyn. Yet the deflation is not permanent, since the vulgar relations between race and class—in which whiteness equals upper class and access to property—that catalyze Buggin Out's ideological excess is recoded in this scene: Clifton, white, owns a property on the block. Next rung down on the social/racial ladder is the Korean owner of the neighborhood grocery store, and then blacks, who occupy the lowest rung. Thus, while Buggin Out may be condemned, his cause must be contextualized.

The film envisions articulation not only as the ruling characteristic of a lived culture but also as a mobilizing strategy. Buggin Out attempts to mobilize the residents to boycott Sal, but as he is told everywhere, his issue and its immediate premises are shallow. When another and evidently more important issue later crops up—the murder of Radio Raheem by the police—the residents practically restructure and *articulate* their differences and present a working united front against a perceived common enemy. Thus, when the Korean grocer shouts "I'm black, I'm black! Me-you, the same!"—the ramifications of which appear hazy to both himself and his auditors—he is expressing a profound truth: a secular articulatory practice as a condition of the liberation of dominated groups.

One "fictions" history on the basis of a political reality that
makes it true, one "fictions" a politics not yet in existence on
the basis of a historical truth.

—Michel Foucault ("The Subject")

The National Association for the Advancement of Colored
People (NAACP), the well-known institutional representative and
national custodian of the project of "race uplift," organizes annual
"Image Awards" during which artists who distinguished themselves through their work, in "uplifting the race" are recognized
with trophies and eloquent citations. In light of my discussion of
both *Coming to America* and *Do the Right Thing,* it is paradoxical then
that Eddie Murphy and Spike Lee have won, without much dis-
criminating judgment, awards for their efforts in both films. One
way to think through this "paradox" is to examine the NAACP's
"theory of representation" as evidenced implicitly by their practices. Particularly problematic for a dominated people and potentially problematizing in relations with the dominant group, effective and successful symbolic representation requires close attention
to *breadth* and *depth.* For the dominated, issues of breadth involve
access to resources and abundance and variety of representations,
while those of depth emphasize evaluation and discursive discern-
ment. I wish to investigate this distinction further in the following
questions: (a) is (1) the dominated group representing itself or is
(2) the dominant group representing the dominated? (b) how is (1)
the dominated group representing itself or (2) the dominant group
representing the dominated?

In the early days of the NAACP's militant opposition of "negative representations" (for its long and valiant struggle against
The Birth of a Nation, see Archer 183–224), the problems it faced
remained relatively clear-cut and mainly a.2 and b.2, the quantity
and quality of "images" of blacks produced by whites. Blacks then
had little to no access to means of theatrical or cinematic self-
representation and thus the NAACP focused its efforts on the critical examination of representations of blacks spawned by the dominant white culture. With the later "democratization" of the "image
industry" and its increased and increasing infiltration (and perfo-
ration, I should say) by blacks, the two problems, a.2 and b.2, still
remain, but the NAACP appears to have shifted its focus almost

exclusively to a.1, at the expense of even its complement, b.2. In other words, the NAACP has become concerned more with the breadth or quantity of black "self-representations" than with their quality or depth. Yet the original aim of the struggle over "negative images" is the "uplift" (a matter of depth) of the "race."

To be sure, a.1, access to and breadth of racial self-representation, is extremely important. In fact, it creates the condition of possibility of b.1, its continuous refinement through self-criticism. Besides, in a context such as that in which the NAACP operated/is operating, ruled by a system(at)ic exclusion of its constituency, a dominated group, a.1 assumes a significance of deep political proportions: hence the need to celebrate without distinction the *existence* of the two movies. Having said this, we must emphasize that it is ultimately self-defeating to ignore b.1 completely. Even as we struggle to wrest the means of self-representation, we also need to remain conscious of *how* we achieve it, of the ramifications of the kinds of dreams we encourage ourselves to dream, the types of worlds we invite ourselves to envision. Reversing insidious subjection, the type so graphically delineated by my epigraph quotations, demands nothing less.

Notes

I am grateful to the Carter G. Woodson Institute for Afro-American and African Studies, University of Virginia, for research support. The original version of this article was first presented under its auspices in the spring of 1991.

1. I am borrowing Foucault's definition of subjection, a nonviolent field of power relations he distinguishes from those characterized by visible force: exploitation and domination ("The Subject" 212–13).

2. Many of these positions appear so natural that we accept them without question (how did we come to recognize ourselves in arbitrary sounds—"James," "Susan," etc.—and even proudly claim them as our own?). Since these are artificial arrangements, nevertheless, the dubious self-congratulation of "autonomy," of "I" the independent," though enabling and reassuring, is therefore already within dependent, circumscribed limits. In other words, representation is not just a process in which the subject is constituted but also in which the subject is self-constituting. One is constituted and constituting in and through one's own subjection. Human subjectivity, Philip Rosen writes in "Text and Subject," "finds itself through a discursive universe which produces and reproduces that subjectivity and, often enough, its constitutive illusions" (156). I have also "signified" Brenkman 141–83; Miller 1–17; Althusser 127–86; Silverman 126–93; and disparate sections of Lacan.

3. The Foucauldian sense of this term, in its emphasis on representation and

subject(ion)ivity, best explains my usage here. To exercise power, Foucault says, is "to structure the possible field of action of others," to act not physically on others but on their actions; "what defines a relationship of power is that it is a mode of action which does not act directly or immediately on others. Instead it acts upon their actions" ("The Subject" 220–21).

4. Concluding his controversial reflections on the state of African American culture in 1959, Harold Cruse reasoned that since African American political and economic dominance seem far-fetched, what remains possible is a revolution in culture, a cultural rehabilitation and refurbishing, as an arsenal against the imperialist centralism of the Anglo-American norm, which he believed was crippling the African American imagination (48–67).

5. There is still a problematic that cannot be ignored. What is the bridge, if any, between edifying symbolic representations and other (more?) important terrains of struggle such as economic and "political"? In other words, will uplifting representations cure poverty and social inequality? Amilcar Cabral was one national liberation fighter and social theorist who once faced this problem. His answer was a complex "yes," for even at the height of a political and military struggle against Portuguese colonialism, he was insistent on the indispensability of all forms of cultural resistance for their *catalytic* effects on other realms—political, economic, and military—even where these were fully controlled by the colonizers (138–54).

6. Some of the more interesting reviews include those by Leavy, Wallace, hooks, Morrison, and Sharkey. For Murphy's response to his critics, see "Murphy Hits" (8). Interesting information on the making of Lee's film is available in Lee with Jones. A point could be raised that given the "constraining" effects of Hollywood as an institution vis-à-vis an "independent" production, is it worth comparing the two films? While we must not underestimate the legitimacy of this question, we must not assume that the hegemony of any institution is total either. And for leading "bankable" black stars like Eddie Murphy, the space of "resistance" could be wide. Murphy thinks otherwise ("Eddie!" 35–36, 97). I put the word resistance in scare quotes to show how less idealistic I am about its precise character, formulated out of context. The important point is to have no illusions about the the limits of the capacious jaws of hegemony but at the same time not to be paralyzed into inertia by it: to study the context of resistance carefully and not to dismiss aforehand gestures that are apparently too "feeble" or too "clearly over-determined" by the dominant. These are what I find lacking in two otherwise interesting criticisms of Spike Lee's work by hooks and Christensen (the latter a response to Mitchell's "The Violence of Public Art"; see Mitchell's sobering and illuminating counterresponse to Christensen, "Seeing *Do the Right Thing*." For a useful general introduction to Spike Lee's work, see McMillan.

7. I have fashioned Debord to my purposes.

8. As Johannes Fabian has beautifully shown, this process involves not only distancing in space, that between America and Zamunda, but also its corollary, distancing in time. Unlike America, Zamunda is still neck-deep in a past "age of tradition," and given Akeem's bizarre show at JFK airport trying to stop a taxi, Zamunda is also pre- the "age of automobile." From where then is the Concorde that brought Akeem to America? A crack in the smooth face of a denial of imbrication of histories?

9. This is an instance of the reason Trinh T. Minh-ha, in her outstanding work *Woman, Native, Other,* insists on calling Bronislaw Malinowski as the "Great Master." I cannot resist citing an example of her usually illuminating but witty and

"irreverent" commentaries (her quoted sections are from Malinowski): "The anthropologist is one of those rare creatures who devotes his time to working for the losing side. He 'has introduced law and order into what seemed chaotic and freakish. [He] has transformed for us the sensational, wild and unaccountable world of "savages" into a number of well-ordered communities governed by law, behaving and thinking according to consistent principles.' Any investigator who claims to be merely 'recording facts' thereby deludes himself, for the Great Master has said it: '*Only laws and generalizations are scientific facts*, and field work consists only and exclusively in the preparation of the chaotic reality, in subordinating it to general rules.' 'Discourse,' 'law,' 'order,' 'generalizations,' 'consistency'—what he values and looks for is, fortunately, what he always finds" (56).

10. "The Indigenous Way of Life" (essentialism) and "The Spirit of the Age" (epochalism) is the bind in which Clifford Geertz locks the postcolonial states in one of his early essays, "After the Revolution: The Fate of Nationalism in the New States." This article is not the space to fully engage Geertz's narrow and disabling formulation but it suffices to say that for the nationalists, in spite of all their parochial and self-defeating formulations, "The Indigenous Way of Life" does not preclude "The Spirit of the Age." The problem arises when an imperializing epoch, an alien dominating "spirit," is perceived in "epochalism." Geertz, like many of the nationalists themselves, refuses to foreground the history of this double bind: its location in the problematics of empire and neo-empire.

11. It is significant that the woman Akeem finds is black. It would have been extremely interesting if she had been white. But of course the squeamishness of the film is defined precisely by its deliberate refusal to rise beyond the expected and the jejune, even if only for the sake of argument. Given the violent history and tabooed nature of black-white sexual relations in this country, it ought to be a legitimate focus of the discourse of "race uplift."

12. For illuminating comments on, and useful extensions of, Mulvey's important essay, see Willeman 210–18, and de Lauretis, Ch. 3.

13. "In any case, the 'business' of anthropology is to get out the merchandise: our astonishing texts. This kind of activity truly belongs to an age of passivity, one that requires no intellectual effort on the part of the 'reader.' Anthropology is in the spectacle business, in a dead heat competition with *Rambo* and pornography to shock the customer. . . . Bali sells because it is a fine text, a spectacle of strange events. It is our sacred circus, our civilized hall of mirrors and chamber of horrors. But it is certainly not theirs. The text of Balinese society is our text. It is moreover fully edited and already interpreted: a complete package ready for immediate consumption" (Friedman 169).

14. I think this is what Houston A. Baker Jr. means when he argues that there should be "no misidentification of *Do The Right Thing*'s opening dancer with passive objects of the male gaze. She is, in fact, an androgynous and almost Amazonian representation of resistance" (170).

15. To understand Radio Raheem as a "critique," consider the usual ads for those boom boxes we see showing easy listening in a voluminous living-room complete with VCR and color TV, or on a picnic in the fields with a man, his wife, and two or three children, just the right number for the size of the latest Grand Am model parked nearby.

16. "STATIC! One hand is always fighting the other. Left Hand Hate is kicking much ass and it looks like Right Hand Love is finished. Hold up. Stop the presses! Love is coming back, yes, it's Love. Love has won. Left Hand KO'ed by Love" (Lee 191).

17. See Paulla Ebron's thoughtful reading of Public Enemy's gender politics (23–27).

18. In other words, I do not share Ed Guerrero's lamentation that at the end of the film, "relations of domination remain exactly the same, while neighborhood consciousness remains unelevated, unchanged by the night's events" (154). The film need not massage desire by showing the revolution. He attributes the failure partly to "the film's slick, color-saturated look [which] has the effect of idealizing or making nostalgic the present, rather than dramatizing any deep sense of social or political urgency" (148). From Guerrero's Olympian height, there is no way to account for the enormous debate generated by the film, a debate whose passion, intensity, and yes, noise, deny precisely Guerrero's claim of a lack of any sense of social or political urgency. And a film does not have to be faded or in black and white to do this. I will respond similarly to Wahneema Lubiano's interesting essay, "But Compared to What?" Her anxiety is that the "general deification" of Spike Lee because of his increasing financial success and sustained media attention "functions to marginalize other African American filmic possibilities—possibilities, for example, such as those offered by independent African-American women filmmakers" (256). While this anxiety is not baseless, it need not be as enervating as Lubiano makes it. This is a result, I suspect, of her overly "denotative" reading of Lee. Influence is never absolutely predictable or unidirectional, as Julie Dash, one of the leading African American women filmmakers, demonstrates in her recent more robust and suggestive assessment of Spike Lee ("Not Without" 160–62). On denotation, see Christian Metz, "Problems of Denotation in the Fiction Film," and a brief but perceptive gloss on Metz by Timothy Murray (2–4).

19. In formulating the secular "model," I have borrowed liberally from Laclau and Mouffe. See also Olaniyan.

20. For all we know, Derrida could be describing the secular principle when he puts forward the idea of a theoretical "jetty" which would be *destabilizing* and *devastating* a "jetty" that "destabilizes the conditions of the possibility of objectivity, the relationship to the object, everything that constitutes and institutes the assurance of subjectivity in the indubitable presence of the cogito, the certainty of self-consciousness, the original project, the relation to the other determined as egological intersubjectivity, the principle of reason and the system of representation associated with it and hence everything that supports a modern concept of theory as objectivity" (86).

21. See Bordwell's useful discussion of Hollywood styles (17–34).

Works Cited

Althusser, Louis. *Lenin and Philosophy and Other Essays*. Trans. Ben Brewster. New York: Monthly Review, 1971.

Andrews, William L., ed. *The American Novel in the Age of Reaction: Three Classics*. New York: Mentor, 1992.

Archer, L. C. *Black Images in the American Theatre: NAACP Protest Campaigns—Stage, Screen, Radio & Television*. Brooklyn: Pageant-Poseidon, 1973.

Baker, Houston A., Jr. "Spike Lee and the Commerce of Culture." *Black American Cinema*. Ed. Manthia Diawara. New York: Routledge, 1993. 154–76.

Baudry, J-L. "The Apparatus: Metapsychological Approaches to the Impression of Reality in the Cinema." Rosen, *Narrative* 299–318.

Bordwell, David. "Classical Hollywood Cinema: Narrational Principles and Procedures." Rosen, *Narrative* 17–34.

Brenkman, John. *Culture and Domination*. Ithaca: Cornell UP, 1987.

Cabral, Amilcar. "National Liberation and Culture." Eduardo Mondlane Memorial Lecture. Syracuse University, Syracuse, N.Y. 20 Feb. 1970. *Unity and Struggle: Speeches and Writings*. Trans. Michael Wolfers. London: Heinemann, 1980. 138–54.

Christensen, Jerome. "Spike Lee, Corporate Populist." *Critical Inquiry* 17.3 (1991): 583–95.

Clifford, James, and George E. Marcus, eds. *The Predicament of Culture: Twentieth Century Ethnography, Literature, and Art*. Cambridge: Harvard UP, 1988.

Coming to America. Dir. John Landis. Eddie Murphy Prods., 1988.

Cruse, Harold. "An Afro-American's Cultural Views." *Rebellion or Revolution?* New York: Morrow, 1968. 48–67.

de Lauretis, Teresa. *Alice Doesn't: Feminism, Semiotics, Cinema*. Bloomington: Indiana UP, 1984.

Debord, Guy. *Society of the Spectacle*. Trans. 1970. Detroit: Black & Red, 1983.

Derrida, Jacques. "Some Statements and Truisms About Neologisms, Newisms, Postisms, Parasitisms, and Other Small Seismisms." *The States of "Theory": History, Art, and Critical Discourse*. Ed. David Carrol. New York: Columbia UP, 1990. 63–94.

Do the Right Thing. Dir. Prod. Spike Lee. Co-Prod. Monty Ross, 1989.

Ebron, Paulla. "Rapping Between Men: Performing Gender." *Radical America* 23.4 (1989) 23–27.

"Eddie! An Exclusive Interview with Eddie Murphy by Spike Lee." *Spin* 6.7 (1990): 33–36, 97–98.

Fabian, Johannes. *Time and the Other: How Anthropology Makes Its Object*. New York: Columbia UP, 1983.

Foucault, Michel. *Discipline and Punish: The Birth of the Prison*. Trans. Alan Sheridan. New York: Vintage, 1979.

———. "The Subject and Power." *Michael Foucault: Beyond Structuralism and Hermeneutics*. Ed. Richard Dreyfus and Paul Rabinow. Chicago: U of Chicago P, 1983. 208–26.

Friedman, Jonathan. "Beyond Otherness or: The Spectacularization of Anthropology." *Telos* 71 (Spring 1987): 161–70.

Geertz, Clifford. "After the Revolution: The Fate of Nationalism in the New States." *The Interpretation of Cultures: Selected Essays*. New York: Basic, 1973. 234–54.

———. *Local Knowledge: Further Essays in Interpretive Anthropology*. New York: Basic, 1983.

Guerrero, Ed, ed. *Framing Blackness: The African American Image in Film*. Philadelphia: Temple UP, 1993.

Hobsbawm, Eric. and Terence Ranger, eds. *The Invention of Tradition*. Cambridge: Cambridge UP, 1983.

hooks, bell. "Counterhegemonic Art: The Right Thing." *Z Magazine* October 1989: 31–36.

Lacan, Jacques. *Ecrits: A Selection*. Trans. Alan Sheridan. New York: Norton, 1977.

Laclau, Ernesto, and Chantal Mouffe. *Hegemony and Socialist Strategy: Towards a Radical Democratic Politics*. London: Verso, 1985.

Leavy, Walter. "Eddie Murphy's Princely Role." *Ebony* July 1988: 31.

Lee, Spike, with Lisa Jones. *Do the Right Thing: A Spike Lee Joint.* New York: Fireside, 1989.

Lubiano, Wahneema. "But Compared to What?: Reading Realism, Representation, and Essentialism in *School Daze, Do the Right Thing,* and the Spike Lee Discourse." *Black American Literature Forum* 25.2 (1991): 253–82.

McMillan, Terry, et al. *Five for Five: The Films of Spike Lee.* New York: S. T. & Chang, 1991.

Metz, Christian. "Problems of Denotation in the Fiction Film." Rosen, *Narrative* 35–65.

Miller, Peter. *Domination and Power.* London: Routledge, 1987.

Minh-ha, Trinh T. *Woman, Native, Other: Writing Postcoloniality and Feminism.* Bloomington: Indiana UP, 1989.

Mitchell, W. J. T. "Seeing *Do the Right Thing*," *Critical Inquiry* 17.3 (1991): 597–608.

———. "The Violence of Public Art: *Do the Right Thing.*" *Critical Inquiry* 16.4 (1990): 880–99.

Morrison, Micah. "The World according to Spike Lee." *National Review* 4 August 1989: 24.

Mulvey, Laura. "Visual Pleasure and Narrative Cinema." *Visual and Other Pleasures.* London: Macmillan, 1989. 14–26.

"Murphy Hits Out at Black Critic's 'Coming to America' Criticism." *Variety* 3 August 1988: 8.

Murray, Timothy. *Like A Film: Ideological Fantasy on Screen, Camera and Canvas.* New York: Routledge, 1993.

"Not Without My *Daughters:* A Conversation With Julie Dash and Houston A. Baker, Jr." *Transition: An International Review* 57 (1992): 150–66.

Olaniyan, Tejumola. "African-American Critical Discourse and the Invention of Cultural Identities." *African American Review* 26.4 (1992): 533–45.

Rabinow, Paul. "Representations Are Social Facts: Modernity and Postmodernity in Anthropology." *Writing Culture: The Poetics and Politics of Ethnography.* Ed. James Clifford and George E. Marcus. Berkeley: U of California P, 1986. 234–261.

Rosen, Philip, ed. *Narrative, Apparatus, Ideology: A Film Theory Reader.* New York: Columbia UP, 1986.

———. "Text and Subject." Rosen, *Narrative* 155–71.

Sharkey, Betsy. "Knocking on Hollywood's Door: Black Filmmakers like Spike Lee Struggle to See and Be Seen." *American Film* July–August 1989: 22+.

Shohat, Ella. "Imaging Terra Incognita: The Disciplinary Gaze of Empire." *Public Culture* 3.2 (1991): 41–70.

Silverman, Kaja. *The Subject of Semiotics.* New York: Oxford UP, 1983.

Thompson, Kristin. "The Concept of Cinematic Excess." Rosen, *Narrative* 130–42.

Wall, James. "*Do the Right Thing:* A Jarring Look at Racism." *Christian Century* 16–23 August 1989: 740.

Wallace, Michelle. "Doing the Right Thing." *Invisibility Blues: From Pop to Theory.* New York: Verso, 1990. 107–10.

Willeman, Paul. "Voyeurism, The Look, and Dwoskin." Rosen, *Narrative* 210–18.

Woodson, Carter G. *The Mis-Education of the Negro.* 1933. New York: AMS Press, 1977.

History and Utopian Desire: Fredric Jameson's Dialectical Tribute to Northrop Frye

Shaobo Xie

The majestic critical system set out in Northrop Frye's *Anatomy of Criticism* appears to be pulled in two self-consciously inconsistent directions. On the one hand, the archetypal critical project announced in the *Anatomy* raises literary creation and criticism to the level of symbolic meditation on human community as a whole. "Archetypal criticism is," Frye declares, "primarily concerned with literature as a social fact and as a mode of communication" (99). Poetry has the social function of expressing "a vision of the goal of work and the forms of desire" (106). From this view, criticism is supposed to chart a certain relationship between literary phenomena and historical life. On the other hand, the historical perspective the *Anatomy* promises is reprivatized in the anagogic moment. The collective content of utopian desire is ultimately internalized and individualized in an ecstatic celebration of unconditioned libidinal freedom. The anagogic view of criticism conceives of literature "as existing in its own universe, no longer a commentary on life or reality, but containing life or reality in a system of verbal relationships" (122). This is the moment when history appears to

© 1996 by *Cultural Critique*. Fall 1996. 0882-4371/96/$5.00.

be completely erased, a moment when the boundary between culture and nature disappears as well.

The inconsistency of Frye's conception of literature can perhaps be traced to a tension between his notion of utopian desire and his model of history as demonic decline. In the first essays in the *Anatomy*, "Theory of Modes" and "Theory of Symbols," he proposes two opposite movements in literature: a displacement of the mythical hero through five historical periods and a mythopoeic imagination. The first movement depicts a degenerative process of losing freedom; the second designates a process of ascendency from bondage to freedom. This polarity, as we shall see, circumscribes Frye's whole conception of culture and history. History takes the form of a torture chamber, an unredeemed, fallen state, while utopian culture, which releases man from demonic history, is a secular version of messianic redemption. If these contradictions crisscross the *Anatomy*, it is difficult to see what appeal Frye's work would have for a Marxist critic such as Fredric Jameson. From the perspective of Jameson's historical materialism, not only is the supersession of history by utopian desire in Frye a gesture of wishful thinking, but his very conception of culture and history seems to be problematic. And yet, the *Anatomy* more than any other book seems to inform Jameson's theorizing in *The Political Unconscious*.

Jameson's relationship with Frye hinges upon the utopian project shared by Marxism and Frye's archetypal criticism. To Marxism, history is one single unfinished narrative about "the collective struggle to wrest a realm of Freedom from a realm of Necessity" (Jameson, *Political Unconscious* 19). This apocalyptic conception of history revalues all sociohistorical movements in terms of a future salvation and presupposes an unceasing critique of the historical present. In a similar manner, Frye's archetypal criticism highlights a utopian vision in which civilization is conceived of "as the process of making a human form out of nature" (*Anatomy* 112). He designates "the idea of complete and classless civilization" as the ultimate goal of human labor (348), and accordingly revises the meaning and value of cultural works. While for Marxism, the oppressed classes assume the role of a messiah to bring about that ideal social formation, for Frye, utopian culture performs a redemptory function, lifting humankind "clear of the bondage of history" (347). Despite his conservative emphasis on cultural unity, however, Frye's revisionary criticism nonetheless implies a rigorous critique of the historical present. To the extent that the utopian imagination is governed by the desire for salvation, the social transfigurations it envisions cannot but pose a radical negation of the alienating reality of day-to-day life. It is in this sense that Frye's archetypal view of literature "shows us literature as a total form and literary experience as a part of the continuum of life, in which one of the poet's functions is to visualize the goals of human work" (115).

In the utopian horizon of criticism, "art becomes no longer an object of aesthetic contemplation but an ethical instrument, participating in the work of civilization" (*Anatomy* 349), and the corresponding moral function of art is to "make one capable of conceiving society as free, classless, and urbane" (347). Frye's conception of ethical criticism evolves from an originary binary structure of culture and nature. Culture figures the "social ideal which we educate and free ourselves by trying to attain, and never do attain" (348). Nature functions as a gathering symbol for all forms of alienating reality. Indeed, as Daniel O'Hara has observed, "All that is not Vision [is] seen as Nature, even when it is really History" (172). From this structural opposition of culture and nature derives a whole set of polarities: vision and history, freedom and bondage, individual and universal, demonic and apocalyptic. In Frye's view, to be caught in nature/history is to be given over to a world of social disunity, class oppression, war, destructive impulses, prejudice, and ideological habits. Since the role of ethical education is to foster both the imaginative capacity and intellectual freedom to transcend these demonic constraints, Frye, like Heidegger before him, takes the work of art to be the most gratifying ethical instrument. The major tasks of ethical criticism are to articulate the vision of the recreation of man, to salvage the utopian potential of the art works of the past, to let the historical "valley of dry bones" take on "the flesh and blood of our vision" (*Anatomy* 345).

It follows that Frye's ethical criticism as such can be more properly termed aesthetic humanism. Insofar as he attributes a unique redemptory function to the work of art, his ethical education no doubt can be taken as a synonym for aesthetic education. The actual world to Frye is what "desire totally rejects: the world

of the nightmare and the scapegoat, of bondage and pain and confusion; the world as it is before the human imagination begins to
work on it" (147). This is a world dominated by an alienating nature, a world yet to be redeemed by the utopian imagination. In
a sense, Frye's aesthetic humanism can be read as a rewriting of
Heidegger's existentialist philosophy of art. For Heidegger, art is
the origin or the "founding of truth" (276), the ideal mediation
between world and earth, which "are always intrinsically and essentially in conflict" (271). The world as being-for-itself always
strives to illuminate the earth as being-in-itself, but the earth rejects every attempt to penetrate it. Therefore, truth is not designated as a determining of what being is, but rather a revealing of
the battle between world and earth. The work of art, as a setting
up of the world and a setting forth of the earth, produces a "lighting," a poetic vision, in which the unity of world and earth is won.
This unity is not the reconciliation of conflict, but "the intimacy
with which opponents belong to each other" (273). For the earth
never surrenders itself to human knowledge; it always remains an
enigma. But beyond what is, Heidegger observes, there occurs an
open place. "This open center is therefore," he goes on to contend,
"not surrounded by what is; rather, the lighting center itself encircles all that is, like the Nothing which we scarcely know" (269).
Heidegger's "open center" is more or less equivalent to Nietzsche's
"perspective" or Frye's utopian vision derived from the will to
knowledge, to freedom.

Indeed, there is a close structural affinity between Heidegger
and Frye on being, art, and truth. The binary opposition between
culture and nature in Frye can be taken as a revision of Heidegger's
world and earth. The privileging of art as redemptory power in
Frye, as in Heidegger, is due to the unbridgeable ontological gap
between culture and nature, or being-for-itself and being-in-itself.
Insofar as the ascending imagination is counterpoised by a degrad-
ing history, utopian desire is always necessitated by and presupposes an ever-alienating reality. The reconciliation of the being-
for-itself and the being-in-itself is not the objective correspondence
between the two, but the imposition of the former's own image
upon the latter. All verbal structures, scientific or philosophical,
according to Frye, are informed or constructed by the same kind
of myth or metaphor as we find in literature, and therefore they

are the epiphanic moments of the utopian desire to humanize the nonhuman. It is in this sense that the aesthetic form constitutes the paradigm or Ur-structure of all cultural constructs and that cultural creativity consummated in art functions as an ethical imperative of doing the impossible. For the purpose of aesthetic education is the creation of a free and classless society, which surely does not exist. If science, granted no ontological priority, is as autoeffective as literature, if the only means of lifting humankind above the bondage of nature/history is the utopian imagination, then art certainly takes on the status of a privileged path to freedom. Aesthetic forms constitute a sanctuary in which man is emancipated, although only temporarily, from alienating reality. Heidegger's remarks on "world" echo Frye's discussion of the function and purpose of culture:

> As a world opens itself, it submits to the decision of historical humanity the question of victory and defeat, blessing and curse, mastery and slavery. The dawning world brings out what is as yet undecided and measureless, and thus discloses the hidden necessity of measure and decisiveness. (Heidegger 272)

In much the same way, the utopian cultural project in the *Anatomy* enables humankind to visualize the outcome of the conflict between vision and reality, freedom and bondage, the apocalyptic and the demonic. Viewed from a dialectical perspective, culture sets forth its own opposite—a chaotic and formless nature. The poetic imagination, as an illumination of culture/world, gives form to what would otherwise have remained "amorphous." Frye's conception of culture, defined as the "process of making a human form out of nature" (112), envisions aesthetic forms as constructs of necessity. Furthermore, in the anagogic moment of imagination, it is reality which imitates art instead of the other way round: "Nature is now inside the mind of an infinite man who builds his cities out of the Milky Way" (119). Here, the "mind of an infinite man," which at the same time stands at the periphery and the center of the universe, can be understood to parallel Heidegger's "lighting center," which encircles what is.

From this perspective, Frye's aesthetic humanism creates a curious double bind: it destroys order and reinvokes it, or in other words, encourages transpersonal and individualistic freedom all at once. On the one hand, it visualizes a universal culture by destroying the divisions between social classes and individuals; on the other, it attempts to redeem individuals from the omnipresent dehumanizing symbolic order of social institutions. From Frye's point of view, this is paradoxical rather than contradictory. If culture is transhistorical, and all social individuals share the transpersonal vision of work, then the battle against alienating order is of course the salvation of individuals, and to achieve individual freedom from that order is, in turn, to confirm the universal order of aesthetic forms. "The work of imagination presents us with a vision," Frye says, "not of the personal greatness of the poet, but of something impersonal and far greater: the vision of a decisive act of spiritual freedom, the vision of the recreation of man" (*Anatomy* 94). Given that the imaginative work of art is to provide a glimpse of a positive alternative to an alienating social reality, the creation of an apocalyptic culture cannot but tend to liberate the individuals as well. So it follows that to create a transpersonal utopian vision of freedom is simultaneously to break up the psychic compartmentalization that has come to characterize a fallen and degraded society. Despite the idealism of Frye's aesthetic humanism, which owes much to Matthew Arnold, it is possible to incorporate its moment of truth into a project of resistance against a dehumanized society. Here it is worthwhile to note that Frye's aesthetic humanism recalls what Max Weber has said on the redeeming power of art. "Art takes over the function of a this-worldly salvation," Weber writes, "no matter how this may be interpreted. It provides a *salvation* from the routines of everyday life, and especially from the increasing pressures of theoretical and practical rationalism" (342). The rationalizing order of late capitalist commodity production and the computer revolution have colonized the last private area of human experience, the unconscious, casting postmodern man into schizophrenic agony and depression. In this context, Frye's antirational aesthetic humanism can be understood to put up a powerful resistance to the omnipresent alienation of industrial and postindustrial society. It is true that the utopian imagination often prefigures the nostalgia for a prelapsarian life of reconciliation with no material effect on reality, but it is no less true that, in some way, the utopian imagination can compensate for the dehumanization of experience and enable humankind to transcend the otherwise intolerable pressures of life.

More than anything else, this utopian vision in Frye's *Anatomy* opens up the possibility of a dialogue with Marxism. Both Frye and Marxism privilege the social function of art, and both rewrite imaginative human work in terms of ultimate salvation. Furthermore, Frye's model of history as demonic decline is not without resemblance to historical materialism. The five epochs of Western literature designated in the *Anatomy* can be interpreted, from a Marxist perspective, as indicative of five phases of the mode of production, which partly determines and subsumes the literary mode of production. In other words, these five modes of narrative, distinguished by degree of the hero/heroine's superiority or inferiority to his/her social and existential environment, can be identified as five modes of consciousness or subjectivity. The mythic mode proper, in which the hero is a divine being, synchronizes somewhat with the least alienating mode of production and accordingly points to a safe although naive phenomenal world. The ironic mode of narrative corresponds to the last phase of history, the epoch of late capitalism, in which man finds himself totally alienated from existential circumstances and social institutions. As Frye notes in "The Theory of Modes," the hero in the ironic mode is "inferior in power or intelligence to ourselves, so that we have the sense of looking down on a scene of bondage, frustration, or absurdity" (34). In the midst of the decentering and deindividualizing industrial bureaucracy, every individual is situated as an ironic hero with little control over personal or social situations. In this sense, Frye's ironic hero finds himself mirrored in Lacan's decentered subject: I am not where I think, and I think where I am not. More importantly, it in part recalls Jameson's Marxist notion of history as a process of alienation, which culminates in late capitalist societies characterized by rationalization and psychic fragmentation. In a sense, Jameson's notion of the schizophrenic subject that he develops in *Postmodernism* corresponds to Frye's conception of the ironic hero whom one can find in most of Kafka's stories.

The abstract parallel that can be drawn between Frye and Marxism in terms of the historical alteration of the subject, however, must not obscure their fundamental difference in concrete terms. Nor is it true that Frye's utopian vision of the goal of human work derives from the same theoretical and historical ground that supports Jameson's Marxist utopian view of history. In fact, the kind of historical perspective that informs the *Anatomy* remains ironically restricted by a Platonic conception of culture, which renders Frye's theorizing short of a historical dialectic and ultimately subverts the collective utopian perspective Frye's archetypal criticism opens up. He proposes a utopian culture unmarked by human history, a conceptualization which fails to grasp that alienation is actually a recurrent necessary phase in the whole utopian process of culture, presupposing the recovery or emancipation of humanity at the other end of historical time.[1] In other words, Frye's view of a demonic historical world does not think human history "positively *and* negatively all at once."[2] Nor does he acknowledge history as a dialectic of the utopian and the demonic, or of alienation and reunification. History, as Georg Lukács points out, "is the history of the unceasing overthrow of the objective forms that shape the life of man" (186). It is a process of both producing and deconstructing the forms of constraint and alienation, since what the development of cultural history overthrows is what is brought about by that history. While Lukács sees history as a dialectic of bondage and freedom, Frye only acknowledges the demonic dimension of history, which is to him the opposite of an innocent culture. In order to construct a purely utopian culture, Frye separates culture from history and history from culture, allowing the whole cultural history of material complexity to slip into a metaphysical romance of desire for freedom. His utopian notion of culture has no place for culture as a material social practice, which in class society has always been a space of struggle, oppression, and resistance.

Furthermore, the ahistorical impulse of Frye's cultural utopianism ultimately deconstructs the distinction between nature and culture. In the anagogic moment, culture merges with nature in the sense that the desire of the libidinal body liberated from any sociohistorical constraints can only belong to a nonhistorical nature. The erasing of the boundary between nature and culture is not a coincidence, but a logical consequence of Frye's binary model of utopian desire and demonic history. If the first levels of symbolism—the literal and descriptive—correspond to the latest modes of literature, namely, realism and ironic satire, then the anagogic phase reengages the mythic mode of narrative. In the mythic mode, the hero or heroine is superior to nature and social environment. Such imaginary superiority of man is known only to the golden age of innocence and freedom lost since man's exile from Eden, and Frye's whole project is of course to recover the imaginative vision of that prelapsarian age. What is problematic is that from the historical perspective, the mythic phase or period of literary symbolism is actually the closest to nature, when man is not yet self-consciously alienated from nature. Therefore, the highest moment of culture in Frye is virtually the closest moment to nature. This contradiction leaves one wondering whether Frye is celebrating or lamenting man's alienation from nature, or whether culture is more imaginative when closer to nature or further removed from it.

As Jameson points out, this is where Frye completely closes off the possibilities of the collective symbolism of culture that his archetypal theory seems to have opened up (*Political Unconscious* 71). In *The Political Unconscious*, Jameson comments on Frye's ahistorical anagogic phase as follows:

> [T]he very concept of apocalypse as the end of history and the culminating struggle of the collectivity is here curiously redirected, rechanneled and indeed recontained, by the image of Blakean absolute "man" and transfigured body projected out upon the universe. . . . being the final "phase" of the allegory, the image of the cosmic body cannot stand for anything further, for anything other than itself. Its figural and political momentum is broken. . . . (73)

Here, we are again confronted with a compelling question: if Frye rewrites the collective into the individual, then why does Frye remain of vital importance to Jameson? How does Jameson propose to appropriate Frye's utopian potential? In the following discussion, I will present the way Jameson redeems the notion of romance developed in the *Anatomy* and therefore rewrites a Marxist genre theory out of Frye's.

To begin with, romance for Frye is "the search of the libido or desiring self for a fulfilment that will deliver it from the anxieties of reality but will still contain that reality" (*Anatomy* 193). Romance represents the fulfilment of desire; it is the secular version of the apocalyptic moment on both the communal and individual level. Similarly, as Michael Sprinker notes, utopia is "one of the decisive categories for all of Jameson's work" (60). Or to borrow terms from Cornel West, the notion of utopian desire which "constitutes the central component of Jameson's notion of freedom" functions as the "center" which "Jameson's Marxist hermeneutics dialectically discloses and decenters" (181). For Jameson to appropriate Frye's notion of desire is to salvage the collective utopian vision it promises, to insert Frye's Platonic model of romance "into history" in order to see "what happens" (*Political Unconscious* 130), or to describe its discontinuous differentiations as historically determinate. If Jameson names his Marxist hermeneutic as "the doctrine of the political unconscious," one can argue that Frye's archetypal criticism is informed by a doctrine of the cultural unconscious. From Frye's perspective of the cultural unconscious, all cultural texts or symbols reflect the unchanging desire for an unalienated, classless social life, and all cultural practice, including literary creation, instantiates the concern with, and symbolic or actual resolution of, existential or social problems confronting humankind. That is, culture is characterized by the utopian longing for collective unity. This is where Frye's critical project fits in with Jameson's and where Jameson must transcend its limits. For while Frye prioritizes the utopian meaning of culture, Jameson sees culture as utopian and ideological all at once.

The opening chapter of *The Political Unconscious* locates this newly politicized genre of romance in three contexts of meaning. In the first, political horizon, the cultural text is construed as an individual symbolic response to social contradictions, projecting a utopian desire for social transformations. Yet the social contradictions, however reconstructed, always remain an absent cause, which refuses to be directly or immediately conceptualized by the text. Therefore, the literary text as a space of ideology turns into a kind of "aporia," which figuratively points to social reality, and yet is not that reality. Jameson's metaphor of "aporia" tends to recall Frye's conception of the literary text, which, like a mathematical construct, "neither is nor is not the reality which it manifests" (*Anatomy* 351). But Jameson's politicized "aporia" rewrites Frye's apolitical metaphor to foreground its capacity to register the ideological closure of the text. Because the subtext of social contradictions is open to different restructurings, each particular restructuring represents an interpretive option that carries with it ideological implications.

In Jameson's second horizon of class discourse, the literary text is restructured as a representative voice of class discourse. Each and every social class, impelled by the desire for secure social dominance or for not-yet-achieved power, rewrites the subtext of experience and history in its own interest. Here Frye's "desire" is approached in class terms.[3] While Frye abstracts a universal desire from heterogeneous cultural texts to prove the continuity between the historical past and the present, and between different individuals and social classes, Jameson, on the contrary, immerses the abstract concept of desire back in concrete semantic and social contexts of the text so as to uncover its historical difference. This is the moment when the utopian becomes ideological in Jameson's dialectical thinking. Just as the utopian asserts universal values and the collective unity of society, so the ideological reflects social contradictions, class struggle, and antagonistic confrontation between hegemony and counterhegemony. Or in Frye's terms, the utopian privileges the primary concerns of human life while the ideological foregrounds its secondary concerns. Primary concerns in Frye are considered in terms of universal and eternal needs and secondary concerns are identified as "patriotic and other attachments of loyalty, religious beliefs, and class conditioned attitudes and behaviour" (*Words* 42).[4] Although Frye defines the utopian and the ideological in similar terms to Jameson's, he does not sanction the dialectic of the contradictory terms, and to him, the greater the artworks, the less they are concerned with ideology. Jameson historicizes Frye's notion of utopian desire by demonstrating its ideological articulations at historical conjunctures. In class societies, or the social formations characterized by conflicted group interests and contending discourses, utopia as a grand vision is always rewritten to justify ideological hegemony or counterhegemony.

The dominant ideology, Jameson argues, "will explore various strategies of the legitimation of its own power position, while an oppositional culture or ideology will, often in covert and disguised strategies, seek to contest and to undermine the dominant 'value system'" (*Political Unconscious* 84). The strategies deployed by the

dominant ideology include not only the argument that "[Y]our social order is not always the way you would have it, but it is the
best you can hope for at the present" (Frye, *Words* 24), but also the
naturalization and universalization of its values and institutions.
For the dominant to legitimate its hegemonic discourse it does and
has to present it as universal and "primary." Insofar as the dominant discourse, "being everywhere, comes from nowhere" (Terdiman 61), it is indeed universal or universalized. However, to assert
class interests in terms of universal values is also to rewrite universal values in class terms. Since universal values in class-conditioned
society always prefigure a Platonic ideal that can never be achieved,
they are used as ideological ruses to contain or bracket social differences. In other words, the dominant always speaks in the name
of the utopian. Similarly, oppositional ideologies also employ such
strategy to contest and undermine the dominant value systems, especially if we consider the terms "covert" and "disguise." For the
oppositional ideology, to cover up and disguise is to neutralize, on
the surface level, its contestative discourse, to use the universal or
primary value code to develop an extra-discourse in an intra-
discursive guise—a process of rewriting the universal in class
terms. This is what Jameson means when he writes that

> the dialogue of class struggle is one in which two opposing
> discourses fight it out within the general unity of a shared
> code. Thus, for instance, the shared master code of religion
> becomes in the 1640s in England the place in which the domi-
> nant formulations of a hegemonic theology are reappropriated
> and polemically modified. (*Political Unconscious* 84)

The concept of a "shared master code" among opposing discourses
certainly subsumes the universal and utopian, or the primary.
Class struggle is dialogical; "the very content of a class ideology is
relational," and its "values" are defined against "the opposing
class" (84). The "dialogical" and "relational" always imply a notion
of sameness as well as of difference, and "sameness" refers to the
ultimate utopian goal as well as the unifying mode of production
in Jameson's sense. The differential relations of social classes primarily consist in their conflicted strategies for realizing that ulti-

mate goal. Therefore, to define class values dialogically is actually to redefine or rewrite the universal values.

Jameson's third, historical horizon, which presents a diachronic view of class struggle, locates utopian desire in cultural revolution, restructuring the narrative romance as a formal reenactment of the coexistence of antagonistic modes of production and ideologies. Every social formation is a "non-synchronic" or retentive and protensive structure of residual and emerging modes of production, for revolution never succeeds in completely repressing previous social formations. This is a genuine "anagogical" (in its medieval sense) phase of meditation on human destiny, in which libidinal revolution always stands for a better community. Different social classes, with different ideologies, desires, and master codes of interpretation, all claim to have the best strategy for the future and the best narrative of history; yet, in Jameson's view, these historical views are all subject to the abrupt reversals of history. For history inexorably rejects individual as well as collective projects to totalize or represent it, ironically defeating their declared intention to twist history to their own interests (*Political Unconscious* 102). As we know, the ideas of freedom, liberty, and equality since the Enlightenment have always been the hallmark the bourgeois ideology; at the same time, however, the Western world has never abolished social hierarchy and class oppression. Modern revolutionary transformation beginning in Russia came as a genuine attempt, in Raymond Williams's terms, to change "the *form* of activity of a society, in its deepest structure of relationships and feelings" (*Modern Tragedy* 76). It promised a total recreation of humanity, which was the end of classes. But ironically, this revolution against human alienation produced new forms of alienation, its institutions constantly breeding disorder and violence. The tragedy of the Soviet revolution now calls for "a new struggle against the new alienation," or a "revolution against the fixed consciousness of revolution" (83). The idea of such historical reversals should in no way confirm the pessimistic view that humankind cannot change its condition; on the contrary, it is a recognition of the dialectical development of history. Paradoxically, the negating of revolution or utopian desire by history implies that revolution or utopian desire remains a continuing reality of human life. For, as Bloch has noted, utopian hope is "the determined negation of that which continually makes the opposite of the hoped-for object possible" (17).

History, as Jameson defines it, is "the experience of Necessity," which assumes the form of "the inexorable logic involved in the determinate failure of all the revolutions that have taken place in human history" (*Political Unconscious* 102). Viewed from the perspective of Necessity, "the contradictory reversal or functional inversion, of this or that local revolutionary process is grasped as 'inevitable,' and as the operation of objective limits" (102). The "inevitable" revolutionary process articulates its "inevitability" twice—its moments of success and· failure. Jameson's nonsynchronic conception of social formation as the "structural coexistence of several modes of production all at once" distances itself from traditional Marxism, which conceives the development of history as the linear "sequence" of modes of production such as tribal society, neolithic society, the Asiatic mode of production, the oligarchical slaveholding society, feudalism, capitalism, and communism (89). The theory of coexistence of modes of production Jameson subscribes to provides a much more dynamic and convincing framework for interpreting the social contradictions of specific historical moments, but nonetheless, Jameson's view of history remains teleological, for the supersession of one mode of production by another is "inevitable." Jameson's notions of "necessity" and "inevitability" as well as Marx's are informed by the utopian vision of ultimate collective unity, which justifies the two moments of any revolutionary process as defined above. Therefore, any dominant mode of production coexisting with antagonistic subordinate modes of production prefigures a step closer to that utopian goal. It is in this sense that Jameson writes,

> all class consciousness of whatever type is Utopian insofar as it expresses the unity of a collectivity. . . . The achieved collectivity or organic group of whatever kind—oppressors fully as much as oppressed—is Utopian not in itself, but only insofar as all such collectivities are themselves *figures* for the ultimate concrete collective life of an achieved Utopian or classless society. (290–91)

Jameson's interpretation of culture is intended as a corrective to the purely negative analysis of culture. Culture has a utopian as well as instrumental or ideological function. All cultures or ideologies, as symbolic or class forms of collective unity, converge toward the forever postponed classless society. To be sure, Frye would not disagree with this conception of utopian culture, but he does not acknowledge culture as simultaneously utopian and ideological. This shortcoming on Frye's part results from his reluctance to take history into account. In his anagogical phase, history is entirely erased to defeat history, and culture and criticism all contract into an ecstatic gesture of libidinal triumph of the human body. Although both Frye and Jameson seem ultimately to obtain a "God's-eye view" of history, Frye empties history of its material reality, whereas Jameson attempts to describe that reality. Jameson appropriates Frye's model of desire, freedom, and narrative in seeing the transformative power of romance in all symbolic acts of culture, yet he is always at pains to uncover the ideology of desire and its ironic relations to history.

In contrast to Jameson, however, Frye persistently refuses to acknowledge the ideology of form. In the *Anatomy* a romance is first of all a story people tell; ideology is something read into it. But even here, Frye's notion of romance has a structural affinity with Jameson's conception of ideology. Hayden White has described Jameson's view of ideology—developed from Louis Althusser—in this way: "Ideology is not, for Jameson, a lie, deception, or distortion of a *perceivable* reality, but rather an attempt to come to terms with and to transcend the unbearable *relationships* of social life" (6). In *The Political Unconscious* ideology figures as the Ur-structure of every cultural and literary construct and therefore allows Jameson to make an identification between "narrative" and "ideologeme":

> The ideologeme is an amphibious formation, whose essential structural characteristic may be described as its possibility to manifest itself either as a pseudoidea—a conceptual or belief system, an abstract value, an opinion or prejudice—or as a protonarrative, a kind of ultimate class fantasy about the "collective characters" which are the classes in opposition. (87)

In defining ideology as the narrative form the political unconscious assumes, Jameson reveals his own position in the Marxist debate on the issue of ideology. The last decades since Althusser have witnessed a number of innovative discourses on ideology within Marxism. Raymond Williams, for example, while rejecting a definition of ideology as false consciousness, identifies it as the material process of social production of meaning.[5] More recently, Stanley Aronowitz argues that even (natural) science is not innocent of ideology. According to Aronowitz, the notion of a disinterested, value-free inquiry is untenable: "[S]ciences are socially and historically constituted by discourses, by professional discourses in particular, and by interest. The object examined is thus inevitably ideological" (531).

These recent discoveries regarding the problem of ideology no doubt reinforce Jameson's effort to mediate between sociopolitical reality and literary forms and structures, and between Marxism and formalism. Inasmuch as every social formation consists of the coexistence of antagonistic modes of production and ideologies, a given cultural text becomes a symbolic miniature of that uneasy and unstable coexistence. A given artistic process is informed by contradictory messages emitted from contending sign systems and, as sedimented content, it carries ideological messages of its own distinct from the manifest content of the text (*Political Unconscious* 99). This is how Jameson's revision of "ideologeme" and "narrative" in each other's terms paves the way for his dialogue with Frye on genre and generic displacement.

Jameson begins his dialogue with Frye on genre theory by dialectically putting in question the fundamental binary opposition that underpins the theory of romance in the *Anatomy*. "Frye's entire discussion of romance," Jameson remarks, "turns on a presupposition—the ethical axis of good and evil—which needs to be historically problematized in its turn, and which will prove to be an ideologeme that articulates a social and historical contradiction" (*Political Unconscious* 110). The basic narrative structure of romance, as Frye defines it, is the conflict between good and evil or white and black magical forces whose imaginary resolution conjures up a lost Eden or an apocalyptic future. But Frye does not take into account the shifting and unstable categories of good and evil in relation to historically changing categories of Otherness. Jameson goes on to comment that evil characterizes, in Nietzschean terms, "whatever is radically different from me, whatever by virtue of precisely that difference seems to constitute a real and urgent threat to my own existence" (115). Therefore, the concept of evil assumes a specific referential meaning which is historically determinate. *The Political Unconscious* uses Frye's model of romance as a starting point "to register a given text's specific deviation from [that model] and thereby to raise the more dialectical and historical issue of this determinate formal difference" (126). Jameson's dialogue with Frye on genre theory launches a threefold argument: the discontinuous displacement of the generic mode, the coexistence of heterogeneous generic modes, and the historical deconstruction of the generic mode.

Both Manzoni's *I Promessi Sposi* and Stendhal's *Le Rouge et le noir*, as representative cases given by Jameson, embody a displaced battle between white and black magic, rewriting the binary structure of good and evil in more realistic, psychological terms. In Manzoni's novel, "the old physical *agon* of the romances of chivalry" is refashioned into "the struggle of Good and Evil for the individual soul" (*Political Unconscious* 132). In Stendhal's novel, the older deep structure of "the 'higher' and 'lower' worlds of white and black magic" is displaced onto a battle between the moral code of Rousseau's natural man and the moral code of the emerging commodity society (*Political Unconscious* 132–33). In both cases, the medieval model of magic, adapted to the new raw material, is reappropriated as an ideologically symbolic response to the sociopolitical anxieties and problems of nascent capitalism. To read a textual deviation from its narrative paradigm is to reveal its historical difference rather than identity. Yet Frye's notion of displacement, on the contrary, only sanctions the typological identity of different textual manifestations of the same narrative model, ignoring their historical specificity and ideological motivations. According to Jameson, any genre emerges as a socially symbolic act, and when older generic forms or narrative paradigms are reappropriated into a later historical context, their original ideologies are rewritten. Consider, for example, the subplot involving Sidney Carton in Dickens's *Tale of Two Cities*. Carton delivers himself to the guillotine out of his love for Lucie and in order to let Darnay be reunited with his family. Frye would see the Christian type of resurrection in the ending of the novel and, in a sense, would identify Carton as belonging to the archetype of Christ. No one would find fault with Frye's typological classification; the problem is that such categorization cancels all the sociohistorical detail. Jameson would take Dickens's creation of Carton as a symbolic response to a historical dilemma. The England of the 1850s was caught up in an increasing antagonism among social classes and a renewed fear that the upheavals of 1848 might happen in England. Within such a context the union of two enemy families made possible by Carton's sacrifice can be interpreted or grasped as an imaginary reconciliation of class contradictions.

In Jameson's assessment, Frye's genre criticism "filter[s] out historical difference and the radical discontinuity of modes of production and of their cultural expressions" (*Political Unconscious* 130). Accordingly, he rewrites Frye's notion of displacement "as a conflict between the older deep-structural form and the contemporary materials and generic systems in which it seeks to inscribe and to reassert itself" (141). This revision of Frye's genre theory is to project a model of the coexistence between conflicting genres or narrative structures, for any given narrative text is an "uneven development" of several distinct generic systems. Eichendorff's *Aus dem Leben eines Taugenichts*, for instance, is made to serve as a case of the internal generic discontinuity. This novella has two diachronically related narrative systems: as a deviation from the mode of comedy of errors, the homosexual comedy diachronically coexists with a plot of a peasant youth courting a porter's niece. Similarly, Manzoni's novel is also taken to embody two generic forms: the heroine's moral and psychological trauma recalls the Gothic narrative structure; the hero's episodic experiences take the shape of the *roman d'aventure*. The generic discontinuities found in the same text, however, make any categorization impossible. The novel is "not so much an organic unity," Jameson argues, "as a symbolic act that must reunite or harmonize heterogeneous narrative paradigms which have their own specific and contradictory ideological meaning" (*Political Unconscious* 144). Each novel as a "layered" structure of "*generic discontinuities*" emerges as a new genre in its own right or as its own narrative paradigm. It is in this sense that Jameson argues that all generic categories function as "experimental constructs, devised for a specific textual occasion and abandoned like so much scaffolding when the analysis has done its work" (145).

Jameson's dialogue with Frye on genre theory ultimately leads to a dialectical *combinatoire*—the relationship among three variables: structural norm, textual deviation, and history. Any systematic change in one term will accordingly give rise to determinate variations in the other two, and thereby articulate the relationships of the whole system. History, the nonrepresentable "absent cause," is to be understood as a historical situation, which "shut[s] down" some "formal possibilities available before," and "open[s] up determinate new ones" (*Political Unconscious* 148). Homer's epic, for example, is not able to reproduce itself in the consumer society which is our own, because the schizophrenia and rationalization of late capitalism would be, in Hegel's terms, "out of tune with the background of life which [Homer's] epic requires" (qtd. in Jameson, *Political Unconscious* 146). Jameson's Marxist genre theory rewrites Frye's elaboration and transformation of literary forms in order to foreground the interaction of texts and social practices. Although Frye's typology of emplotment derives from what Paul Ricoeur has called the "dialectic of sedimentation and change," which "gives rise to a whole range of combinations" (3), his notion of "combinations" only describes a two-term process of norm and deviation, leaving out the greater complexity of the dialectic of historical change and literary form.

What Jameson has done with Frye is, in Terry Eagleton's terms, "to rescue the academicist category of genre for a materialist criticism. Genre, [Jameson] persuades us, is an indispensable mediation between immanent textual analysis, the history of cultural forms and the evolution of social life" (62). His historical materialism ironically reveals Frye's ahistorical genre theory to be a romance par excellence. What is at stake in Frye is the utopian unity of culture. Yet it seems that to approach the difference between Jameson and Frye in terms of the utopian unity of culture is to leave the problem of their relationship unexhausted, for Jameson's theory of the political unconscious is nonetheless informed by the utopian unity of history as a single great narrative. In fact, to move from Frye to Jameson is to move from model to history and ultimately transcend their opposition. Jameson opens *The Political Unconscious* with a strategic imperative against all kinds of formalism: "Always historicize!" To historicize a model or concept is to restore the historical specificity ideologically repressed or transformed, to uncover the constitutive relationship between history and ideology. If every generic or theoretical model is an ideologically symbolic response to a certain historical dilemma, then one might have to agree with Jameson that to affirm the primacy of theory is to recognize the primacy of history itself as well. While Frye consciously separates literary creativity from sociopolitical life, Jameson tries to mediate these two realities dialectically. History speaks through symbolic forms of culture; the changes of aesthetic taste and narrativity are to be studied in relation to sociopolitical movements. The *Anatomy* moves from difference to unity or from fact to category in drawing mythical archetypes from historically different literary images. *The Political Unconscious* proceeds in the opposite direction, problematizing conceptual identity in terms of historical *différance*. Totalizing conceptuality, from Jameson's point of view, no doubt impoverishes the rich differentiated experience, but it is an inevitable consequence, or the first step in dialectical thinking. By setting the regressive cycle of unity and difference in constant motion, Jameson dialectically bridges concept and history. Obviously, his genre criticism takes the form of the Hegelian dialectic: Frye's abstract model functions as a thesis, which in turn is used to introduce its antithesis, namely, the ideologically motivated deviation from a certain model; the dialectical synthesis is the historically modified mode of knowledge. This is what Jameson means when he says that Marxist dialectics transcends the opposition between theory and literary history, and this again accounts for how he "subsumes," or cancels and preserves, the non-Marxist models of literary theory, including Frye's. While criticizing Frye's "still," abstract notions of desire and narrative, Jameson preserves them as one necessary phase for his own dialectical thinking.

The highest tribute Jameson pays to Frye is his privileging of Frye's "views of romance as the displaced expression of a utopian desire for fundamental revolutionary changes" (O'Hara 188). In Jameson's own terms, "The association of Marxism and romance therefore does not discredit the former so much as it explains the persistence and vitality of the latter, which Frye takes to be the ultimate source and paradigm of all storytelling" (*Political Unconscious* 105). Frye's conception of romance designates a paradigm of all different discourses, which, constructive or deconstructive, conservative or radical, ultimately end up being a political romance with its own strategy of containment. Paradoxically, *The Political Unconscious* might be as much a romance of interpretation as the *Anatomy*. In this regard, Frye indeed functions as a mirror image of Jameson's own "interpretive persona" (O'Hara 193).

The constant return of Frye in Jameson seems to demand that the latter have to share the burden of the former's idealism. History to Frye is a dehumanizing underworld, yet at the same time his hermeneutic romance "barbarously" (in Walter Benjamin's sense of the word) conquers that alienating material history. A similar idealistic impulse could be detected in Jameson's historical materialism. On the one hand, Jameson says that "History is what hurts, it is what refuses desire," inexorably frustrating any project of theorization, individual or collective—a revision of Lacan's argument that the Real resists symbolization absolutely—but, on the other hand, Jameson's own Marxist romance of interpretation claims to be able to grasp the true movements of history. Moreover, the return of Frye's visionary idealism also finds expression in the over-emphasized utopian notion of "collective unity," which informs the final chapter of *The Political Unconscious*. As White points out, Jameson's notion of "master-narratives" may be invoked by "representatives of official culture" to "justify the sacrifices and sufferings of the citizenry" (13). White goes on to observe that "one alternative to 'collective unity' is anarchy, and this alternative becomes more attractive as an ideal, the more 'collective unity' is enforced upon us by a combination of 'master-narratives' and instruments of control backed by weapons" (13). If this is so, then it would indeed seem to be a grisly reversal of utopian potential.

In assigning to all dominant classes the goal of collective solidarity, Jameson ends up with a "utopianism gone mad" (195), to borrow a phase from Cornel West, which both grounds and derives from the anxieties to overcome ethics by going beyond the binary opposition of good and evil (188–89). West identifies Jameson's utopianism as "mad" because it embraces every conceivable historical force as potentially capable of actualizing it, underplaying dynamic class conflicts and therefore precluding any political agenda for transforming social praxis. Jameson attempts to transcend the binary oppositions of good and evil, progressive and conservative, and revolutionary and reactionary, with a view to creating a "new logic" by "linking the Nietzschean quest beyond good and evil to Marxist theory and praxis" (Jameson, *Political Unconscious* 194–95). But from West's perspective, Jameson has perversely misread both Nietzsche and Marx. For Nietzsche's attempt to go beyond good and evil is not aimed to transcend moral categories, but "to unmask them, disclose what they conceal," and "to debunk and demystify in order to build anew" (West 190). Nor does Marxism intend to go beyond "metaphysical, epistemological, and ethical discourses" in attempting to transform present social practices "against the backdrop of previous discursive and political practices" (West 193). Jameson twists Nietzsche and Marx for the purpose of asserting his reconciliatory utopianism in a more acceptable terminology, but at the same time he loses the politically significant legacy from both. Similarly, in a recent critique of Jameson, Kathleen Martindale approaches Jameson's "mad" utopianism from a Marxist-feminist-deconstructive perspective. She charges Jameson with an "ethico-political failure" (34), for his hermeneutics is not sensitive to the issues of gender and race. Calling for a "feminist materialist ethics" (41), Martindale considers it premature and politically disempowering to attempt to think beyond ethical binary structures as Jameson does. In her assessment, Jameson's fundamental error is "to have been seduced by poststructuralism into believing that bourgeois theory could take the place of praxis" (36).

As I have argued, Jameson's use of Frye brings him back to the literary universe from politics, enabling him to shift Marxist politics from the social to the literary realm, to mediate between history and text. He appropriates Frye's four-level model of interpretation—the ingenious rewriting of the medieval Christian allegorical method—because this model allows him to "come to terms with the persistent problem for Marxism: the problem of mediation, the task of specifying the relationship between various levels" of a literal or cultural work in regard to social life (West 185). His use of Frye for a reconstructed Marxist hermeneutics brings him a politicized version of the relationship among desire, freedom, and narrative, a theory of the political unconscious that is equivalent to Frye's anagogic vision of literary expression (White 3). Frye's conception of literature as a "symbolic meditation on the destiny of community" (*Political Unconscious* 70) not only is congenial to a

Marxist perspective, but facilitates Jameson's investigation of the single "collective struggle to wrest a realm of Freedom from a realm of Necessity" in literary texts not obviously informed by political interests. This is how he appropriates Frye and turns him to the service of his own project, opening up new possibilities for a Marxist hermeneutics.

However, Jameson's rapport with Frye returns with a vengeance, for it blunts the critical edge of a negative Marxism whose prime purpose is to change social praxis, rendering Jameson intellectually detached from the actual scenes of confrontation between embattled social forces. The kind of rational thinking displayed by Jameson can be well traced to Frye's claim to produce a scientific anatomy of culture. His intellectual detachment comes closest to Frye's critical distance when he is brought to see through Frye's anagogic lens the utopian will to collective unity in all cultures and all social classes. If this is what prompts West to diagnose in Jameson a "utopianism gone mad," then paradoxically, this moment of madness is also a moment of intellectual transcendence. For such a utopian view of history presupposes the transcending of ethical binary oppositions as well. This is where and why Martindale charges Jameson with "an ethico-political failure." Apparently, Jameson's attempt to move beyond the binary opposition of good and evil derives from his rapport with Nietzschean deconstruction, but to anyone familiar with his historicist hermeneutic, this can be read equally as a desire resulting from his utopianism.

Ironically enough, in attempting to mediate between politics and literature, Jameson sometimes only manages to separate them, and regrettably his efforts to rethink Marxism for an era of late capitalism have often alienated it from those whose genuine historical need for such radical critique is the greatest. The intellectual prowess of his "too theoretical" texts (West 196) is ironically counterpoised by the resultant political ambivalence or impotence, for his texts tend to preclude the possibility of "ethico-political agendas" (Martindale 38) and have little bearing on political praxis (West 196). This is perhaps the price Jameson has to pay for turning Marxism from a theory of class struggle into a model of reading, a move primarily facilitated by his appropriation of Frye. At some moments Jameson's dialectical thinking is indeed too circumspect and comprehensive to foster political action. His innovative effort to think culture as simultaneously utopian and ideological has unquestionably proved the perspective of Frye inadequate, but the endless circling of dialectical utopia and ideology could prove as politically impotent as Frye's apolitical liberalism. It could even short-circuit the kind of Gramscian countercultural struggle Jameson himself champions, for an overemphasized utopianism could indeed lead, as White has pointed out, to an ultimately repressive solidarity within society.

Jameson's idealist impulse and excessive play of utopianism are symptomatic not only of the "major political shortcoming of his work," as West argues (196), but of the sociohistorical conjuncture at which he relaunches Hegelian Marxism. Taking into account the historical situation in which *The Political Unconscious* was written, Jameson's polemical emphasis on the utopian dimension of cultural works should not be unquestioningly identified with Frye's anagogical conception of utopian culture. Actually, Jameson's cultural analysis is intended as a corrective to both Frye's purely utopian hermeneutic and the purely negative cultural criticism upheld by traditional Marxism and Derridean deconstruction, which tend to focus on the ideological dimension of culture. From this perspective, Jameson's notion of the dialectic of utopia and ideology may not give a real chance to the "representatives of official culture" to justify the silencing of the marginalized "collectivities," although they might seize on certain moments of Jameson's cultural analysis for that purpose. Indeed, Jameson's dialectic of utopia and ideology reveals his own political and historical milieu. The commodity logic of late capitalism tremendously democratizes Western social life in the culture and entertainment industry, in the use and convenience of technology, in television-mediated ideas, and in monadic living spaces. While the leveling technology of the commodity brings about a choking sense of artificiality and psychic schizophrenia, the democratization of consumer society generates a collective self-congratulation for the majority within Western societies (we Western democracies are much closer to the ideal society sketched by Marx than so-called communist countries). This not only makes impossible the old-fashioned class struggle with the proletariat as the leading force of resistance, but urges cultural critics like Jameson to explore the utopian dimension of capital and technology. Western consumer society, characterized by placeless freedom, nonclass social relations, and domination by hegemony, has an unprecedented capacity to neutralize all oppositional discourses, including Marxism, by assigning them a limited space—a textual realm—for exercising their political energy. That is why Jameson as well as New French Theory advocates a "Long March" through institution, in Jameson's terms the Marxist class struggle in the superstructure. That is also why Western Marxism, along with other forces of opposition allowed to carry on counterhegemonic politics only on a symbolic or formal level, grows increasingly sophisticated in theory. When Eagleton asks, "[H]ow is a Marxist structuralist analysis of a minor novel of Balzac to help shake the foundations of capitalism?" this is actually a question posed for all groups and individuals of oppositional politics.

Jameson's insistence on the utopian character of all cultures and ideologies, however, does not seem to prevent his anxiety from conceiving and developing new collectivities in opposition to the sophisticated, penetrating cultural logic of late capitalism. The difference between the hegemonic ideology of consumer society and the contestatory collective consciousness may be summarized thus: the former justifies the present in light of a utopian future, whereas the latter uses the utopian as a negative standpoint from which to critique and challenge the present. Aware of the political and theoretical consequences of the overemphasized notion of "collective unity" promised by his doctrine of the political unconscious, Jameson reintroduces Walter Benjamin's identification of culture and barbarism in his final chapter to remind his readers of the ideology inscribed within all utopian symbolisms. All the cultural texts of class history, Jameson paraphrases Benjamin, "are in one way or another profoundly ideological, have all had a vested interest in and a functional relationship to social formations based on violence and exploitation," and "within the symbolic power of art and culture the will to domination perseveres intact" (*Political Unconscious* 299). Jameson's dialectical mode of thought never seems to allow him to retire for good from any argument; instead, he has to stand on guard for the restless reversals of the dialectic. So he concludes *The Political Unconscious* with the statement that it is only at the price of "the simultaneous recognition of the ideological and Utopian functions of the artistic text" that "a Marxist cultural study can hope to play its part in political praxis" (299). The idealistic impulse in Jameson, which grasps the utopian vision in culture and history, indeed has a curious affinity with Frye, but that utopian vision is ultimately recontained within the conceptual framework of the historical dialectic. Still, there is no doubt that Jameson's revision of Marxist criticism owes much to Frye's theories of desire, narrative, and genre. The importance of the *Anatomy* for the theorizing in *The Political Unconscious* is testimony to the continuing significance of Frye's writing for literary and cultural studies.

Notes

I owe an immense debt of gratitude to Professor Pamela McCallum for the numerous conversations I had with her during the writing of this article. She read closely all the previous drafts and generously provided expert criticism.

1. See Jameson, "Imaginary and Symbolic in Lacan," in *Situations of Theory* (75–115); and "*History and Class Consciousness* as an 'Unfinished Project'" (49–72).

2. See Jameson, *Postmodernism, or, The Cultural Logic of Late Capitalism* (47). Jameson celebrates Marx's historical dialectic that "capitalism is at one and the same time the best thing that has ever happened to the human race, and the worst," encouraging "some effort to think the cultural evolution of late capitalism dialectically, as catastrophe and progress all together" (47). This dialectical view of cultural history can be taken as a proper critique of Frye's idealistic notion of history as totally negative or culture as totally positive. Although Marx's remark relayed by Jameson is focused on the particular case of capitalism, it should apply to cultural history in general as well.

3. One can make a formal mediation between Frye's archetypal phase and Jameson's horizon of class discourse in terms of Saussure's model of *langue* and *parole*. In Frye, who attempts to write a grammar of images, this model is transcoded into the relationship of the archetype and its variations. In Jameson this model is revised in terms of the relationship between class discourse and its individual utterances; the individual text is refocused as a *parole* of the "vaster system, or *langue*, of class discourse" (*Political Unconscious* 85). In both critics the individual subject is decentered: it is not the individual consciousness, but the literary or political unconscious, which writes the text. Yet what Jameson reveals in reappropriating the Saussurean model is the ideological confrontation between social classes, whereas what Frye highlights is "the continuum of life" (*Anatomy* 115).

4. In *Words with Power* (1990), Frye rethinks the problem of ideology, obviously modifying his previous position on this issue articulated in *Anatomy of Criticism*. He argues that there are two dimensions to ideology, the active and the passive. The actively ideological includes "structures of social authority"; the actively ideological is where the tactics of rhetoric are deployed to "articulate and rationalize authority," to "persuade and create a response of *conviction*" (*Words* 16–17). The passively ideological is "where every verbal structure, simply by being conditioned by its social and historical environment, reflects that conditioning" (18). However,

Frye's conception of ideology remains consistent to the assumption that myth is first of all a story, and ideology is something added to it (Salusinszky, *Criticism in Society* 31).

5. Raymond Williams refutes the traditional notion of ideology as false consciousness; instead, he agrees with Volosinov that ideology is "the process of the production of meaning through signs, and 'ideology' [should] be taken as the dimension of social experience in which meanings and values are produced" (*Marxism* 70). Although the uncertainty of "ideology" hovering between a system of class beliefs and a system of false ideas has never been resolved in Marxism, Williams argues, the thrust of Marx's whole argument on ideology is: "Consciousness is seen from the beginning as part of the human material social process, and its products in 'ideas' are then as much part of this process as material products themselves" (59–60).

Works Cited

Aronowitz, Stanley. "The Production of Scientific Knowledge: Science, Ideology, and Marxism." *Marxism and the Interpretation of Culture.* Ed. Cary Nelson and Lawrence Grossberg. Urbana: U of Illinois P, 1988. 519–41.

Bloch, Ernst. *The Utopian Function of Art and Literature.* Trans. Jack Zipes and Frank Mecklenburg. Cambridge: MIT P, 1988.

Eagleton, Terry. "The Idealism of American Criticism." *New Left Review* 127 (1981): 53–65.

Frye, Northrop. *Anatomy of Criticism.* New York: Atheneum, 1969.

——. *Words with Power.* San Diego: Harcourt, 1990.

Heidegger, Martin. "The Origin of the Work of Art." 1971. Rpt. in *Deconstruction in Context: Literature and Philosophy.* Ed. Mark C. Taylor. Chicago: U of Chicago P, 1986. 242–79.

Jameson, Fredric. "*History and Class Consciousness* as an 'Unfinished Project.'" *Rethinking Marxism* 1.1 (1988): 49–72.

——. *The Political Unconscious.* Ithaca: Cornell UP, 1981.

——. *Postmodernism, or, The Cultural Logic of Late Capitalism.* Durham: Duke UP, 1991.

——. *Situations of Theory.* Minneapolis: U of Minnesota P, 1988. Vol. 1 of *The Ideologies of Theory.* 2 vols.

Lukács, Georg. *History and Class Consciousness.* Trans. Rodney Livingstone. Massachusetts: MIT P, 1971.

Martindale, Kathleen. "Fredric Jameson's Critique of Ethical Criticism: A Deconstructed Marxist Feminist Response." *Feminist Critical Negotiations.* Ed. Alice A. Parker and Elizabeth A Meese. Amsterdam: Benjamins, 1992. 33–43.

O'Hara, Daniel T. *The Romance of Interpretation: Visionary Criticism from Pater to de Man.* New York: Columbia UP, 1985.

Ricoeur, Paul. "*Anatomy of Criticism* or the Order of Paradigms." *Centre and Labyrinth: Essays in Honour of Northrop Frye.* Ed. Eleanor Cook, Chaviva Hosek, Jay Macpherson, Patricia Parker, and Julian Patrick. Toronto: U of Toronto P, 1983. 1–13.

Salusinszky, Imre. *Criticism in Society: Interviews with Jacques Derrida, Northrop Frye, Harold Bloom, Geoffrey Hartman, Frank Kermode, Edward Said, Barbara Johnson, Frank Lentriccia, J. Hillis Miller.* New York: Methuen, 1987.

Sprinker, Michael. "The Part and the Whole." *Diacritics* (Fall 1982): 57–71.

Terdiman, Richard. *Discourse/Counter-Discourse*. Ithaca: Cornell UP, 1985.

Weber, Max. *From Max Weber.* Ed. and trans. H. H. Gerth and C. Wright Mills. New York: Oxford UP, 1946.

West, Cornel. "Fredric Jameson's Marxist Hermeneutics." *Boundary 2* 11.1–11.2 (1983): 177–200.

White, Hayden. "Getting Out of History." *Diacritics* (Fall 1982): 2–12.

Williams, Raymond. *Marxism and Literature*. Oxford: Oxford UP, 1977.

———. *Modern Tragedy.* London: Chatto, 1966.

Baudrillard, *After Hours,* and the Postmodern Suppression of Socio-Sexual Conflict

Cynthia Willett

There was a time when Hollywood films could end happily and yet make socially progressive contributions to conflicts that afflict American culture (Willett, "Hollywood" 15). This, however, is no longer the prevailing view regarding the classical Hollywood films. Most critics now argue that the screwball comedies of the 1930s and 1940s, or what Stanley Cavell terms "the comedies of remarriage," create a magical escape from very real class and gender struggles of the Depression. My claim, on the contrary, is that screwball comedies such as Howard Hawks' *Bringing Up Baby* (1938), George Cukor's *The Philadelphia Story* (1940), Preston Sturges's *The Lady Eve* (1941), and Frank Capra's *It Happened One Night* (1934) effectively and pragmatically educate their audiences to reinterpret what liberal America terms the "pursuit of happiness."

Contemporary suspicions of such a claim arise predominantly from postmodernist critiques of classical structures of plot and character development. In this essay, I focus on the postmodern theory of French sociologist Jean Baudrillard and an exemplary postmodern film, Martin Scorsese's *After Hours* (1985), in order to

© 1996 by *Cultural Critique*. Fall 1996. 0882-4371/96/$5.00.

argue that postmodern culture does not so much critique as suppress the socio-sexual agons (i.e., the conflicts that instigate plot and character development) of classical Hollywood comedy, and thus blocks the possibility for progressive social change.

Screwball comedy exhibits a dialectic that can be dubbed "Neo-Aristotelian." As a genre, these films represent middle-class America's cultural debt to a classical ethical principle that has become known as "the golden mean." The Hollywood films portray heterosexual marriage as a unity of two extreme characters—often drawn from upper and lower classes and frequently arranged in binary oppositions such as artist vs. yuppie, jock vs. intellectual, or scientist vs. artist—where each character moderates some dimension of his or her personality in order to learn to communicate with a prospective mate. Most often, the comic film juxtaposes the values of practical but rigid to free but irresponsible. This genre of comedy emphasizes that each of the opposite-type characters learns from the other and that it is this double education that justifies the happy ending.

For example, *Bringing Up Baby* opposes a rigid and excessively rationalistic[1] scientist played by Cary Grant to the screwball, or, to use the postmodernist language of Deleuze and Guattari, the "schizophrenic"[2] Katharine Hepburn. Both Grant and Hepburn play comic characters precisely to the degree that they verge from an ethics of moderation, the ethics originally conceptualized by Aristotle as necessary to the happiness of the human being as a social animal. The comedy ends happily only when the hyper-rationalist Grant learns to become more flexible, that is, more open to the surprises as well as the pleasures of erotic desire, and when Hepburn's "feminine negativity," as Julia Kristeva terms the transgressive pleasures of "schizoid subversion," yields to a certain measure of social responsibility.[3]

This mutual transformation is evident in the final scene of *Bringing Up Baby*. Hepburn approaches Grant in his lab, where he is piecing together the skeletal remains of a brontosaurus. While throughout the film Hepburn gleefully displaces one thing after another, at last she returns something to its rightful place, namely, the missing tailbone of the brontosaurus. Grant, on the other hand, allows the rather phallic bone to fall and the entire lifeless structure of the dinosaur to collapse in order to embrace the fully living Hepburn. The rigor mortis of a masculine rationalism, no less than the transgressive eroticism of "feminine negativity," gives way before a renewed vision of community. Both opposed characters learn something.[4] And it is this double education—this way of "being brought up"—that produces a nonhierarchical vision of social exchange, what Northrop Frye in his discussion of comedy terms a "pragmatically free society," and that thereby legitimates an otherwise unearned happy ending (169).

My defense of screwball comedy, however, is not motivated simply by a nostalgia for traditional films. The films of the 1930s and 1940s clearly contain images that are regressive by contemporary standards. *The Philadelphia Story*, which centers around a haughty heiress (played by Katharine Hepburn) and her alcoholic ex-husband (played by Cary Grant) serves as an excellent example of the limitations of this genre of comedy. In the final scene of the film Grant stands behind Hepburn, who in puppetlike fashion repeats the words that Grant gives her to say before an audience expecting a wedding ceremony. The image of a woman who has become "easy to handle" and therefore "ready for marriage" is not what the contemporary feminist would want to call a happy ending. My interest in screwball comedy lies in the dialectic that animates the plot. In *The Philadelphia Story*, this dialectic moves the overly rigid Katharine Hepburn to recognize her own imperfections and forgive those of others while Cary Grant learns to moderate his frivolity and accept his various social responsibilities.

Here again, the mutual transformation of opposite-type characters provides a basis for a pragmatic model of community. Much of the laughter of screwball comedy depends on misunderstandings between eccentric main characters. As the characters moderate the vices that are destructive to both themselves and others, they engender necessary conditions for communication. At the same time, the end of the film does not typically show these characters as having lost their distinctive differences. The final laughter usually comes from an affirmation of those idiosyncrasies of character that, in turn, are productive of the open-ended values of a pluralistic community. For example, in the final scene of *Bringing Up Baby*, the ever-exuberant Hepburn returns the missing bone only to effect the collapse of the entire skeletal remains of the brontosaurus. The resolution of the main conflict of the film does not require that Hepburn lose core dimensions of her eccentric self. Nor does comic resolution require that Grant and Hepburn adopt the same styles of self-expression. On the contrary, the final scene celebrates residual differences between Grant and Hepburn and thereby suggests that comic dialectic does not anchor communication or community in shared concepts, or in what postmodern critics term the logic of the same, but in shared laughter over the playful exchanges between idiosyncratic human beings.

Hollywood screwball comedy restages the agons of dialectic derived from a fundamentally tragic conception of social change that originates in Hegel and is appropriated by Marxist philosophies (Willett, "Hegel"). The constant ironies and eventual recognitions that emplot Hegelian dialectic grow out of Hegel's reinterpretation of classical Greek tragedy. Hegel argued that classical tragedy should not be viewed as a static and one-sided human transgression against transcendent law but as a fully human struggle between partial and intertwined perspectives of a dynamic ethical society. According to Hegelian dialectic, the struggle between opposed perspectives intensifies into tragic violence until each side recognizes its interdependence on the other. The reversals and recognitions enlisted by German idealism, however, subordinate human claims for happiness to an abstract notion of truth. Notoriously, Hegelian dialectic leaves behind social and political spheres in order to locate truth tentatively in a cathartic art—art whose function is defined in terms of purging the emotions of the spectator—and finally in a purely concept-based philosophy.

My suggestion is that dialectic reconceived by way of classical American film comedy rather than classical European tragedy promotes the struggles and reconciliations required of an ethical society without finally sacrificing human desire to a cathartic or otherwise overly abstract truth. As in tragic dialectic, the agonistic characters that define comic dialectic grow to recognize both their own limitations and the virtues of those who are different. In this sense, comic dialectic parts from what Northrop Frye identifies as the traditional principle of comedy, namely, "unincremental repetition, the literary imitation of ritual bondage" (168). The audience does not so much laugh at those who fail to transform themselves as laugh with idiosyncratic characters who learn to moderate pre-

cisely those eccentricities that are destructive to self and Other before these differences escalate into all-out war.

Comic dialectic works only when social differences approach
mediation through *moderation* rather than the *polarization* of differences characteristic of tragic agon. This distinction with regard to
means can, in part, be accounted for by way of the different aims
informing comic and tragic dialectic. Comic dialectic aims toward
the horizontal interrelation of individuals in a pragmatically free
community and not the vertical subordination of individual happiness for the sake of a more abstract concept of truth. On the contrary, a typical comic plot transforms the life of the socially and
sexually repressed thinker into the less predictable but more liberated life of the lover. *Bringing Up Baby* exemplifies such a transformation. Nerdy Cary Grant first appears before the camera alone
in the pose of Rodin's *The Thinker* while the final scene brings Grant
and Hepburn together in an embrace that mimes Rodin's *The Kiss*.

My argument is that if comic dialectic breaks down in postmodern film, it is not because classical Hollywood films produce
"fairy tale" illusions of happiness and therefore are not credible,
but rather because they invoke an ethical dynamic that is overlooked by postmodern critics. Scorsese's *After Hours* depicts what
happens *after* the dialectic—the plot progression—of Hollywood
comedy *no longer works*. The film sets up the same oppositions between male rationality and female irony that animate *Bringing Up
Baby*. However, while in the screwball comedy an agonistic encounter between male and female values leads to mutual transformation for both characters, *After Hours* preempts any dialectical
exchange between the so-called opposite sexes. With the preemp-
tion of dialectic, the American postmodern scene is literally "after
hours."

Baudrillard accounts for the failure of postmodern culture to
generate social progress in terms of the rise of new forms of power.
His argument depends on the premise that he shares with a broad
range of post–World War II European and American philoso-
phers, including poststructuralists and Wittgensteinians. According to this view, subjectivity is an effect of language: the implication is that meanings are grounded in external communication
networks and not in personal or private subjective experiences.

These networks are constituted by a web of external signifying relations, or matrices, whose endpoint, as Bill Martin points out in *Matrix and Line,* can be an "asocial 'textualism'" (27). For Baudrillard, in postmodern culture these matrices of power take the form of the global information net, which reaches into every aspect of our personal lives. Not emotion-laden language games but emotionless computer chips store memory and determine subjectivity. Power is no longer experienced as repressive of subconscious desire and, therefore, does not lead to agonistic opposition. In Baudrillard's terms, the agonistic scenes of classical drama reverberate into postmodern "obscene," or the visual equivalent of postmodern noise, failing to produce a vision for social change.

Scorsese's *After Hours* exemplifies the "hi-tech postmodernism" of Baudrillard and so can be interpreted as a direct attack on the emancipatory claims implicit within comic dialectic. Paul Hackett (played by Griffin Dunne) presents a postmodern update of the classic comic role of the bore, in this case a computer hack (hence Hackett's name) with a banal desk job in upper Manhattan. Just as the opening shot of *Bringing Up Baby* fixes the nerdy paleontologist behind an elaborate matrix of skeletal remains, so the first shot of Paul Hackett locates him within an equally lifeless maze of office desks topped with computer monitors. In both films, male characters are positioned within structures of power that are indifferent to social and expressive dimensions of the self. Also in both, the plot is set in motion by the machinations of a female character. But if Hepburn transforms the stiff Grant into a flesh-and-blood human being at the end, the female characters that Dunne encounters only serve to harden the defenses of an ever more paranoid male subject. In screwball comedy, an encounter with an Other brings about the emancipation or, I am arguing, the pragmatic reeducation of desire. For the narcissistic subject, defined by postmodernism as an effect of power, an encounter with an Other outside that system of power can only pose a threat to self-identity.

Paul Hackett's nightmarish encounters with a series of threatening women occur in downtown Soho. After work, he runs into a seemingly innocent and seductive blond named Marcy (played by Rosanna Arquette). The two characters discover a mutual interest in Henry Miller's *Tropic of Cancer.* After briefly discussing the book, which is interpreted as a statement that art is dead, Marcy mentions that she shares a loft with an authentic Soho artist whose specialty is bagel and cream cheese paperweights. Hackett uses the bagel and cream cheese sculpture as a ploy for pursuing his more obvious interest in Marcy. Later that night, he shows up at her loft and finds her roommate, the kinky sculptress Kiki Bridges at work on a papier-mâché figure that recasts Edvard Munch's expressionistic *The Scream* in the style of George Segal's bland and expressionless mummies. Significantly, the papier-mâché sculpture serves as a central figure in the film, immediately signaling a central difference between dialectical and postmodern experiences of alienation. The blank postmodern figure, unlike its expressionistic predecessor, exhibits a subjectivity that is not so much repressed as socially and sexually empty.

The almost obligatory flirtation between Hackett and Kiki leads nowhere as Kiki falls asleep just as Hackett is about to seduce her. Meanwhile, Marcy returns to the loft to discover Kiki asleep in Hackett's arms. After Marcy is satisfied that nothing happened between Hackett and Kiki, she promises Hackett an evening of wild fun, all the while intimating that due to some kind of accident her body may be covered with burn marks. The image of burn marks not only turns Hackett off but solicits his worst fears of mutilation.

Hackett then runs out on Marcy, who, discovering that she has no one to listen to her, commits suicide. Meanwhile, finding himself without money and trapped in Soho for the night, Hackett makes his way to a bar where the bartender offers subway fare if Hackett retrieves a key for the cash register from the bartender's apartment. However, the apartment residents mistake Hackett for a thief, and he finds himself chased through the streets of Soho by a vigilante mob threatening to either burn him alive or tear him to shreds. During the chase, Hackett encounters three more blond women—a bar waitress, a driver of an ice cream truck, and an old customer of a music club, Club Berlin, where he also seeks a haven from the threatening mob. However, Hackett's "escape" from the mob into the club turns out to be yet one more trap. The older blond at the club saves Hackett from the mob only by wrapping him in a papier-mâché figure that exactly resembles Kiki's version of *The Scream*.

The fact that the bouncer at Club Berlin recalls the doorkeeper in Kafka's *Before the Law* only serves to underscore that Hackett has fallen into a Kafkaesque-style maze of paranoid proportions, but with a difference. In yuppie America, there is one way out of terror, namely to return to work. By chance, the real thieves in the film mistake the papier-mâchéd Hackett for Kiki's sculpture and cart Hackett away. Fittingly, Hackett as sculpture falls out of the thieves' van in front of the gates of his company the next morning.

Classic Hollywood oppositions reappear in the differences between uptown and downtown Manhattan. *After Hours* plays on Soho's reputation as a free zone for avant-garde art and unsanctioned sexual encounters.[5] If upper Manhattan profits from what dialectical thinkers would diagnose as the appropriation of libido to the productive tasks of instrumental reasoning, the lower East Side promises to desublimate desire and liberate the imagination. In classic screwball comedy, an agonistic encounter between the two worlds would have been *both* productive *and* liberating. But while Dunne seeks a liberating reversal in his life, the ironies in Soho escalate without end. The result is a nightmare of repetitions and reversals without dialectical advance until Dunne is by chance returned home (for the yuppie, work is home) exactly on time for work.

After Hours parodies the nightmare of leaving home in *Wizard of Oz*. For example, Dunne's dizzyingly fast taxi ride to Soho simulates tornadolike winds. More significantly, like *Wizard of Oz*, Scorsese's film solicits the conservative sentiment that there is no place like home. In *After Hours,* however, the discovery that there is no place like home turns out to be the parody of a real discovery. Dunne finds himself anxious to return to a home that is no place, or no *real* place, but rather an abstract work space. Even the minimalist decor of his apartment duplicates the sterile, geometric style of his office building. In sharp contrast to the existential black of Soho, uptown interiors come in blank industrial white. Both work space and living space in upper Manhattan center around modern technologies of communication: computer, telephone, cable television. But Dunne's inability to converse with his new colleague at work or to resist grazing the TV via the remote control underscores the idea that upper Manhattan, while offering security, cannot offer the playful dialectic that screwball films taught viewers to demand from what they called home.

As a postmodernist, Baudrillard argues in terms more devastating to dialectical progression than do, for example, even the most pessimistic critical theorists. According to Baudrillard, the new devices for exchanging information do not block the human potentialities for self-expression and social exchange in the reified object of the commercial system but substitute the simulacra for these potentialities. Since the simulacra of communication do not frustrate, but instead pacify, desire, they dissipate any impetus for personal or political change. Thus, the simulacra of communication, in effect, preempt any interchange between dialectically opposed characters or positions. As a typically postmodern film, *After Hours* preserves and even intensifies two of the traditional elements of dialectical development: ironic reversal and repetition. But because the film cancels the communication of opposites, of "opposite sexes" for example, it also expunges the elements of self-discovery and mutual recognition that enable dialectical advance and a happy ending.[6]

Repeatedly Griffin Dunne finds himself staring at a mirror and yet unable to pull himself together or otherwise discover a cogent sense of self. At the end of the film, Dunne is the same narcissistic bore that he was in the beginning. The adventures of the yuppie do not lead to new powers of self-expression or mutual understanding. In effect, scenes are repeated and reversed; tensions mount but nothing happens. If classical dialectic measures the advance of plot by way of reversals and moments of recognition, *After Hours* deconstructs plot and cancels the linear component of temporal advance.

But then if postmodern America stands at the end of time, *After Hours* demonstrates that it is not because the United States has attained the final goals of history (cf. Fukuyama). Nor, if Baudrillard is right, can we mourn the "failure" of historical progress. For failure, like progress, presupposes the possibility of human goals, purposes, or desires, whereas the postmodern screen displays instead scintillating electron beams. It is the power of these scintillations to redefine subjectivity as an effect of electronic communication networks and abstract information systems that paralyzes dramatic progression and dissipates historical dialectic.

After Hours depicts the inescapable networks of power that dismiss modern dialectic as boring, lifeless, and emasculating. The occupation of computer operator identifies Dunne with that which

Baudrillard has characterized in his "Ecstasy of Communication" as a "pure screen, a switching center for . . . networks of influences" (133). The paradigmatic postmodern subject exists as a node in the circuits of information, the endless connections that relay information and instrumentalize knowledge. Hi-tech postmodernity transforms the first premise of modernism, knowledge is power, from the "hot universe" of passion, desire, and will into the "cold universe" depicted by Baudrillard as the "smooth operational surface of communication" (127). The pathos that initiates dialectical history or even the will that impels Nietzschean-style genealogies of power has disappeared, seemingly without a trace.

Unlike "true" power, Baudrillard explains, the power of the cold universe produces not a strategy or a stake, but simulations that take their profit from mass consumption. Politicians, for instance, are transformed into media stars. And thus the political as such no longer exists. "Likewise with work. The spark of production, the violence of its stake no longer exists" (*Simulations* 47). If the Enlightenment and the Industrial Revolution locate the origin of value in labor, postmodern capitalism, Baudrillard argues, has not redefined but disavowed both labor and value. There are only simulacra, "dedicated exclusively" "to their recurrence as signs, and no longer to their 'real' goal at all" (41).

If Baudrillard is right, the unsatisfying relation between the characters and values of Soho and upper Manhattan does not illustrate implacable forces resistant to mutual accommodation. *After Hours,* then, does not leave erotic impulses repressed and resistant to the requirements of labor in a stalled dialectic. As Baudrillard explains, "Not so long ago sex and work were savagely opposed terms: today both are dissolved into the same type of demand" (*Simulations* 36). It is precisely because Griffin Dunne is not libidinally repressed that Soho can provide no cure for him. The classic polarities repeat, intensify, and then disperse; for "only capital," Baudrillard writes, "takes pleasure" (35).

After Hours ends by returning an unemancipated Dunne to his solitary post at the computer terminal. Although his position is solitary, there is no alienation in the classical sense. Computer networking deletes the agonistic difference between self and other. For example, his workplace shows no evidence of the traditionally oppressive hierarchy in relations of power. There is no struggle for recognition between employer and employee as Dunne answers to no one. The only encounter between employees occurs in the opening scene when he instructs a new trainee. And the trainee's attempt to communicate to Dunne his fantasies of becoming a writer meets with neither sympathy nor hostility but only distraction. Art is dead, and neither dreams nor fantasies register in postmodern memory banks. The new trainee must yield to what Griffin Dunne already accepts: dramatic encounters have made their exit from what Baudrillard unveils as the "empty stage of the social" (*Simulations* 48).

In a critique of Marxist dialectic, Baudrillard argues that the transmissions of the communication industry, or media space, are

> anti-mediatory. They fabricate non-communication—this is, what characterizes them, if one agrees to define communication as an exchange, as a reciprocal space of a speech and a response and thus of a *responsibility*, . . . *they are what always prevent response,* making all processes of exchange impossible (except in the various forms of response *simulation,* themselves integrated in the transmission process, thus leaving the unilateral nature of communication intact). This is the real abstraction of the media. And the system of social control and power is rooted in it. (Baudrillard, *For a Critique* 167–70)[7]

Once the communication industry infiltrates social discourse, the mechanism of preprogrammed responses emerges. Thoughts count for no more than what can be recorded on the computer-read data sheets of the opinion poll. Emotions become electrical discharges And between the sexes, person-to-person connection is not possible (Poster 77). For example, a disinterested Dunne accepts the six digits that the lonely Soho barmaid (played by Teri Garr) gives out as her telephone number even though he realizes that the number is incomplete. Meanwhile, the barmaid, who is so to speak not quite "properly wired," insists that those six digits make up her complete telephone number. Postindustrial networks put out of play the elements of reciprocal exchange necessary for ethical comedy.

A social nexus without reciprocal exchange, however, is not a society deprived of information. On the contrary, Baudrillard portrays postmodern society as a society without secrets. From census takers, poll takers, data collectors of all kinds, the sheer quantity of information accumulated today is "obscene." Baudrillard describes this state of positive communication as a place where "all secrets [are] abolished in a single dimension of information . . . [and where there is] an extermination of interstitial and protective spaces" ("Ecstasy" 131). Whatever postindustrial communication would fail to register has no status as fact and, therefore, could not be a secret. In the opening scene, Dunne is demonstrating to the new trainee the steps required for storing files in the computer memory. Whatever fails to make it into the file is irretrievably lost. Similarly, as the new trainee finds no register, in Dunne or in his new occupation, of his dreams of being a writer, Dunne will find that the electron beams that wrap his daylight world cannot record his nightmare in Soho. The final scene of the film returns Dunne from his nightmare in Soho to a preprogrammed greeting on his computer screen. The programmed greeting is completely indifferent to viewer response as the information systems of postmodernism cannot register traces of the secret night, "after hours."

And yet another premise of postmodern culture, at least as it is represented in the ethical moments of Derridean deconstruction, leads the postmodern critic to suspect that no system of power is total. As Derrida argues, it is necessarily the case that every system is perturbed by the residues of what it would exclude. And so, it is the case that a deconstructive reading of *After Hours* yields what the theories and programs of Jean Baudrillard would elide, for in the final scene, Dunne appears at work with the telltale traces of the other world of Soho still on him. The plaster dust that speckles his suit and tie thus suggests what otherwise the film would erase. There is a remainder of secret desire not neatly programmable into the sterile networks of technological power. Not all pleasures belong, as Baudrillard hypothesizes, to capital and its simulacra. The expression of a desire superfluous to the demands of the new institutions of power can and does occur.

So too, the sense of distraction or irony that characterizes Griffin Dunne's performance at work testifies to hidden pockets of friction in the system. This friction—this difference within the interstices of any conglomeration of the same—enables dialectical critique and accounts for the possibility of resistance to capitalist

forms of power.[8] The redefinition of the human being beyond interiority into terms that are operational is never clean.

Thus, a deconstructive interpretation of *After Hours* could
serve to rehabilitate avant-garde efforts to oppose, and even, I believe, dialectical aims to overcome, the debilitating effects of institutions of power. Of course, Derrida poses dialectic as a primary
target of deconstructive practices. Nonetheless, deconstructive
theory could locate a basis for difference in the margins of what
Baudrillard theorizes as the totalizing power of the new technology. For example, the remainder depicted in *After Hours* between
power and its other could serve to reengender dialectical change.

Scorsese's film, however, poses a second stumbling block for
ethical advance. For even if a deconstructive interpretation of the
film could make possible, in theory, a basis for radical difference,
the film itself continues to frighten its yuppie viewer away from any
kind of an encounter with extreme difference. Even though *After
Hours* reveals the emptiness of the culture of information, it also
represents the impulses of the avant-garde as pathological and bizarre. Dunne's escape from the culture of information to the culture of expression is represented as a relapse into a nightmare of
sadomasochistic violence. If Baudrillard on occasion romanticizes
graffiti art and the speech of the streets as the only surviving forms
of reciprocal, agonistic communication, *After Hours* demythologizes
that dream as insipid fantasy (*For a Critique* 176). The pervasive
evidence of the commercialization, or death, of art, as well as the
castration images that characterize the graffiti of Soho, supports
Douglas Kellner's rebuke to Baudrillard: that the so-called free
"communication [of the street] can be just as manipulative, distorted, reified as the rest of media communication" (Kellner 67).

The Soho of *After Hours* recalls in part the Paris of Henry
Miller's *Tropic of Cancer*, the book that Dunne is reading in the first
scene in Soho and that initially attracts the attention of Rosanna
Arquette. But if, as Shapiro argues in his introduction to *Tropic of
Cancer*, the streets of Miller's Paris—the city that Miller describes
as a whore—"flow with the healthy fluids of life (xxix)," the series
of women who appear in Scorsese's Soho tease, frustrate, and finally cancel the desire that they promise to set free. *After Hours* may
not succeed in erasing all traces of libidinal communication outside

of systems of power, but it does succeed in conjuring fear for what
is alien.

This paranoia may be justified if it is the case that unrepressed
desire—at least as it is exhibited in the manipulative behavior of
Griffin Dunne in *After Hours* or in the characters of Henry Miller's
Tropic of Cancer—is without responsibility, without the possibility of
reciprocal exchange.[9] Throughout the film any interest that
Dunne shows in the "opposite sex," not to mention in the value of
art (e.g., the bagel and cream cheese paperweights), proves to be
an alibi for narcissistic sexual gratification. Dunne journeys to
Soho not, as he pretends, to appreciate the work of a Soho artist
but to pursue the artist's attractive if strangely troubled roommate,
Arquette. Further, he interprets Arquette's desire for a heart-to-
heart discussion of her problems as an obstacle to his advances.
And throughout the various chase scenes of the film, Dunne shows
that he is incapable of caring for another person.

Arquette finally and unfortunately stops stalling when she
mistakes Dunne's sexual interest as sympathy. But just at the point
when Arquette becomes receptive to Dunne's advances, he con-
vinces himself that her anxiety is an attempt to conceal a badly
burned body. A phobia of burn scars prompts Dunne to leave and
anticipates the hell-like night to follow. If Dunne appears in Soho
on the prowl, the pursuer becomes the pursued. He is chased first
by women who seem to seek only some understanding, but finally
by a vigilante, almost bacchanalian mob led by the driver of the ice
cream truck. The mob mistakes him for a thief and, more appropriately, an intruder and threatens in Dionysian fashion to tear him
to bits.

Dunne's encounters with a weird series of demanding women,
emasculated gays, and thieving Latinos reinforce middle-class
male phobias of life outside of the "normal" channels of success.
The central focus of the film is on the series of blonds, all of whom
fit stereotypes of misogynist culture. The move from uptown to
downtown is also a move from a world centered around men to
one that is depicted as female. The series of blonds degen-
erate from Arquette, whose attractiveness depends on her self-
presentation as victim, to the clinging and nagging (thus wifely)
barmaid, to the bitchy driver of the ice cream truck, and finally, at
Club Berlin, to the cradling arms of the overprotective mother-

type. Moreover, each blond comes from an older generation than the former, thus identifying yet another object of repulsion, the aging woman. Numerous castration images—for example, bathroom graffiti exposing a penis to the jaws of a shark and the mousetraps surrounding the barmaid's netted bed—define the clear danger that women with power represent.

Dunne survives the vigilante mob only with the help of the last woman, the motherly one, who shelters him within a papier-mâché figure in her womblike salon. The fact that the figure resembles the sculpture of the artist whose work he originally sought to purchase not only satirizes the countercultural drive to transform life into a work of art but underscores Dunne's regression from active consumer to passive object. Wrapped in shreds of newsprint, the emasculated Dunne literally vanishes into the bits of information that constitute the communications networks. The stiff, fetal figure pulled from the dark subterranean world of Soho suggests that the muted Dunne is about to be, not reborn, but stillborn to the labor force, or what Baudrillard terms "the deepfrozen infantile world" once known as the real (*Simulations* 24).

Dunne, however, does not escape from his nightmare intact. Near the end, while Dunne is dancing with the last of the blonds and the words of the musical refrain repeat, "Is that all there is?" he mumbles that all he wants is to live. In effect, this allegedly advanced society at the end of history reduces the human being to a most elemental impulse; drained of speech and desire, it seems that the *animal laborans* wants to subsist.[10] Nothing more is at stake.

After Hours elicits a sense of uneasiness with the system and yet mocks the impotence of the yuppie to change it. The film promises, frustrates, and finally paralyzes a paranoid male subject in webs of power that are depicted as castrating, all consuming, and female. The aging motherly blond saves Dunne from the Dionysian mob by virtually entombing him in shredded newspaper. The resulting figure of the muted Dunne aptly anticipates not his recovery as a speaking subject, but his return to the entombing matrices of the postmodern communication network. The paralyzing arms of the communications network extend into the Soho art world and thus suggest significantly that, like the character Dorothy in *Wizard of Oz*, Dunne has never really left home (for Dunne, the labyrinthine systems of power).

In contemporary use, the word "matrix" signifies a network of intersections between input and output leads in a computer, sometimes referred to as the "motherboard." This contemporary figuration of the switchboard of the computer as maternal reflects the etymological root of the postmodern term "matrix" in the Latin *matrix*. The Latin term signifies womb and stems from *mater*, or mother. *After Hours* then figures Dunne's return to the security of his computer station as one to a kind of womb. But if Baudrillard is right, the matrices of postmodern power lack the "secret pockets"—the interstices of either existential desire or interpersonal alterity—that might resist dominant sources of power and engender narratives of subversion and social change. As long as postmodernists like Baudrillard and Scorsese project images of power as castrating and castrated matrices, as images of maternal origin missing not a penis but the folds of a womb, no tale of ethical and political change is possible. The disfiguring and disenabling "hysterectomy" performed by hi-tech postmodernism does not so much re-envision as remove the sources of desire.

Baudrillardian theory would suggest that Dunne is no more a passive object than his Soho female tormenters are aggressive subjects. There is no agon of classical polarities because there are no more poles. The "pacification" that characterizes postindustrial societies stems from the fact that "the two differential poles [of classic dialectic] implode into each other . . . [producing] a simultaneity of contradictions that is both the parody and the end of all dialectic" (*Simulations* 70). If comic dialectic moderates rigid characters via encounters with their equally excessive opposites, postmodern farce would dismantle the freezone that exceeds the grids of power and engenders dialectical advance. No longer free, Soho appears as the product of reactionary imagination, stereotypes constructed out of regressive, narcissistic, middle-class phobias. The final diminution of Griffin Dunne to an image of fetal passivity prepares him to function in power structures that are depicted not in terms of a masculine economy of mastery but rather as emasculating matrices of preprogrammed technology. In postmodernity, power is not phallic; it is maternal. This new image of power, however, is not friendly to women, at least not as long as major artists and theorists like Scorsese and Baudrillard schematize power by way of reactionary images of the feminine.

I suspect, however, that the web of emasculating and emasculated powers envisioned in *After Hours* is not real. If Oz turns out to be nothing but a dream and Dorothy has never left Kansas, then Soho is woven out of the paranoid projections of the yuppie male imagination. Dialectic requires some minimal opening to a flesh-and-blood Other. For Dunne's character, there is none. In *Bringing Up Baby*, Cary Grant encounters a woman beyond his imagination and outside of the projections of male phobia. *After Hours* places Dunne in the presence of castrated victims or castrating powers but never outside of paranoid projections of female power. Scorsese's film should be interpreted as an indictment of the hardened narcissism that, Baudrillard admits, characterizes postmodernism. Once the "opposite sex" is approached as a person and not a barren object, power—especially as Baudrillard theorizes the matrices of power in the postmodern era—will no longer be figured as a woman without secret pockets. It is not, as Derrida argues, radical alterity that obstructs dialectical movement, at least not in this case. It is rather that postmodernism, appearing to have deconstructed the happy endings of comic dialectic, in fact falls short of those classic scenes.

Notes

1. I use the term "rationalistic" to align Grant's character with a modernist formulation of a masculine reason. For an interpretation of Cartesian rationality in terms of a modernist construal of masculinity, see Bordo 114.

2. I use the term "schizophrenic" to indicate that orientation in postmodernism that celebrates freedom from the dominant, phallogocentric codes. See, for example, Deleuze and Guattari.

3. I am agreeing here with Drucilla Cornell and Adam Thurschwell, who argue that "[t]here is an irony in an unbridled feminine negativity that Kristeva does not note explicitly. . . . The striving for absolute freedom in the form of abstract negation denies its relation to the Other" (153).

4. The double education that occurs in the dialectical comedies of Hollywood contrasts sharply with the comic dynamic that is the focus of Bakhtin's studies. Bakhtin argues for the existence of a comic laughter that derives from the lower classes and, thus, brings down whoever might claim a higher status. For this genre of comedy, "there is nothing for memory . . . to do. One ridicules in order to forget" (23).

5. For a Baudrillardian characterization of the aesthetic sensibility of the Soho of the mid- to late-1980s, see Danto 44–48.

6. Cf. Gallop on Baudrillard's use of ironic reversal. According to Gallop, while

Baudrillard never allows reversals to be sublated, he does forestall the complete reversal of at least one position—namely, his hostility to feminism.

7. On the "possibility of 'responsible' or 'emancipatory' media communication," see Kellner 67.

8. For a similar argument, see Jochen Schulte-Sasse's foreword to Bürger.

9. In the great "anti-epiphany" of the *Tropic of Cancer*, the narrator chants "I made up my mind that I would hold on to nothing, that I would expect nothing, that henceforth I would live as animal, a beast of prey, a rover, a plunderer. . . . And if rape were the order of the day then rape I would, and with a vengeance. . . . [For] at the extreme limits of his spiritual being man finds himself again naked as a savage. . . . Morally I am free" (98–99). And later "I haven't any allegiance, any responsibilities" (153).

10. See Fraser for an analysis of the claim that technological societies vanquish the political in favor of an "economic-socio-techno-cultural complex" characterized by the "triumph of the *animal laborans*" and a common life "governed by considerations pertaining to subsistence" (84).

Works Cited

After Hours. Dir. Martin Scorsese. Perf. Griffin Dunne and Rosanna Arquette. Prod. Amy Robinson, Griffin Dunne, and Robert F. Colesberry. 1985.

Bakhtin, Mikhail. *The Dialogic Imagination.* Austin: U of Texas P, 1983.

Baudrillard, Jean. "The Ecstasy of Communication." *The Anti-Aesthetic: Essays on Postmodern Culture.* Ed. Hal Foster. Seattle: Bay, 1983. 126–34.

———. *For a Critique of the Political Economy of the Sign.* Trans. Charles Levin. St. Louis: Telos, 1981.

———. *Simulations.* Trans. Paul Foss, Paul Patton, and Philip Beitchman. New York: Semiotext(e), 1983.

Bordo, Susan. *The Flight to Objectivity.* Albany: SUNY P, 1987.

Bringing Up Baby. Dir. Howard Hawks. Perf. Cary Grant and Katharine Hepburn. Prod. Howard Hawks. 1938.

Cavell, Stanley. *Pursuits of Happiness.* Cambridge: Harvard UP, 1981.

Cornell, Drucilla, and Adam Thurschwell. "Feminism, Negativity, Intersubjectivity." *Feminism as Critique.* Ed. Selya Benhabib and Drucilla Cornell. Minneapolis: U of Minnesota P, 1987. 143–62.

Danto, Arthur C. "The Hyper-Intellectual." *New Republic* 10 and 17 Sept. 1990: 44–48.

Deleuze, Gilles, and Felix Guattari. *Kafka: Toward a Minor Literature.* Trans. Dana Polan. Minneapolis: U of Minnesota P, 1986.

Fraser, Nancy. *Unruly Practices.* Minneapolis: U of Minnesota P, 1989.

Frye, Northrop. *Anatomy of Criticism.* Princeton: Princeton UP, 1957.

Fukuyama, Francis. "The End of History?" *National Interest* 16 (1989): 44–48.

Gallop, Jane. "French Theory and the Seduction of Feminism." *Men in Feminism.* Ed. Alice Jardine and Paul Smith. New York: Routledge, 1989. 111–15.

Kellner, Douglass. *Jean Baudrillard: From Marxism to Postmodernism and Beyond.* Stanford: Stanford UP, 1989.

Martin, Bill. *Matrix and Line: Derrida and the Possibilities of Postmodern Social Theory.* Albany: SUNY P, 1992.

Miller, Henry. *Tropic of Cancer*. Introd. Karl Shapiro. New York: Grove, 1961.

The Philadelphia Story. Dir. George Cukor. Perf. Cary Grant and Katharine Hepburn. Prod. Joseph L. Mankiewicz. 1940.

Poster, Mark. "Words Without Things: The Mode of Information." *October* 53 (1990): 63–77.

Schulte-Sasse, Jochen. Foreword. *Theory of the Avant-Garde*. By Peter Bürger. Trans. Michael Shaw. Minneapolis: U of Minnesota P, 1984.

Willett, Cynthia. "Hegel, Antigone, and the Possibility of Ecstatic Dialectic." *Philosophy and Literature* 14 (1990): 268–83.

———. "Hollywood Comedy and Aristotelian Ethics: Reconciling Differences." *Sexual Politics and Popular Culture*. Ed. Diane Raymond. Bowling Green: Popular P, 1990. 15–24.

Nintendo and Telos: Will You Ever Reach the End?

Peter Buse

Ｗe live in the "cybernetic age." The presence of machines and technological devices in our culture is so pervasive that it no longer makes sense to talk of technology as separate from the general sphere of human activity. In *The Soft-Machine: Cybernetic Fiction,* David Porush says we need look no further than today's children to find a telling barometer of the shift into this new age. Here is the sinister picture he paints of the local video arcade where the offspring of the new age are to be found:

> In their off hours, their fingers play over the controls of video games and "micros," their faces lit up by the light of CRT screens, bodies moving in rhythm to a complex feedback mechanism, eyes, minds and hands locked in a looped circuit of reflex and reward with a more-than-mere-game. In the video arcade, the machines are united by a single principle: ultimately, hardware defeats exhaustible and vulnerable organs and intelligences grown in flesh and housed in bone. Next time you're there, watch the players hitched to their boxes and ask who controls what. Or what controls whom (1–2)

© 1996 by *Cultural Critique*. Fall 1996. 0882-4371/96/$5.00.

Parents, it seems, should no longer ask where their children are, but what they are. In any case, the rapid advent of Sega and Nintendo "home entertainment systems" ensures the datedness of Porush's "futuristic" scenario, with video arcades sadly vacant and going the way of the Amstrad: cybernetic obsolescence. In the past five to ten years, the video game context has altered radically and vid-kids (still primarily boys, if *i-D* magazine and innumerable other sources are to be trusted) can be found sublimating their aggression in the safety of their bedrooms and TV rooms instead of lurking in dark and dingy arcades.

Although *The Soft-Machine* leaves video games after the dramatic vision of the arcade, going on to discuss novelists like Barth, Pynchon, Calvino, and Coover, the passage just quoted is representative of Porush's main thesis: cybernetic fiction is pitted against science in a contest where "literature actually has the means to meet science on its own territory" (373). Porush claims to be ushering in a new epistemology, attempting to break down the opposition that separates "human" and "machine," but in doing so he clings to a very old paradigm, maintaining a wariness toward a cold hard science that erodes our "humaneness." More specifically, Porush describes an ideal "postmodern science" that allows for the human element in science (377). This is a bit like the pop psychology idea of men recognizing their feminine side and women recognizing their masculine side. It maintains the categories as discrete, but says they can exist harmoniously within a single subject.

This is not the place to re-rehearse the critique of the Enlightenment subject. Suffice it to say that Porush's ominous question about "who controls what or what controls whom" in the arcade invokes a potentially autonomous human consciousness engaged in a struggle with technology; and in the case of video games, technology appears to have the upper hand. To posit the relationship between technology and its users as a conflict for control amounts to inserting an old debate about free will versus determinism into a contemporary frame. Such a frame reduces discussion of technology to the absolutes of technophiles singing the praises of useful new tools and technophobes who cite Chaplin's *Modern Times* as the most telling commentary on the dehumanizing capacity of the mechanical age. With the introduction of such a limiting frame, Porush excludes any possible analysis of video games in terms of desire and subjectivity. For him, the vexed problem is whether we control the machines or whether they control us, when he could be asking what the *implications* of technology are for the subject. I think Porush is right: video games *are* potentially revealing indicators of a paradigm shift, but I would like to reorient the mode of analysis. Rather than thinking of video games as machines with manipulative capacities, "minds of their own," it might be more useful to see them as narrative machines, providing for their players stories in which to participate. Participation, as a term, has the advantage of skirting the bounds of both free will and determinism, and should be taken to have at least two meanings here: first, the literal playing of the game, and second, the "enunciation" of the game/narrative by the viewer/player. What is so fascinating about video games is the possibility for overlap in these two meanings. In the following discussion I first attempt to trace and account for that overlap and then try to place video games within a wider cultural context.

Doing Things with Video Games

Thinking of video games in terms of narrative may seem like a paradoxical operation, an encounter between an old-fashioned concept and a thoroughly modern phenomenon. Paradoxical or not, video games without fail deploy some variety of skeleton plot, usually culled from the adventure genre, and indeed, Marsha Kinder has fruitfully explored, in *Playing with Power,* their insertion into the wider signifying network of children's entertainment, including film and Saturday morning television. But the structure of video game narratives also merits closer attention on its own. A trip to the (abandoned) local (British) arcade yields four random examples: *Streetfighter II, AeroFighters, Seibu-Cup Soccer,* and *Undercover Cops.* The emphasis on combat and competition is not as random as the choice, because video and computer games generally thrive on narratives based on belligerence. *Streetfighter II* involves hand-to-hand combat between various colorful characters in exotic locales, ranging from an American airbase to a temple in India and a street in China. A similar international flavor predominates in *AeroFighters,* in which lone pilots from the U.S.A., Sweden, Japan,

or the U.K. engage in air battles with the ultimate aim of destroying the enemy's base.[1] The soccer game uses as its narrative the
World Cup and the player has the choice of one of the globe's leading sides. *Undercover Cops*, meanwhile, is, like *Streetfighter II*, a hand-
to-hand combat game, but this time the plot involves tracking
down and eliminating uncharismatic drug dealers. The games all
go to some length to provide background information on the plot
scenario or on the traits of the characters. In *Undercover Cops*, then,
the opening credits of the game explain that a plague of drugs is
ravaging the city and it is up to the special drug squad (that's you:
the player) to squash the ring; in *AeroFighters*, names and faces, not
to mention nationalities, are assigned to the choices of pilot.[2]

None of these narratives are particularly remarkable: innumerable similar examples could be found in more elaborated and
expanded forms in war comics and Kung-Fu movies, and analyzing
their aggressive project would be neither difficult nor particularly
illuminating.[3] Equally, video game narratives are predictable and
depressing when it comes to sexual politics: with a few notable exceptions, like *Tetris* and other nongendered games, they rather
crudely reproduce the worst-case scenario of patriarchal gender
relations.[4] What *is* remarkable about the games is not so much the
stories they tell, or even the way in which they tell them, but the
actual process of telling and reading or, alternatively, of playing.
The notion of "playing a narrative" is not entirely satisfactory, but
is preferable to "reading," because, as Paul Virilio says when he
comments on the speed of propaganda transmission, "Reading implies time for reflection, a slowing-down" (5). Video games accelerate narrative beyond any possibility of "reading" in a traditional
sense. They do for narrative what the microwave does for cooking.

In *Story and Situation*, Ross Chambers identifies two major
strands of inquiry in contemporary narratology: on the one hand,
the examination of narrative structure, and on the other, analysis
of the discursive presentation of events. These two forms of study
yield, respectively, a "grammar" and a "rhetoric" of narrative (4).
In the case of video games, ascertaining a fine grammar would
involve labeling elements common to all games, such as the hero
figure, the progression through stages or levels, the scoring system,
and so on. Analyzing the rhetoric of a game, on the other hand,
would entail examining the basic narrative ("story") in relation to

its mode of presentation ("discourse"), that is, the visual, or more precisely, graphic, format. However, in addition to these two critical approaches to narrative, Chambers suggests a third, largely neglected, possibility for inquiry: the function of telling. Claiming that "literary criticism and theory have paid little attention to the performative function of storytelling," he proposes a narratology concerned primarily with the "event" of storytelling (4). Chambers draws on the speech-act theory elaborated by J. L. Austin, who distinguished, in *How to Do Things with Words*, between constative utterances, which simply convey information, and performative utterances, which "do things." The same division can be applied to the utterance of narratives. Each telling or reading of a "story" is not simply the safe transmission of a content, but also a performance.

Video games attempt to collapse the distinction between narrative as story and narrative as performance. In Chambers's discussion of nineteenth-century short stories, he foregrounds storytelling as performance, but in a video game narrative there is no evident narrator or storyteller. In a video game the playing process both constitutes the narrative and "performs" the text. The plot proceeds only by dint of the player participating in the game, bringing the main protagonist to life, and directing it/him/her through the hazardous fictional world. If *Pac-Man* is a story about a round yellow creature which makes its way around mazes eating little dots and avoiding nasty creatures, then that story is realized only when the playing enacts the situation. And each performance is different, elaborating a different plot, with Pac-Man following different patterns in the maze and living for shorter or longer durations. A poor player might last only twenty seconds; another story might be abruptly ended due to unnecessary risks on the part of the protagonist; yet another might play for hours on end. But this is not some highly refined form of reader-response whereby a skeleton plot is left to the whims of the players' expressivity. Success in a video game demands a rigorous interpretative process: not a hermeneutics aimed at unveiling the truth, but a rapid scanning of specific signs and situations prompting the best possible "moves," which in turn guarantee the continuation of the story. How, then, do these video games differ from games like chess, or even Monopoly for that matter? Those games also require interpretative acumen and a selection of "moves" that can range from brilliant to disastrous. The element of speed has already been touched upon, and certainly board games do not require the conditioning of reflexes and high levels of hand-eye coordination. There is at least one other important distinction to be made between the two game forms: in one the player faces a board and another player, while in the other the player faces a screen.[5] The presence of the screen inevitably suggests that video games be submitted to the discoveries of film theory.

Ross Chambers emphasizes the need "not simply to read texts in situation (which is inevitable) but also to read, in the texts, the situation that they *produce*" (4). Such reading occurs in film theory, particularly as elaborated in *Screen*, which dedicated much energy in the 1970s to questions of modes of address and how cinematic "texts" *produce* for the spectator a position (or positions) from which to "enounce" or "utter" the film. It seems to me that Chambers's interest lies in very much the same questions about narrative, albeit from within a different theoretical framework; whereas *Story and Situation* draws on speech-act theory, the work done in *Screen* sets out from theories of ideology and psychoanalysis. Both approaches are germane to this project, which hopes to chart the configurations of both performance *and* subjectivity in video games.

A speculative reading of video games through classical film theory would probably proceed by way of the player's Imaginary. Questions of the spectator's Imaginary investment in the cinema are most famously addressed by Christian Metz in such essays as "The Imaginary Signifier," where he extrapolates from the work of Jacques Lacan on the mirror-stage. Lacan memorably argues in "The Mirror-Stage" that the infant perceiving itself in the mirror is "caught up in the lure of spatial identification, the succession of phantasies that extends from a fragmented body-image to a form of its totality" (4). The perceiving proto-subject finds security in its stable image and an attendant object world, but is simultaneously alienated from itself as it identifies with an imaginary object in the mirror image. Metz reorients Lacan's theory and applies it to the cinema, claiming that the screen is like a mirror in which "everything may come to be projected," except for one essential thing: the spectator's own body (48). Since there is no body to identify with, Metz reasons that the spectator may identify with a character, but that above all, "the spectator *identifies with himself* [*sic*], with himself as pure act of perception" (51). Here Metz invokes the scopic drive, concluding that the spectator achieves a position of plenitude, of power within the field of vision, by identifying with the camera, which presumably can see everyone and freeze and control the object world.

Despite the obvious difference that there is no literal camera in video games, we can still bring Metz's arguments to bear on them. It little matters how images are provided to the subject: it is the very provision of images that is important. We might say that the video graphics simulate the activity of the camera, or, so as not to give priority to one technique over another, we could equally say that the activity of the camera has the capacity to simulate the generation of computer graphics. They both frame time and space within a limited field of vision. In any case, the kind of projection of interest here is psychic and not cinematic. As far as the Lacanian infant is concerned, Jacqueline Rose explains, "The early emphasis by Lacan on *Gestalt,* on the child's ability to represent its body to itself, is . . . not simply a notion of some comforting illusory poise, but is directly linked at this stage in his theory to its ability to control its world in a physical sense" (172). The mirror confirms the proto-subject's own motor coordination, by sending back a falsely totalizing image of a fragmented and incoordinate body. The structural relation here is metonymic (image: part; body: whole), and all video games employ this very same screen device, providing the player with an icon, which has a metonymic function in relation to the player's body. The player manipulates the icon on the screen with a joystick and/or various buttons, completing the circuit of specularity. Following Metz's argument, the player sees herself or himself seeing herself or himself and, through this actual physical participation, gains control over the physical world as well as the image one. Video games, it seems, incarnate the perfection of the mirror, inserting the subject into a narrative in which she or he sees herself or himself projected as the hero and potential master.

This happy and insouciant subject, linked merrily to an imago machine, is, of course, a caricature, and headed for a fall. As it turns out, the seeing subject in a Lacanian schema never achieves plenitude and is doomed to be duped, not satisfied. When Lacan treats the gaze, he speaks of the subject "who apprehends something that is one of the essential correlates of consciousness in its relation to representation, and which is designated as *I see myself seeing myself* . . . correlative with that fundamental mode to which we referred in the Cartesian *cogito,* by which the subject apprehends himself as thought" (*Four Concepts* 80). But Lacan dismisses the specular claims of the cogito and refers instead to "the illusion of the consciousness of *seeing oneself seeing oneself*" (83). The cogito is undermined by the intervention of desire in the "domain of seeing" (85).

In *Sexuality in the Field of Vision,* Jacqueline Rose criticizes Metz's formulations of the spectator's imaginary identifications precisely on the question of desire, which always disrupts plenitude or satisfaction. Rose points out that in Lacan, as well as Freud, identification is only temporary and never complete, instead slipping constantly. She wants to emphasize "the presence or insistence of desire inside these very forms which are designed to reproduce or guarantee the specular illusion itself (image, screen, spectator)" (190). Even if the player experiences a moment of jubilation at the control wielded over the little yellow Pac-Man, that moment is predicated on the possibility of another such moment (the next dot eaten, the next level cleared). And at the end of the day, even if you imagine you have won the simulated World Cup of *Seibu-Cup Soccer,* you are still playing a game designed to be lost. This is not the gambler's complaint of the rigged table that impairs the fairness of the odds. Fairness is not at issue here. The inevitable loss is the condition of the desire set up by the game format. However, this desire is set up along the axis of narrative enunciation, and not necessarily within the scopic regime. Indeed, as Gillian Skirrow has observed, video games may in fact constitute a "break with television's traditional role as world-window" and the screen as suturing device, because they "unhook the aerial" (121). Therefore, in order to begin to understand the movements of this desire, it is best to leave film theory and return again to the narrative.

Will You Ever Reach the End?

In its glossy, visually dazzling, and aggressive adverts, the Nintendo corporation, as represented by a booming and scornful voice, tempts prospective buyers of a new video game with the tantalizing slogan, "The Ultimate Challenge Has Arrived." Following this in dramatic lettering, as the rhetorical coup de grace, is the challenge, "Will You Ever Reach the End?" After a suitable pause additional letters join the word "End" to form "Super Nintendo." In equally technically mind-boggling and fast-paced advertisements, the competition, Sega, offers its incentive: "To Be This Good Takes AGES." The final moments of each advert see Sega pulling a page from the Nintendo guide to creative advertising (or is it the other way around?), with the "AGES" spinning on its axis to reveal the source of *this* Ultimate Challenge. A few things become clear from these simple, up-front visual prompts.[6] The narrative on offer in these video games is not going to be an easy read. The first time you play it, you will quickly lose your icon, or character, or "life," or what you will. This first loss may be frustrating or upsetting, and the frustration may be compounded if you keep on dying at a tricky part of the game. But do not worry if you cannot get past a particularly nasty monster; after all, you can always go back and start again, and if you repeat the process enough times, you will eventually defeat that monster and move ever closer to that elusive End. Whatever you do, don't give up: you can die a thousand deaths before you do that. When you are skillful enough, but only then, you will attain that triumphant moment of completion, having mastered every danger and trap in the long narrative adventure, and the sweet taste of victory will more than compensate for the time, trouble, and struggle. Bask in the glory for awhile, tell all your friends (who still haven't reached even Level 4), and if you get bored, don't worry, your parents are an easy touch for a new game.

The story just recounted is not a new one. It goes back at least as far as 1920 when Freud told it in *Beyond the Pleasure Principle*. That text arose from his inability to account for the repetition compulsion marked in some of his patients, a compulsion that flew in the face of the dominance of the pleasure principle previously thought to be supreme. Intervening in the domain of pleasure is the reality principle, which "demands and carries into effect the postponement of satisfaction and the temporary toleration of unpleasure as a step on the long indirect road to pleasure" (278). This psychic economy of the detour acts as a device for managing trauma. A subject will unconsciously repeat a painful experience, not for pleasure evidently, but so as to master that experience: "by

repeating it, unpleasurable though it was, as a game, he took an
active part. These efforts might be put down to an instinct for mastery that was acting independently of whether the memory was in
itself pleasurable or not" (285). Freud then extrapolates from this
account of the Fort/Da game to attribute to humanity "an urge . . .
to restore an earlier state of things" (308). This is the infamous
death drive, which has it that "the aim of all life is death" (311).
However, we are not forever throwing ourselves off cliffs because
of the prevalence of the reality principle (or is it the pleasure principle?),[7] which causes "the still surviving substance to diverge ever
more widely from its original course of life and to make even more
complicated *detours* before reaching its aim of death. These circu-
itous paths to death . . ." (311).

In *Beyond the Pleasure Principle,* Freud makes certain formulations about deferral, delay, and the impossibility of presence, but
then he relays his discoveries into a metaphysical conclusion. In
his close and extended reading of *Beyond* in *The Post-Card,* Jacques
Derrida suspends Freud's conclusions and puts them off slightly
longer, emphasizing the double deferral of the pleasure principle,
which "submits itself, provisionally and to a certain extent, to its
own lieutenant" (288), and "the enigmatic death drive which appears, disappears, appears to disappear, appears in order to disappear" (262). In the "Envoi" section of *The Post-Card,* Derrida rewrites *Beyond* in terms of postal systems, those networks designed
to send letters to their proper destinations, but by way of relays
and way stations where the letters could, and do, go astray. The
post links destination to identity, but identity (reciprocity, the self-
same) is always sent down the trail of desire instead (192). A postal
coordinator who would master and monitor very post-box and office and carrier, would always be one step away from that mastery.
Mastery, like death, has no fixed address.

The parallels between Freud's paper and the video game–
playing process can be readily recognized, and Marsha Kinder has
already made the connection with *Beyond the Pleasure Principle,* or
rather, she reads video games through Peter Brooks's version of
Freud's "master plot" in *Reading for the Plot:*

> players are constantly threatened by short circuiting and pre-
> mature deaths (which indeed are called "deaths"), while their

compulsive repetitions are rewarded (for this is the only means of advancing in the game). Spatialized as detours and warp zones, the narrative elaborations serve to postpone and intensify the final gratification: mastering the game (Kinder 111).

In Kinder's version though, the result is a somewhat rosier outlook on play, narrative, and repetition, where the tensions between reality and pleasure principles are resolved and Eros and Thanatos exist in a complementarity they never achieve in Freud's text. Of the narrative-play process she describes, she concludes, "Such a structure is bound to lead to cognitive development, for, like drinking milk or doing daily aerobics, the compulsive consumption of video games appears to accelerate growth" (111). Comparison of aerobics and video games must give either one or the other a bad name, and as for milk, one would not have to look far to find a parent or equivalent moral arbiter to protest that games constitute something more toxic, or at least less wholesome.

What Kinder leaves out is the darker side of Freud's paper; for one thing, a trauma is the necessary starting kernel for compulsive repetition, and games produce for their players that trauma. Furthermore, "mastery," whether achieved or not, is never pursued without costs. As Kinder herself is quick to emphasize, video games have always courted and supported a masculinist culture (103–8); and it is safe to say that mastery has traditionally been a masculine preoccupation. If the games do offer and expect mastery from players, this certainly squares with the charge frequently made that video game playing not only is a predominantly male practice but is gendered masculine. Leslie Haddon has usefully charted the development of video games as a male preserve, from their prehistory in the all-male MIT computer labs of the 1960s to the arcade culture of the 1970s and early 1980s. He argues that the insertion of video games into an arcade setting meant they were "slotted into an existing nexus of social relations" with marginalized girls (61) and adds that the "coin-op context may have contributed to the development of the games as 'masculine texts', but it also structured games playing as a collective male activity" (65). However, the masculinity cultivated in arcades must be qualified as ambivalent at best. Gone are the days of the Tom Brown or Boy Scout–style entry into the symbolic order, for video games drag growing boys away from their natural healthy habitat—the sporting fields—and into the dark arcade where all other muscles atrophy at the expense of wrist and retina. The development of a youth male culture around video and computer games may not constitute an erosion of the masculine, but it at least signals a re-configuration of gender around technology.

In any case, is it really valid to claim, as Kinder does, that players achieve "the final gratification: mastery of the game"? In the video game situation, mastery through repetition is indeed on offer. In fact, the games not only offer mastery to the player but demand it; but it is a mastery that is always just delayed or de-ferred. It is important to note in this context a minor but signifi-cant difference between the video game played in the arcade and the one played at home. Although the playing paradigm remains for the most part consistent in both situations, one difference is striking: an arcade game is interminable, the home game termina-ble, at least at a superficial level. Nintendo and Sega games both offer the lure of "completing" all the levels of one of their games, of reaching the end, whereas in the arcade, there are an infinite number of levels to play. In the old-style arcade game with the interminable narrative, the lure consists in reaching yet another level or stage of the game, with outright "victory" over the machine impossible. Mastery, then, is understood as only temporary in the arcade, and the challenge consists in getting as much playing time out of one coin as possible; as in Freud's *Beyond,* the player repeats persistently the drive toward ending the game but perversely and simultaneously does the utmost to prolong the struggle, and to de-fer and delay the end.

Computer games played in the home originally deployed the same strategy of interminable narratives, until Sega and Nintendo corporations transformed game playing with terminable game narratives. For instance, *Sonic the Hedgehog,* released in 1991, seems potentially endless to the uninitiated and unskillful, but in fact it is possible to "conquer" the game, to "reach the End," at least after playing the game many times over and discovering and avoiding progressively more traps and dangers the second, third, fourth, and nth time round. Repetition here seems to promise more than just more of the same: there are potential "returns" at a material level, in the form of closure. Closure in this case is also temporary, of course, because the player will repeat the same process with a "different" game.

It is obviously very much in the the interests of Sega and Nintendo to provide games with terminus points, because when players finish one game, master it, they will most likely want to head right out and buy another. It is also impossible to overestimate the impact of Nintendo and Sega and their "entertainment systems" on the the very paradigms and culture of video game playing. Even before Nintendo's entry into the market in the mid-1980s, arcade games were phenomenally lucrative, straddling the top of the culture industry in financial terms. In 1982 these games grossed 8 billion dollars, outstripping both pop music (4 billion) and Hollywood films (3 billion); revenue from *Pac-Man* alone is thought to have surpassed even *Star Wars* (Haddon 53). It is sobering to think that among the leading youth icons of the late 1970s and early 1980s, Luke Skywalker might have come second to a little yellow "icon." But 1982 marked the peak of the arcade game successes, and when Nintendo arrived on the American scene in 1985, the industry was generally thought to be in decline; in three years the bottom had fallen out of Atari's market (Kinder 88). Nevertheless, within five years, Nintendo had remarkably taken a firm grip on the entire industry and had effected the transition of high quality video games from arcade to living room. They achieved this coup partly by virtue of "superior technology and close control over compatible software" (Kinder 91). Equally crucial to their success was their expansion into what Marsha Kinder calls the "commercial supersystem of transmedia intertextuality" (92). Nintendo does not limit itself to video games, but casts its nets widely, incorporating cartoons, magazines, clothing, games programs, and countless other product tie-ins, all copyrighted under the Nintendo trademark (Kinder 92–93). In other words, they deftly combine the twin magic of merchandising and the microchip. The big video game corporations benefit constantly from the high visibility of their names and the continual reinforcement of their consumerist message in spheres other than simply game playing.

Nintendo and Sega can never be extricated from the culture industry complex and the consumerist apparatus they inhabit. However, although it is true that the circuit of desire in video games is set up, in the crudest terms, to make money, there is by no means a one-to-one correlation between the financial and libidinal investments made in the games by their players, because the significance of these narratives at the cultural level exceeds any reduction to the economy. Video games, after all, are not necessarily a money-making proposition (like all software, they can be copied and therefore require electronic protection); and it takes the marketing wizardry of Nintendo's commercial infrastructure to make them viable. In the remainder of this article I shall suggest how one might start to think about these video game narratives in terms of a more general economy of desire and expenditure.

Kiddie Cocaine

In the January 1993 "screen issue" of *i-D* magazine, whose cover is graced by none other than "Sonic the Hedgehog, game hero," a panel of "experts" on computer games are brought together to discuss the significance and impact of the boom in computer games in the United Kingdom. The very first question addressed to the forum includes the term "kiddie cocaine," which apparently was coined by the *Sunday Times* to describe the effects of games on fourteen-year-olds. The phrase has a potent emotive charge, juxtaposing the supposedly innocent with the absolutely tarnished. Members of the panel jumped at this bait and were quick to downplay the potential addictive powers of computer games. However, the topic did not so quickly go away, and one panel member proposed that the games were "compulsive," while another suggested that "[m]ost games incorporate obsessive patterns." Guy Nisbett summarizes most succinctly the cocaine effect:

> [T]he object of the game is to elevate you to an adrenalised state which is where the cocaine analogy comes in. You're encouraged to continually project your excitement forwards and imagine you're about to get to something really interesting. Of course there's a constant denial of resolution which keeps you obsessively projecting forwards. ("i-D's Forum" 16)

Already there is a hint of a Freudian formula, but it is only when the panel must answer criticism about the pervasive violence in the games that the drug equation emerges fully. Claire Bowen points out that "there are no controls . . . to prevent young people being *exposed* to what could be called *harmful material*," and Vivienne Baker claims that "[g]ames are designed to *create altered states* and as powerful ones as possible" (16; my emphasis). On the reverse side of this concern, the ITV program *Bad Influence,* which reviews new games, consciously exploits in its title the same metaphorics of drugs.

The analogies made between narcotics and computer games and addiction and obsessive playing are not particularly satisfying, at least not within the current understanding of "narcotics" and "addiction." Besides bearing the great weight of moral censure, a weight exploited by the *Sunday Times* in their "kiddie cocaine" phrase, drugs and addiction are also overinscribed and overanalyzed by both the legal and medical institutions. Therefore, it is almost impossible to speak of "drugs" without invoking an entire set of values and prohibitions, both moral and legal. Nor is it possible to speak of "addiction" without assuming in that use a primarily biological and physiological state. Nor does a simple reversal of the antidrugs stance, in the form of a sixties-style celebration of "experimentation" and addiction, escape the dominant logic about drugs. What is needed is an analysis of "drugs" that suspends the naive choice of "for" or "against" and promotes a wider exploration of the implications of narcotics. This is precisely what Avital Ronell attempts to do in *Crack Wars: Literature Addiction Mania,* preferring to think about addiction in terms of desire and subjectivity rather than physiology and morality.

While Ronell does not ignore the various explanatory systems brought to bear on "drugs," she points out that rarely do these systems succeed in accounting for drugs, which have a great capacity to "resist conceptual arrest" (51). No discipline deals with them comprehensively:

> Drugs cannot be placed securely within the frontiers of traditional disciplines: anthropology, biology, chemistry, politics, medicine, or law could not, solely on the strength of their respective epistemologies, claim to contain or counteract them. While everywhere dealt with, drugs act as a radically nomadic parasite let loose from the will of language. (52)

It is drugs' potential to be substituted and re-contextualized so easily which allows the phrase "kiddie cocaine" to work so smoothly in relation to video games. Ronell's point is that the signifier, or the substance "drugs," is, beyond any explanatory analysis, libidinally invested: "To get off drugs, or alcohol (major narcissistic crisis), the addict has to shift dependency to a person, an ideal, or to the procedure itself of cure" (25). In other words, anything can act "as a drug," as an other that will provide temporary gratification. And just as an understanding of desire must go beyond the naive single object "sex," so Ronell includes in her "Narcoanalysis" "soft" drugs like caffeine and literature, as well as hard ones like cocaine, heroin, and crack.

What is at stake in "drugs"? "More so perhaps than any other 'substance,' whether real or imagined, drugs thematize the dissociation of autonomy and responsibility that has marked our epoch since Kant" (Ronell 59). *Crack Wars* at every turn resists summary, but this statement may be plucked out of the text as a sort of thetic pronouncement. Drugs introduce the specter of dependency into the Enlightenment model of the autonomous, independent subject. Dependency has a bad name: in spheres other than drug use it is equally to be avoided at all costs. In relationships, for instance, dependency is seen as a poor substitute for "love," understood as equal, reciprocal, democratic. Dependency is the realm of the addict, who is controlled and driven by substances and urges outside his or her agency. With addiction, culture can establish a mode of existence that is abnormal, because dependent, and thereby reaffirm that in general independence and autonomy are the rule. But drugs are never entirely excluded, and are subject instead to categorization: "good" drugs and "bad" drugs. Metaphysics in fact embraces drugs in small doses: "Precisely due to the promise of exteriority they are thought to extend, drugs have been redeemed by the conditions of transcendancy and revelation with which they are not uncommonly associated" (Ronell 61). If taken within reason, or so the argument goes, drugs can be a reassuring supplement whose "exteriority" acts as a guarantee of our interiority. Ultimately though, drugs in their more general sense radically throw into doubt the possibility of such a thing as "nondependency."

How does a "narcoanalysis" relate to the countless fourteen-year-olds "hooked" on their video games? To begin, it might be useful to remember that aside from the "kiddie cocaine" analogy, drugs and video games share a certain history. Video arcades are notorious as haunts of drug dealers, and many adolescents' first encounters with illegal drugs may coincide with the playing of video games. Ironically though, the appearance of games in the arcade, which was already an established setting for youth culture, was partly heralded as an opportunity to "clean up" the poor reputation of arcades. According to Leslie Haddon, "Amusement park owners adopted electronic games as part of a wider attempt to shed the sleazy image of the arcade . . . the electronic hi-tech form of the new games signalled a cleaner, more modern image" (59–60). Such a position corresponds to the conception of technology as panacea and locates the games firmly within the scope of drugs, albeit "good" ones.

Video games, like drugs, also promote a sort of expenditure without reserve: the player, like the addict, will divert all resources to the financing of the habit, and even be parasitic on the family—parasitic in the sense that there is no "return" on money put toward the habit. The substitution of the living room for the arcade as the dominant context for video games may have removed the immediate specter of drugs, but the boom in Nintendo and Sega has, if anything, increased the extraordinary capacity for video games to empty the pockets of their players. The rate of expenditure has, however, taken on a somewhat different complexion: arcade games take endless streams of small currency to ensure continued play, while home systems require large layouts of money at staggered intervals, with the guarantee of virtually endless play.

The *Sunday Times* hardly achieved a great journalistic insight by stigmatizing video games with the epithet "kiddie cocaine." It was more a case of reinventing the wheel, since the accusations leveled at the industry reach back to its inception: the debate is as old as the invention. In the late 1970s not only did a Labour MP in the United Kingdom attempt to pass a bill regulating *Space Invaders* and other games, on the grounds they were addictive, but the surgeon general in the United States warned that the games were potentially dangerous and addictive to children (Haddon 60). The mass media and government are not alone in producing reactions to the video game phenomenon; video games have also come increasingly under scrutiny by the disciplines that monitor antisocial behavior in general. A quick survey of *Sociofile* yields many examples of empirical research on "the effects" of video games on

"social behavior," with titles such as "Video Games and Leisure Behaviour: A Report on an Empirical Study," "Video Arcades, Youth,
and Trouble," "Videogames, Television Violence, and Aggression
in Teenagers," and "The Effects of Prosocial and Aggressive Videogames on Children's Donating and Helping." The last example
in this short list hints that video games might be "good" as well as
"bad" drugs, if more attention is paid to their "content." In the
Sociofile survey, there are also examples of video games seen as potentially instrumental, as "good" supplements to education: "Play
as Acquisition of Mental Structures: The Case of Video Games"
and "Educational and Recreational Uses of Computer Technology:
Computer Instruction and Video Games." These two modes of
analysis seem at odds; they read the absolutely contrary lessons of
danger and utility from the games. However, they share a similar
totalizing view of supplementarity as an "adding on" that can and
should be controlled. Patricia Marks Greenfield, writing on child
development theory, is representative of this train of thought.
While rejecting the addiction thesis in favor of an optimistic evaluation of the games' "use" value, she repeats the classic poison/
cure dilemma:

> [T]oo much control over the fantasy worlds of video games
> could bring about impatience with the messy uncontrollable
> world of real life. This possible danger must, however, be
> weighed against the positive effects of achievement and con-
> trol for children who, for whatever reasons, lack a sense of
> competence and predictability in other domains of life (114).

It is not insignificant that while relatively speaking not a great deal
has been written about games from the point of view of cultural
studies, there is an ever-growing literature from cognitive psychology, skills acquisition theory, sociology, and so on. The assumption
prevails that video games are an inherently neutral medium and
can be discussed in terms of behavior and socialization instead of
culture and signifying practices. Equally telling is the bracketing of
children and youth in the same category of scrutiny (and anxiety)
as addiction; the potential of addiction, which lets loose dependent, nonautonomous subjects on the world, is to be most feared
among those individuals who have not yet acceded legally, physi-

cally, or psychically to "full" subjectivity, and who are therefore still dependent beings.

Video games are a by-product of the much larger realm of computer technology, and computers are the technological prostheses par excellence of the late twentieth century. They act as mnemonic aids, as calculating devices, as writing machines, and have countless other "uses." "User" is the apparently transparent term applied to any operator of a computer, and a "user-friendly" computer is one whose operation is so simple it is almost natural. But much more is implied by "user" than mere utility. With use comes wear and tear, repetition, erosion and loss, and of course an addict is also known as a "user." "Use" cannot be easily detached from dependency even though it immediately signifies activity and manipulation on the part of the user. The unfixing of the simple association of computers with utility goes hand in hand with a more general interrogation of the technology-progress link, usually taken as self- evident. This is a good point at which to refer directly to the first part of the double title of this paper, already alluded to silently throughout the section on video game narratives and the death drive. In order to prise technology, and therefore the supplement, away from its connection to the meta-narrative of progress (whose "end" is understood as telos), maybe we need to propose, tentatively, a teleology without a definite telos. Is such a thing possible? In Freud it may be, for what does *Beyond the Pleasure Principle* suggest if not a certain teleological operation—drives, desires, instincts—in which telos has become blurred to the point of indeterminacy, even irrelevance? Perhaps the appropriate answer to Nintendo's question cum provocative challenge, "Will You Ever Reach the End?" is neither the "yes" of mastery nor the "no" of the perpetually duped subject-player, but "Who cares?" or "Does it even matter?"

When Derrida announces in *The Post-Card* that "a letter can always—and therefore must—never arrive at its destination," this is not a source of frustration, "not something negative, it's good, and is the condition . . . that something does arrive" (121). Something arrives, but the arrival is not subject entirely to intention or consciousness. In the video game narrative of repetition I have just told, that which is intended never arrives, and this *is* a source of frustration. But where are the slippages, if any, within this seamless desiring (or addictive) network I have detailed? The answer, I think, is in the playing/reading process initially outlined. If a video game is a narrative that is performance-contingent, and each performance diverges or detours, then the traditional humanist manner of securing the stable meaning of a text in a proper name that stands in for the full consciousness of the intender/author no longer holds. This is the radical implication of the new narrative process that does not assume a transmission of full information from one consciousness to another. If we borrow Michel de Certeau's formulation of "reading as poaching" in everyday narrative practices, and substitute "playing" for reading, we can speak of a process where

> The reader takes neither the position of the author nor an author's position. He [*sic*] invents in texts something different from what they "intended." He detaches them from their (lost or accessory) origin. He combines their fragments and creates something unknown in the space organized by their capacity for allowing an indefinite plurality of meanings. (169)

As de Certeau points out, such a reading activity is nothing new to literary critics well versed in the protocols of poststructuralism, but in this case the escape from passivity in reading is not limited to a privileged and enlightened group of professional intellectuals. However, the radical implications of the process are contained in video games as the narratives produce for their players a position of specularity to take up and provide for them the dangling carrot of potential presence as figured in the mastery of the game never quite attained. Take the cocaine analogy: if we are to see video games as analogous to cocaine in the spectrum of drugs, soft and hard, we might do well to remember that cocaine, which provides its user with a rush of aggressive confidence and buoyancy, has been described as a Republican drug in the United States (in contrast to marijuana, which Bill Clinton can attest is a Democratic narcotic).

Notes

I would like to thank Sara Ahmed, Catherine Belsey, Fred Botting, Natalka Freeland, Jane Moore, Hugh Osborne, and Simon O'Sullivan for their comments and help on this article in its various stages.

1. Terri Toles reflects on the militaristic implications of video games in "Video Games."

2. This anthropomorphic trend in more recent games is partly a function of improved graphics, but the desire for games with human protagonists may have other sources. Whereas in the past players more often than not manipulated spaceships or other "devices," or icons, there seems to be a tendency lately toward providing human or humanoid figures for the player to manipulate. Hence the popularity of the streetfighting genre.

3. For a social scientific take on this question, see Graybill et al. (1985) and Graybill et al. (1987). Marsha Kinder argues that the violence in video games "was not inevitable, but was partly determined by cultural coding and marketing decisions tailored specifically to the United States" (102).

4. In *Playing With Power*, Kinder most successfully addresses the gendering processes at work in video games without naturalizing the games as necessarily gender-specific. Just as I examine video narratives in terms of enunciation, Kinder focuses on the positioning of players: "In the world of Nintendo and its rival systems, players are almost inevitably positioned as active, growing, male consumers—whether they identify with the voracious Pac-Man, who is empowered to devour more enemies whenever he munches fruity energizers; or with the humble Mario and Luigi, who are instantly transformed into giant Super Brothers whenever they consume a Super Mushroom" (85–86). See Gillian Skirrow for a darker view of games and masculinity seen through Kleinian psychoanalysis. Meanwhile, the debate about gender and technology continues, and will not abate in the near future. The volume of work on gender and video games is sizable, particularly in the social sciences. See Kaplan (1983); Trinkaus (1983); McClure and Mears (1984); Morlock, Yando, and Nigolean (1985); Braun et al. (1986); Haddon (1988); Braun and Giroux (1989).

5. Another crucial difference has to do with the respective "goals," or more aptly, "ends" of the games. In chess the aim is to capture the opponent's king and in Monopoly the victorious capitalist owns everything. There is no such definite telos in a video game, for there is no ideal conclusion to the plot; the player aims simply to extend the narrative as long as possible. I will return to this aspect of the narratives later.

6. In Britain, Sega first began using their catchphrase in June 1991; according to Nintendo's marketing office in London, the "Will You Ever Reach the End?" advertising campaign ran on British screens from October 1992 to February 1993. I am, however, unsure of the reliability of this information since I recall the catchphrase being employed both prior to and after the dates given to me by Nintendo.

7. To be precise, the subject of the passage in *Beyond* which follows is the vague "decisive external influences."

Works Cited

Austin, J. L. *How to Do Things with Words*. Oxford: Oxford UP, 1975.

Braun, Claude M., Georgette Goupil, Josette Giroux, and Yves Chagnon. "Adolescents and Microcomputers: Sex Differences, Proxemics, Task and Stimulus Variables." *Journal of Psychology* 120.6 (1986): 529–42.

Braun, Claude M., and Josette Giroux. "Arcade Video Games: Proxemic, Cognitive, and Content Analyses." *Journal of Leisure Research* 21.2 (1989): 92–105.

184   *Peter Buse*

Brooks, Peter. *Reading for the Plot: Design and Intention in Narrative.* New York: Vintage, 1984.

Chambers, Ross. *Story and Situation: Narrative Seduction and the Power of Fiction.* Minneapolis: U of Minnesota P, 1984.

de Certeau, Michel. *The Practice of Everyday Life.* Trans. Steven Randall. Berkeley: U of California P, 1984.

Derrida, Jacques. *The Post-Card from Socrates to Freud and Beyond.* Trans. Alan Bass. Chicago: U of Chicago P, 1987.

Freud, Sigmund. *Beyond the Pleasure Principle. On Metapsychology.* Trans. James Strachey. Ed. Angela Richards. London: Penguin, 1984. 275–338.

Graybill, Daniel, Janis Kirsch, and Edward Esselman. "Effects of Playing Violent Versus Nonviolent Video Games on the Aggressive Ideation of Aggressive and Non-Aggressive Children." *Child Study Journal* 15.3 (1985): 199–205.

Graybill, Daniel, Maryellen Strawniak, Teri Hunter, and Margaret O'Leary. "Effects of Playing Versus Observing Violent Versus Nonviolent Video Games on Children's Aggression." *Psychology* 24.3 (1987): 1–8.

Greenfield, Patricia Marks. *Mind and Media: The Effects of Television, Computers, and Video Games.* Cambridge: Harvard UP, 1984.

Haddon, Leslie. "Electronic and Computer Games: The History of an Interactive Medium." *Screen* 29.2 (1988): 52–73.

"i-D's Computer Games Forum." *i-D* 112 (January 1993): 14–17.

Kaplan, S. J. "The Image of Amusement Arcades and Differences in Male and Female Videogame Playing." *Journal of Popular Culture* 17.1 (1983): 93–98.

Kinder, Marsha. *Playing with Power in Movies, Television, and Video Games: From Muppet Babies to Teenage Mutant Ninja Turtles.* Berkeley: U of California P, 1991.

Lacan, Jacques. "The mirror stage as formative of the function of the I as revealed in psychoanalytic experience." *Ecrits.* Trans. Alan Sheridan. London: Tavistock, 1977. 1–7.

———. *The Four Fundamental Concepts of Psychoanalysis.* Trans. Alan Sheridan. London: Penguin, 1979.

McClure, Robert F., and Gary F. Mears. "Video Game Players: Personality Characteristics and Demographic Variables," *Psychological Reports* 55.1 (1984): 271–76.

Metz, Christian. "The Imaginary Signifier." *Screen* 16.2 (1975): 14–76.

Morlock, Henry, Todd Yando, and Karen Nigolean. "Motivation of Video Game Players," *Psychological Reports* 57.1 (1985): 247–50.

Porush, David. *The Soft-Machine: Cybernetic Fiction.* New York: Methuen, 1985.

Ronell, Avital. *Crack Wars: Literature Addiction Mania.* Lincoln: U of Nebraska P, 1992.

Rose, Jacqueline. *Sexuality in the Field of Vision.* London: Verso, 1986.

Skirrow, Gillian. "Hellivision: An Analysis of Video Games." *High Theory/Low Culture: Analysing Popular Television and Film.* Ed. Colin MacCabe. Manchester: Manchester UP, 1986. 115–42.

Toles, Terri. "Video Games and American Military Ideology." *The Critical Communications Review, vol III: Popular Culture and Media Events.* Ed. Vincent Mosco and Janet Wasko. Norwood: Ablex, 1985. 207–23.

Trinkaus, John W. "Arcade Video Games: An Informal Look." *Psychological Reports* 52.2 (1983): 586.

Virilio, Paul. *Speed and Politics: An Essay on Dromology.* Trans. Mark Polizzotti. New York: Semiotext(e), 1986.

A Shock Therapy of the Social Consciousness: The Nature and Cultural Function of Russian Necrorealism

Ellen E. Berry and Anesa Miller-Pogacar

We're not living, we're living out.

—Gleb Aleinikov

On our corpses there keep munching
hoards of fattened beetle-bugs
Yes, boys, it's only after death
you get life like it's s'pozed to be!
            —Song from "The Woodcutter" by Oleg Kotelnikov
                                        and Evgeny Iufit

In attempting to situate Soviet underground art of the 1980s in the context of experiments from previous eras, Mikhail Epstein comments:

> Our old avant-garde which flourished in the teens and twenties ... was a utopian avant-garde. It tried to invent patterns for the future: the suprematism of Malevich or the futurism of Mayakovsky and Khlebnikov; constructivism, surrealism in

© 1996 by *Cultural Critique*. Fall 1996. 0882-4371/96/$5.00.

France, and so on. They tried to bring the future into the present, or to move the present into the future and all of their schemes and constructions fit some kind of normative intention or else assumed a very critical distance from the existing society which is the other side of utopian consciousness: to undermine, destroy and to ridicule. The early decades of this century were possessed by a superiority complex. Then, on the edge of exhaustion, the century began to appreciate lack of form; inferiority was just the thing. The all-accepting bottom of the universe swallows the sublime forms and great ideas of previous epochs. They've been digested and then expelled as in a lavatory pan and this bottom becomes the top of our rear-garde art. It is post-utopian or anti-utopian and it doesn't proclaim any communistic "shining heights". . . . Art is now tired both of realism, which tries to coincide with reality, and of the avant-garde which rushes forward and leaves reality behind. . . . Genuine art . . . shouldn't try to compete with the fast pace of history and the art of the rear-garde refuses to do so. It falls behind deliberately, inventing aesthetic forms of backwardness. Art lags behind, collecting the remainders of the accelerated historical process, its trash, dust and excrement. Among the examples of rear-garde prose writing are the novel *Sushkov* by Igor Shevelev and the narratives "Equilibrium of Day and Night Starlight" by Valeria Narbikova and "Prism-cinema" by Ruslan Marsovich. Trash and excrement become the most common images in the art of the End. In the so-called parallel or rear-garde cinema, there are sequences of people soiling each other. This is a parody of the sublime gesture with which, in the beginning of the century, all artists wanted to be anointed, to become a king in the kingdom of his own projects. From the eschatological perspective, as distinct from the historical, to be last is more creative, more fertile, a more productive position than first. Not to proclaim loudly, but to mumble; not to lead, but to lag behind. (Berry, Johnson, and Miller-Pogacar 116–17)

Epstein does not elaborate a complete aesthetics of the rear-garde, but his comments do suggest an orientation within which to explore aspects of the underground or parallel culture that flourished during the years leading up to the dissolution of the Soviet Union as a national entity. In this article, we wish to elaborate some specific strategies of this rear-garde and to analyze their cultural significance through a study of one of the rear-garde's most vivid manifestations, in which its eschatological and scatological orientations are extravagantly evident: necrorealism.

The necrorealists themselves are a loosely connected group of painters, filmmakers, and performance artists who emerged from the St. Petersburg underground or second culture during the mid-1980s. Unofficially led by Evgeny Iufit and Andre Mertevey, they share with other rear-garde artists[1] an aesthetic vision and an attitude that has been referred to as pure or "heroic idiocy." This term signifies a blatant rejection of both the uncritical affirmations demanded by the official state aesthetic of socialist realism and the reasoned semantic critique of official ideology evident in conceptualist art.[2] To effect this distinction, necrorealism offers a harsh tragicomic vision suffused with traces of black humor, surrealism, slapstick, and a punk industrial style, dramatizing the "living death" of subjects in a post-utopian society at the end of the twentieth century.

Although individual artists express the necrorealist aesthetic in a variety of ways, all use it to launch a biting social critique by performing a cultural autopsy on a moribund yet not fully expended social system. In so doing, they help to exhaust the forces of this social inertia by offering a survival strategy of sorts for the marginalized imagination of individuals in a still tightly controlled society. Necrorealism remains committed to an extreme process of de-idealization; it dramatizes the inverse of a will to power. As cinema critic Sergei Dobrotvorsky notes, necrorealism is a direct challenge to the Soviet myth of social immortality. "Conceived within the rotting body of socialism, necrorealism returned to the Empire [a mockery of] its most hallowed stereotypes: homosexuality as the flip side of an exaggerated masculinity, idiocy as an extreme parody of heroic pathos, and disdain for death as a natural consequence of collective ethics" (Miller-Pogacar and Nathan 15). In short, it represents not a stance of active resistance but rather the assumption of forms profoundly antipathetic to the existing social formation.

Necrorealist films, the particular focus of this essay, were created in amateur and unofficial studios in St. Petersburg between 1984 and 1989, as were many other "parallel" films, those made outside the Goskino State Cinema system as an alternative to its monopoly of the cinematic means of production. Such films as *Medic Werewolves* (1985), *Spring* (1987), and *Urine-Crazed Body-snatchers* (1989) have heavily influenced the parallel film movement as a whole; indeed, one critic considers their impact equivalent to that exerted by *An Andalusian Dog* (I. Aleinikov 7) on an earlier generation of filmmakers.[3] Necrorealist films had virtually no public showings before 1987, although a growing community of St. Petersburg and Moscow filmmakers continued to share their works with each other. By now, however, the necrospirit as well as some of its thematic and stylistic preoccupations has wafted into more official spheres of establishment art. As Gleb Aleinikov remarks in regard to *Repentance*, (1986) one of the first major perestroika films, "many so-called professional filmmakers are drawn to the tempting scent of corpse, as if they had served an apprenticeship with the necrorealist artists of Leningrad" (37).

Described as existing somewhere between an abstract joke and a sadistic ditty, necrofilms are short, largely silent, 16mm black-and-white works that are deliberately primitive stylistically.[4] They are frequently hectic, even chaotic, in their pacing or else slow and lugubrious; in either case, traditional narrative elements are minimized in favor of an emphasis on the spectacle of necro-existence itself. In *Virility* (1988), for example, the action consists of one man very deliberately helping another into a hole in the ground. After doing so, the first man throws a pan of scalding water in the other's face (which we are shown in close-up), calmly covers the hole with a board, and walks away. Neither man resists or appears to consider the action remarkable in any way. *Medic Werewolves* (1984) features a sailor who gets off a train in the dead of winter and walks purposefully into the woods. He is followed by spasmodically writhing corpses who crawl after him and running corpses shot in fast motion. When the sailor reaches his destination—a large tree that he climbs and jumps from—the corpses crowd around him, roll him in a blanket, and beat him with a shovel.

Necrofilms are all set in a nonspecified post-apocalyptic realm of urban detritus, claustrophobic interiors, or desolate rural landscapes. They are also temporally vague—meant to reflect and critique the entirety of post-1917 Soviet history. In films such as *Spring* (1987) or *The Knights of Heaven* (1989), stereotypically posi-

tive images from state-produced films of the 1940s and 1950s—
such as children dancing on a beach, a white steamship cruising
out to sea, or Soviet gymnasts performing—appear in ironic juxta-
position to frames portraying the grotesque corporeal reality of
necro-existence itself. This strategy effectively lowers the abstract
ideals of socialism's "bright future" by logically extending the materialist premises of Marxism to include the material fate of the
body. That is, in necrofilms, the social is not represented outside
its inscription on bodies—the site through which relations of
power and resistance are played out.

The grotesque state of necro-existence—of excremental assault, self-mutilation, and futile spasmodic actions—suggests a
moment in which the death of the social body and, by extension,
its failure to sustain the lives of its members, become accomplished
facts. With an ironic detachment appropriate to the "resistance of
the object," the subjects of necrofilms avoid recognizing the reality
of ideological indoctrination as such, but by actually reveling in the
hellish state of living death, they radiate a negativity inimical to
social order. In aligning the individual with a realm of socially excluded or tabooed objects—filth and decomposition or what Julia
Kristeva has called the "abject"—necrorealism deconstructs the
stability of both nature and culture. The post-abject necrosubject
does not "live" but persists like a slow wasting disease or a decomposing object, and, in embracing this "impossible" state of living
death, achieves a molecule of freedom—not by actively resisting
sociopolitical oppression but by choosing a state of knowing numbness, by passively refusing the role the system would assign as a
blind and happy automation. Thus, necrofilms do not present a
positive critique that would seek to renew or revitalize an out-
moded cultural order. Instead, the pure idiocy of the living dead,
the utter lack of being and meaning presented in these films, ex-
pose the excluded underground history of the Soviet era, thus dis-
playing the bankruptcy of its narrative of social renewal and revealing the hollowness and banality of the images that continue to
reflect this ideology.

In the following discussion, we draw upon the work of Jean
Baudrillard, Julia Kristeva, and Mikhail Epstein to elaborate further aspects of the necrophenomenon and to illuminate its cultural
functioning in a society on the brink of the third millennium. We

begin, however, with the work of a theorist whose interest in the grotesque and the scatological immediately suggest an affinity with necrorealism: that of M. M. Bakhtin.

Bakhtin located Rabelais's genius in his ability to integrate the vitality of folk humor, based on the carnival spirit, into works of high art. The carnival nucleus of folk culture exists, as Bakhtin explains, on the "borderline between life and art" (7), where many trends in parallel culture also originate. The performance aspect of necrorealism—popularized in Sergei Kuriokhin's *Pop Mechanics,* in which the actors and directors of many necrofilms participate— serves as one example of this improvisational, interactive border-line. That is to say, necrorealism is not just a set of stylistic devices encountered in films and paintings but rather reflects a basic atti-tude shared by contemporary artists and their audiences. The ex-aggerated depiction in necroperformances of behaviors typical in a Soviet lifestyle—tedious repetition of seemingly pointless actions, performed, as if compulsively, for no apparent reason—further in-dicates the roots of the necromentality in popular life.

More importantly, however, necro-aesthetics shares with the folk culture of Bakhtin's description an ambivalent type of humor based on internally heterogeneous, grotesque imagery that serves to "lower . . . all that is high, spiritual, ideal, abstract . . . to the material level, to the sphere of earth and body" (19–20). In Rabe-lais's time, such humor was achieved by juxtaposing images of state or ecclesiastical authority with the crudest elements of secular, ma-terial existence, especially images of the "bodily principle . . . with its food, drink, defecation and sexual life" (18). According to Bakh-tin, such humor was innately egalitarian in that it equalized the socially well-placed and the humble.

As with the grotesque humor of the medieval carnival, the viewer of necrofilms may become both a participant in laughter and simultaneously its object. But this laughter differs in its nature and function from what Bakhtin found all-pervasive in Rabelais's world. Viewers purchase the ability to see a laughable absurdity in their eventual necrocondition by viewing this "life" from another vantage point, before or beyond a senseless immersion in it. But it is difficult to call this a "deeply positive" laughter that "revives and renews," as Bakhtin writes of the carnival (19). For him, the wastes of the body and the body itself as a wasted corpse represent refertilizing organic matter, ready to bring forth new life. Despite Gleb Aleinikov's assertion in *Cine-Fantom* that "the medic-werewolves and woodcutter are humanitarians. They tell us that life is death, death is life" (54), the "positive pole of the grotesque image" (Bakhtin 24) does not clearly emerge in necro-art. The medieval sculptures of toothless old women with large pregnant bellies described by Bakhtin (25) find an analogue in the necrotext about a pregnant school teacher who dies to provide her pupil with flesh to feed on. But while the former shows aged decrepitude ready to give birth to the new, the latter depicts a young, fertile woman, teaching a child to thrive on death. In *Urine-Crazed Bodysnatchers* the figure of a small boy stands bewildered beside a basin where a man is urinating, while above, a corpse hangs from the ceiling, joyfully decomposing. A segment then follows in which the man licks the torso of a corpse, which quivers in satisfied "response."

These images of youth alongside a wealth of bodily fluids convey none of the organics of regeneration that Bakhtin discusses. Rather, they suggest that youth has no future other than an existence in which the juices of life and death are equally worthless—both end up in the toilet, in a horrid cycle of repetition that never leads to improvement, but only to more of the same. The senseless repetition of violent and patently futile or unmotivated behaviors is a hallmark of all necrofilms—corpses spy on each other, drag one another from place to place, crawl in circles, stand and fall repeatedly—a trait further underscored by the form of the films, in which actions unfold and are repeated without constituting themselves or contributing to any narrative or even pictorial development.

While the grotesque carnivalized body theorized by Bakhtin appears to threaten social norms, it finally acts to reinscribe them. The inversion of sacred and profane operating in the medieval carnival is an authorized and temporary transgression involving a carefully circumscribed time and place after which social and religious hierarchies are reestablished. Such a preservationist function is also appropriate for rituals designed to confront and expel what Kristeva calls the abject, a category of excluded acts or objects which, in an even more extreme sense than Bakhtin's carnivalesque, acts to threaten the social order.[5] Kristeva explores the ways in which abjection—as a source of horror—works to reinforce the security of the social contract by providing a mechanism for distinguishing human from nonhuman, the living subject from all that threatens it with extinction.

Abjection refers to an individual and collective reflex or psychic dynamic that seems to achieve an impossible confrontation with what might be called absolute otherness. It is not, properly speaking, experienced in relation to an object; rather, abjection is experienced as an absolute loss of the ability to construct any subject-object relation whatsoever, an ability on which construction of a "normal" subjectivity depends. From the perspective of a coherent subject, the place of the abject is impossible, intolerable, unthinkable: "the place where meaning collapses, where I am not" (Kristeva 2). It is a violent, dark revolt against being, a "something" that cannot be recognized as a thing. "A weight of meaninglessness about which there is nothing insignificant and which crushes me on the edge of non-existence and hallucination of a reality that, if I acknowledge it, annihilates me" (Kristeva 2). As a radical threat to the integrity of the self and the social, that which is identified as abject must be removed from the body and deposited in a taboo space beyond it. This act of pathologization and banishment establishes not only the boundaries of individual subjectivity but also the foundations of collective existence. Culture itself is renewed, Kristeva argues, in the process whereby the abject element that "transgresses borders, positions, and rules" (Kristeva 7) is approached with fascinated horror and safely removed. However, while this rite of confrontation and expulsion may *renew* culture, it does not necessarily transform it, since, in reinscribing the parameters of the existing social symbolic, it acts as a safety valve through which threats to the integrity of that order are safely drained off and purged.

With its iconography of corpses, mutilation, and the expulsion of bodily wastes, necrorealist films would appear to reside in Kristeva's "place" of abjection and to function ritually to purge the abject element through a descent into the foundations of the symbolic construct, as Barbara Creed argues is true of the ideological project of Western horror films. Indeed, the therapeutic nature of necrofilms may be an important aspect of their cultural functioning, at least for some audiences, but it is necessary to examine also the broader historical and social context in which they function before fully applying this interpretation to Soviet reality. This examination is particularly crucial since Kristeva's model is articulated in relation to an earlier Western historical moment and implies a stable social symbolic that could be firmly reestablished through expulsion of the abject element. Yet it is precisely the lack of psychic, social, political, or perhaps even species stability which may be the clearest distinguishing feature of a contemporary postmodernity, in which—as Lacan and Jameson, among others, have argued—we are all pulverized, schizophrenic subjects wandering through a ruined landscape at the end of history. This conclusion would be true in the case of both a Western postmodernism and the postcommunist postmodernism operative in the former Soviet Union, although the reasons for this instability differ, as we will discuss. Even if we argue that the stability of the social symbolic has always been a fiction—why else would it require elaborate rituals of reassurance?—the postmodern forces the exposure, if not the full acknowledgment, of its tenuousness by focusing on the collapse of a rational foundation for power within it.

In order to theorize some key aspects of the postmodern social symbolic and to speculate on the possibilities of resistance and regeneration within it—as these possibilities are figured in necrofilms—one should consider the work of Jean Baudrillard. Whereas modernism was distinguished by production, the development of industrial capitalism, expansion, energy, and movement, Baudrillard characterizes postmodernism as entropy, implosion, inertia, and, crucially, by reproduction of models without referents. The Baudrillardian scheme posits that in advanced capitalist cultures, most especially in the United States, reality itself has disappeared, dissolved in an incessant proliferation and dissemination of media simulations of reality, of signs that refer only to other signs. This implosion of sign and referent indicates for Baudrillard a radical breakpoint in the social symbolic that definitively and permanently alters previous conceptions of individual subjectivity and social relations and negates the possibility of an effective oppositional stance (Baudrillard 35–44).

Subjects in hyperreality are neither explosive in a revolutionary sense nor critical in a traditional sense, but remain implosive and blind, according to Baudrillard. Rather than being motivated by any real stance of critical agency, they proceed by sensation-seeking or lapsing into inertia. The system of capitalist production attempts to fight this erosion of the real, this catastrophic spiral of simulation, by "secreting through the media one last glimmer of reality in which to found one last glimmer of power." But in so doing, capitalism only multiplies and accelerates the play of simulation. Thus, Baudrillard concludes, within an American postmodern moment, while everything happens as if we were continuing to produce history, in "reality we are only feeding the end of history by accumulating the signs of the social, the signs of the political, the signs of progress and change. The Year 2000 has already happened" (43).

Baudrillard's analysis of simulation in contemporary Western culture resonates strongly with the postcommunist temporality theorized by Mikhail Epstein in which the utopian final event—Baudrillard's year 2000—has swung from the future to the past, has already happened/will never happen. This paradoxical temporality strongly informs necrofilms, which, on the one hand, deliberately blur references to any specific historical era or location and, on the other, incorporate images of a "historical" past in the form of Stalinist-era film footage (through inclusion of uplifting images of socialism's current superiority and its "bright future"). But of course—and this is the point—these images are simulations of a history that never existed.

In "The Origins and Meaning of Russian Postmodernism," Epstein explicitly argues that postmodernism need not be considered solely an outgrowth of global capitalism, as it is often understood in the work of Western theorists. Rather, in the former Soviet Union, a postmodernization of cultural and political life has arisen in large part from the ways in which ideology operated in Soviet society. In such a society, the postmodern extinction of history and temporality and the proliferation of ideological simulations that mask reality and substitute for it create a distinctly Soviet version of postmodernism. For Baudrillard, simulation appears to be a purely Western and relatively recent phenomenon. In his reworking of the term, Epstein suggests that it has been historically and "ironically accomplished" in Russia. "Throughout the course of Russian History, reality has been subjected to a gradual process of disappearance. Realities have always been produced in Russia from the minds of the ruling elite, but once produced, they were imposed with such force and determination that these ideological constructions became hyperrealities" (Berry and Miller-Pogacar 38–39). In various ways, throughout Russian history, reality was forced to coincide with those ideas by which it was described; it thus effectively became nothing more than a creation, a simulation of those ideas. In this case, signs cannot be said to refer to reality but rather to conceal a fundamental lack of reference, becoming "labels pulled off of emptiness." In the Soviet context, ideas denuded of a material referent and vacuous signs in a world of "spectral annulled realities" were, in fact, the only true and genuine substance of the Soviet lifestyle (Berry and Miller-Pogacar 40–41).

The particular Russian variant of simulational logic operates at all levels of society from everyday life to the sociogovernmental. In Epstein's words:

> Long before Western video technology began to produce an overabundance of "authentic" images of an absent reality, this problem was already being solved in Russia by our ideology, by our press, and by statistics that calculated crops that would never be harvested to the hundredths of a percentage point. . . . Roads lead to villages that have disappeared; villages are located where there are no roads; construction sites do not become buildings; house builders have nowhere to live. A civilization of this type can be defined as a system with a meaningful absence of essential elements, "a society of deficit." (Berry and Miller-Pogacar 36).

In a contemporary moment, the once secure referents of communist ideology implode, becoming detached from their previous meanings. A postcommunist politics emerges in which, as Epstein puts it, "ideology can name all phenomena in any way it deems necessary," creating a continuous, complete ideological environment that is ultimately trans-ideological, in that no particular positions remain consistent or comprehensible. Postcommunist politics, like Baudrillardian postmodernism, is a play of signs and gestures that have no stable referents, that lead to pure simulation on the level of political events and to the "universal deconstruction of meaning" in a hyperreal social reality characterized by a profound loss of affect. In Epstein's words, "Postcommunism is the zero level of being: empty being, empty writing, so that now we live in a vacuum, in empty space where all words, all actions seem to have no meaning of all. They can only be traced on the level of surfaces, with no depth, no truth standing behind them (Berry, Johnson, and Miller-Pogacar 103–04).

One of the most extensive and disturbing analyses of this postcommunist waning of meaning and affect, the repressed other side of communism's "bright future," is Ilya Kabakov's essay "On Emptiness." Like Epstein, Kabakov traces this state of being throughout Russian history. For Europeans, Kabakov argues, emptiness is a space waiting to be filled by means of human labor while Russian emptiness is an ongoing condition, an antinatural state that eludes European rationalist consciousness. As the "absolute antipode of any living existence," a special form of absence, emptiness involves the transference of "active being into active non-being" (Berry and Miller-Pogacar 111). Emptiness then is the "other, antithetical side of any question. . . . the opposite, the eternal no beneath everything small and large," that, like Epstein's simulational consciousness, renders futile any constrictive impulse (Berry and Miller-Pogacar 112). Citizens living in a culture of emptiness acquire a particular psychic mold or cultural pathology marked by excitedness, apathy, causeless terror, absurdity, and impermanence, a structure of feeling perfectly reflected in the ground tone, pacing, and iconography of necrorealist cinema.

This distinctly Russian loss of affect appears to have been particularly profound among the youth subculture, the inheritors of a future that will never come, and, significantly, the necrorealists are among this generation. As Ekaterina Dobrotvorskaya explains in her analysis of the role of Western rock music among Russian youth culture: "At some point in the 1970s there came a moment when the dual processes of debunking [communist] ideals in social and individual psychologies coincided within the mind of the typical teenager to form a new and enduring nihilism with respect to all the 'positive' values of the social system" (147). The result was "a generation ripe for suicide" characterized by aggressiveness, despair, loss of stable moral values, and loss of affect. "In a totalitarian state if you do not want to be a conformist it is best to appear dead," as Dobrotvorskaya puts it (148). Clearly, the characteristics developed to account for modes of subjectivity arising from within a hyperreal Western culture of media simulations and information overload must be recontextualized to take into account the Russian context. Nonetheless, the characteristics of a postcommunist subjectivity as explored by Epstein, Kabakov, and Dobrotvorskaya share features with the forms of subjectivity analyzed by Baudrillard and others as particularly postmodern: a fragmented schizophrenic subject who oscillates between blankness or autism (Jameson's loss of affect) and blind sensation-seeking or viciousness for fun (the explosive frenzy of Baudrillard's masses).

Baudrillard's follower, the Canadian theorist Arthur Kroker, attributes that all-too-familiar event of contemporary life, "viciousness for fun," to a desperate attempt at a "revival of the real." This viciousness results from an oxymoronic "panic boredom" that is the residue of a postmodern loss of affect. Boredom, which has been called "a deconstruction of the emotions" (Berry, Johnson, and Miller-Pogacar, 117), combines with panic because affects act first on the body, even though consciousness is too overburdened to react to it, that is, register it in the real. In other words, the body does not escape the effects of an affect that may well be lost to consciousness. If this is cause for panic in the affluent West, how much more so it must be in a society known for chronic shortages of those things the body craves most: bread, alcohol, tobacco, affection. Kroker asserts that "panic boredom" fuels a "howling spirit of revenge," which blames its ills on whatever symbolic representatives of social authority it can recognize. It confronts the ideological system with a mirror image of its own sick logic, reflected in the behaviors and misbehaviors of the masses of subject that ideology has produced (Kroker 170–88).

This postmodern, postcommunist loss of affect appears in the necrosubject's analytical detachment as it tediously constructs meticulous apparatuses for self-mutilation, and in the ubiquitous instances of senseless, or at best unexplained, assault—instances of "viciousness for fun." Pure idiocy, the Soviet equivalent of panic boredom, fuels this spirit of revenge in the form of a resistance of the object: the rebellion or refusal of the corpse. In *Repentance*, the corpse will not stay buried, just as the stinking fish of abuses committed in the name of Stalin's personality cult will not politely go away. In underground necrofilms, the logic of a sadistic ideological system is mirrored back in sadomasochistic behaviors that seem to correspond to impossible varying levels of deadness. Since the loss of affect has rendered emotion meaningless in its impotence to produce real connections on the grids of cause and effect, there ensues an attempt at reviving the real in the form of desperate efforts to elicit any response whatsoever. The fully dead social body makes no accommodation; so necrosubjects go to work on one another.

The most active, or seemingly "least dead," of the characters in necrofilms enact sadism, forcing a response from others through invasion of the body, in the form of sodomy; imposition, in various forms of assault; and consumption, particularly cannibalism. Descending the scale of deadness into the area of excremental imposition, we find the passive-aggressive necrosubject that urinates or defecates at odd times and in inappropriate places, sometimes provoking a violent reaction, either of anger or arousal, from its peers. These types of active "subjects" are ruled by passions and appetites analogous to those of the living, but even more powerful in their obsessive force. Normal hunger becomes a lust for consuming bodily fluids; the need for sensory stimulation becomes a compulsion to experience or inflict injury (one hesitates to call it pain, since the loss of affect places this result in question). Sexual desire is enacted almost exclusively as male sodomy, perhaps because any heterosexual contact would violate the precepts of death by suggesting the possibility—however remote—of a reproductive, life-engendering activity. The two sexes seem to have hostile, or more often purely accidental, relations with each other. Among male necrosubjects, however, there develops an interesting complementarity through the interaction of partially and more fully dead entities. Just as sadomasochism itself is predicated on a complementarity of active and passive roles, so the necroworld functions with the cooperation of masochistic subjects that approach the lower levels of deadness. These creatures compensate their less dead comrades—those still tormented by active urges—for the powerlessness occasioned by the death of the social and for the meaninglessness occasioned by the loss of affect through their willing accommodation of sadistic desires. They exude fluids or excrement, present their orifices in an unabashed surrender of waning bodily energies, apparently begrudging their senselessly compulsive brothers nothing. But, amazingly, it is at the last level of deadness evident in necrofilms, in the arrested state of adipocere, "fat wax," that life processes slow down enough for the subject to reestablish affect and, thereby, the real: an individual, subjective reality, replete with both duration and consequence. While undergoing the processes of passive decomposition, the corpse appears to experience an almost sexual pleasure, as seen in *Urine-Crazed Bodysnatchers*, or feels putrefaction as a prolonged, seemingly endless state of bliss, as in "The Woodcutter."

It is tempting here to return to the Middle Ages for an analogue that brings us back to Bakhtin's model of the grotesque body in carnival humor. Bakhtin emphasizes that the positive, regenerating force emerges in images of death and decay by virtue of the collective nature of the social body. The problem of *individual* suffering or pleasure does not arise. Kroker provides a useful description of the condition called *acedia,* which, he reports, "in medieval times . . . meant a sudden loss of the will to go on, a mutiny of the living body against a cynical power" (Kroker 85). In the case of necrorealism, we have the mutiny of a dead body against the inevitable. As Sergei Dobrotvorsky has pointed out, in necrofilms, we never see the moment of death that would have to include the moment of final dissolution of the decomposing corpse. The end takes place—or doesn't—off camera, as if the corpse refuses to go the last mile to the point of total annihilation. The ability to experience affect gives the corpse the stature of an individual reality from which it refuses to sacrifice itself for the regeneration of the collective social body. The process of decay is so pleasurable in and of itself, so rich in consequence for the "subject," that it remains indefinitely on this rudimentary level of meaning, cheating the insatiable earth—or the consuming collectivity of an oppressive society—of its final victory.

The sarcopho-consciousness of necrofilms does not, however, participate in a renewal of the social. It is not concerned with a mode of production but rather is obsessed by a mode of disappearance, staging in its unique and highly stylized way the disappearance of a particular social order. The strategic blankness and knowing numbness of the necroperformance might be among the only strategies of critique possible within a hyperreal culture of simulation in which an explosion of information, an overproduction of speech, and the omnipresence of an ideological system capable of appropriating any idea in its power scheme have led to an implosion of shared systems of meaning. This implosion produces what Mikhail Zolotonosov calls a moment of cultural "zero time"— the moment of the rear-garde—in which "there is nothing to take from history into the future and nothing to be proud of in the past. . . . When there is simply no faith left in an ideal concord, there is nothing left to defend, and the artistic world, based on the imaginary, disintegrates on its own" (Berry and Miller-Pogacar 196).

Distinct from an earlier modernist avant-garde moment in which a historical subject could assume a positive line of strategic resistance through liberation, emancipation, or self-expression, within a postmodern/postcommunist era of simulation, a strategic refusal of meaning and the word and the ironic and neutral resistance of the object turn out to be most appropriate. As an art of the rear-garde, necrofilms depict the dark side of a failed communist sociality, a breakpoint in the social symbolic. With their tone of hilarious horror, flatline numbness, overt refusal of meaning, and punk acts of viciousness for fun, these films reflect to the system the ultimate result of its own logic. It remains to be seen whether the strategies of necrorealist art—which require a hyperconformist simulation of the very mechanisms of the system it seeks to refuse—are effective forms of nonreception, or whether they will prove fatally ineffective by recontaining and thus reinforcing the status quo. Further, it is not clear yet whether they will lead to the development of new conceptual fields for the displaced contemporary Russian consciousness.

Fat Wax*
A Song from "The Woodcutter"
by Oleg Kotelnikov and Evgeny Iufit

Strolling once down by the woods,
I snagged a bullet in the brain.
I thought that death would put an end
to me, but no—"fat wax" set in.

---

*The English equivalent of this term, *adipocere*, meaning a waxy substance produced by decomposing animal bodies, lacks the graphic expressiveness and conversational stylistic tone of the Russian. The neologistic translation, "fat wax," attempts to convey the literal meaning and the suggestiveness of the Russian *zhirovosk*.

There I lay for some two weeks
one warm August in the woods,
broken out in little bubbles,
with white foam all up my nose.

Then, one morning, just about the crack of dawn,
it chanced to pass: an old man,
hunting mushrooms with his son
and grandson, found me there.

And now we're lying here together,
decomposing in our glory.
It's such fun: the old man's more puffed up,
but I'm the rotten one.

Out beyond the nearest village
we heard guns begin to fire.
It's the hunters and a herder
killing off the extra stock.

They drove them out here to the forest,
half the herd gave up the ghost.
Cats made off with all the meat,
but we're still here—so what's the beef?

Now the fall is coming on,
the ageless forest turns to gold,
little birds fly by above us,
still we just keep gaining weight.

On our corpse there keep munching
hordes of fattened beetle-bugs.
Yes, boys, it's only after death,
you get life like it's s'pozed to be!

Notes

Portions of this essay appeared in the exhibition catalogue for the British tour of several parallel cinema artists, among them the necrorealists, under the title "Iufit's Necrorealist Cinema and Resistance Postmodernism" (*New Leningrad Eccentrics* [London: British Film Institute/Watershed Media Center, February 1991], 11–17). This essay represents a substantially revised and expanded version of the earlier piece.

1. Necrorealism shares with certain contemporary Russian cinematic and literary works a dark grotesque vision that has been termed the "chernuka" style. Its expression of this dark and absurd vision in terms of "actual" living corpses appears to be unique among the art of the rear-garde.

2. Conceptualism as an art form appropriates the worn-out signs of communist ideology and manipulates them to critique that ideology. Sots art—a form of conceptualism—takes as its subject the quotidian aspects of Soviet daily life. In a manner similar to American pop art, which ironically appropriates the clichés of commercial culture, sots artists react to the "advertising" of socialism. Epstein considers the conceptualist strategies of poets such as Dmitry Prigov to be awkward empty gestures rather than effective critiques: "How is it possible to hold up for ridicule an ideology . . . that has long been laughing at itself. . . . What is ideological in conceptualism is out of date, a relic of anti-communism in the epoch of postcommunism" (Berry, Johnson, and Miller-Pogacar 112).

3. In noting this connection, Aleinikov refers to the celebration of irrationality and the nihilistic stance that necrorealism shares with dada, surrealism, and other movements in the historical avant-garde. However, as a late-twentieth-century rear-garde movement, necrorealism offers no possibility of future social renewal as we would argue these earlier movements do.

4. While Iufit acknowledges the deliberateness of the primitivism in necrofilms, constraints on cinematic production in the Soviet Union during this period must also be considered when describing them. Sixteen mm equipment and synch-sound cameras were difficult to obtain, film stock was often damaged by the time the filmmaker received it, and only a few studios in the country would process the work of parallel directors. Although parallel cinema helped to put a crack in the monopoly of Goskino and, at the present moment, small self-financing and cooperative film studios are being formed, funding is still difficult to obtain and distribution is still a problem. While necrorealist films have been shown at a number of independent film festivals in both the U.S. and Europe, they are not, to our knowledge, currently available for distribution. Iufit currently works at Lenfilm Studios in St. Petersburg and may be reached there.

5. The dynamics of resistance in necrofilms might be compared to those operating in masochistic behaviors among men which, by making pain visible, dramatize and objectify the workings of sadistic power and thus operate through negation as a discourse of resistance. Freud's writings on masochism do not necessarily allow for this conclusion, although contemporary revisions of Freud's work—most notably those developed by Gilles Deleuze and Kaja Silverman—do. Freud posits that under certain circumstances of prohibition and denial, the superego promotes a pure culture of the death drive. Deleuze extends this insight by arguing that male masochism not only exposes the losses and divisions upon which cultural identity is constructed but also works insistently to negate the foundations of the cultural contract: paternal power and privilege.

Works Cited

Aleinikov, Gleb. *Cine-Fantom*. Moscow: Samizdat. 7/8. 1987.
Aleinikov, Igor. *Redfish in America Exhibition Catalogue*. Cambridge: The Arts, 1990.
Bakhtin, Mikhail. *Rabelais and His World*. Boston: MIT P, 1968.

Baudrillard, Jean. "The Year 2000 Has Already Happened." *Body Invaders*. Ed. Arthur and Marilouise Kroker. New York: St. Martin's, 1987. 35–44.

Berry, Ellen E., Kent Johnson, and Anesa Miller-Pogacar. "Postcommunist Postmodernism—An Interview with Mikhail Epstein." *Common Knowledge* Winter 1993: 103–118.

Berry, Ellen E., and Anesa Miller-Pogacar, eds. *Re-Entering the Sign: Articulating New Russian Culture*. Ann Arbor: U of Michigan P, 1994.

Creed, Barbara. "Horror and the Monstrous Feminine: An Imaginary Abjection." *Screen* 27 (1986): 44–70.

Deleuze, Gilles. *Masochism: An Interpretation of Coldness and Cruelty*. Trans. Jean McNeil. New York: Braziller, 1971.

Dobrotvorskaya, Ekaterina. "Soviet Teens of the 1970s: Rock Generation, Rock Refusal, Rock Context." *Journal of Popular Culture* 26.3 (1993): 146–154.

Epstein, Mikhail. "The Origins and Meaning of Russian Postmodernism." Berry and Miller-Pogacar 25–47.

Freud, Sigmund. "The Economic Problem of Masochism." *Standard Edition of the Complete Psychological Works of Sigmund Freud*. Vol. 19. London: Hogarth, 1924. 159–70.

Kabakov, Ilya. "On Emptiness." Berry and Miller-Pogacar 91–98.

Kristeva, Julia. *The Powers of Horror: An Essay on Abjection*. New York: Columbia UP, 1986.

Kroker, Arthur. "Baudrillard's Marx." *The Postmodern Scene*. New York: St. Martin's, 1986. 170–88.

Miller-Pogacar, Anesa, and Jacqueline Nathan, eds. *Russian Necrorealism: Shock Therapy for a New Culture*. Exhibition Catalogue, Dorothy Uber Bryan Gallery. Bowling Green, Ohio, 1992.

BOOKS RECEIVED

Adelson, Leslie A. *Making Bodies, Making History: Feminism and German Identity.* Lincoln: U of Nebraska P, 1993.

Ahearne, Jeremy. *Michel de Certeau: Interpretation and Its Other.* Stanford: Stanford UP, 1995.

Bahti, Timothy. *Allegories of History: Literary Historiography after Hegel.* Baltimore: Johns Hopkins UP, 1992.

Balibar, Etienne. *The Philosophy of Marx.* Trans. Chris Turner. New York: Verso, 1995.

Balsamo, Anne. *Technologies of the Gendered Body: Reading Cyborg Women.* Durham: Duke UP, 1996.

Barker, Deborah E., and Ivo Kamps, eds. *Shakespeare and Gender: A History.* New York: Verso, 1995.

Barker, Francis. *The Tremulous Private Body: Essays on Subjection.* Ann Arbor: U of Michigan P, 1995.

Barry, Peter. *Beginning Theory: An Introduction to Literary and Cultural Theory.* New York: Manchester UP, 1995.

Baruch, Elaine Hoffman, and Lucienne Juliette Serrano. *She Speaks He Listens: Women on the French Analyst's Couch.* New York: Routledge, 1996.

Bathrick, David. *The Powers of Speech: The Politics of Culture in the GDR.* Lincoln: U of Nebraska P, 1995

Baudrillard, Jean. *The Gulf War Did Not Take Place.* Trans. Paul Patton. Indianapolis: Indiana UP, 1995.

Behar, Ruth, ed. *Bridges to Cuba / Puentes a Cuba: Cuban and Cuban American Artists, Writers, and Scholars Explore Identity, Nationality, and Homeland.* Ann Arbor: U of Michigan P, 1995.

Bell, Elizabeth, Lynda Haas, and Laura Sells, eds. *From Mouse to Mermaid: The Politics of Film, Gender, and Culture.* Indianapolis: Indiana UP, 1995.

Bentham, Jeremy. *The Panopticon Writings.* Ed. Miram Bozovic. New York: Verso, 1995.

Berger, Bennett M. *An Essay on Culture: Symbolic Structure and Social Structure.* Berkeley: U of California P, 1995.

Biagioli, Mario. *Galileo Courtier: The Practice of Science in the Culture of Absolutism.* Chicago: U of Chicago P, 1993.

Black, Edwin. *Rhetorical Questions: Studies of Public Discourse*. Chicago: U of Chicago P, 1992.

Black Public Sphere Collective, ed. *The Black Public Sphere: A Public Culture Book*. Chicago: U of Chicago P, 1995.

Blundell, Valda, John Sheperd, and Ian Taylor, eds. *Relocating Cultural Studies: Developments in Theory and Research*. New York: Routledge, 1993.

Bové, Paul A., ed. *Early Postmodernism: Foundational Essays*. Durham: Duke UP, 1995.

Brett, Phillip, Elizabeth Wood, and Gary C. Thomas, eds. *Queering the Pitch: The New Gay and Lesbian Musicology*. New York: Routledge, 1994.

Browning, Barbara. *SAMBA: Resistance in Motion*. Indianapolis: Indiana UP, 1995.

Burnett, Ron. *Cultures of Vision: Images, Media, and the Imaginary*. Indianapolis: Indiana UP, 1995.

Canclini, Nestor García. *Hybrid Cultures: Strategies for Entering and Leaving Modernity*. Trans. Christopher L. Chiappari and Silvia L. Lopez. Minneapolis: U of Minnesota P, 1995.

Castronovo, Russ. *Fathering the Nation: American Genealogies of Slavery and Freedom*. Berkeley: U of California P, 1995.

Chaloupka, William. *Knowing Nukes: The Politics and Culture of the Atom*. Minneapolis: U of Minnesota P, 1992.

Coetzee, J. M. *The Master of Petersburg: A Novel*. New York: Penguin, 1994.

Cross, Gary. *Time and Money: The Making of Consumer Culture*. New York: Routledge, 1993.

Certeau, Michel de. *The Writing of History*. Trans. Tom Conley. New York: Columbia UP, 1988.

Dery, Mark, ed. *Flame Wars: The Discourse of Cyberculture*. Durham: Duke UP, 1993.

Descombes, Vincent. *Proust: Philosophy of the Novel*. Trans. Catherine Chance Macksey. Stanford: Stanford UP, 1992.

Dixon, R. M. W., W. S. Ramson, and Mandy Thomas. *Australian ABORIGINAL WORDS in English: Their Origin and Meaning*. New York: Oxford UP, 1990.

Dollimore, Jonathan. *Radical Tragedy: Religion, Ideology, and Power in the Drama of Shakespeare and His Contemporaries*. 2nd ed. Durham: Duke UP, 1993.

Doty, Alexander. *Making Things Perfectly Queer: Interpreting Mass Culture*. Minneapolis: U of Minnesota P, 1993.

Drinker, Sophie. *Music and Women: The Story of Women in Their Relation to Music*. 1948. New York: Feminist, 1995.

Du Bois, Page. *Sappho Is Burning*. Chicago: U of Chicago P, 1995.

Duggan, Lisa, and Nan D. Hunter. *Sex Wars: Sexual Dissent and Political Culture*. New York: Routledge, 1995.

Dyson, Michael Eric. *Between GOD and Gangsta RAP: Bearing Witness to Black Culture.* New York: Oxford UP, 1996.

Enzensberger, Hans Magnus. *Mediocrity & Delusion.* Trans. Martin Chalmers. New York: Verso: 1992.

Epstein, Julia, and Kristina Straub. *Body Guards: The Cultural Politics of Gender Ambiguity.* New York: Routledge, 1991.

Fairclough, Norman. *Media Discourse.* New York: Edward Arnold, 1995.

Folger Collective on Early Women Critics, eds. *Women Critics 1660–1820: An Anthology.* Indianapolis: Indiana UP, 1995.

Foluke, Gyasi A. *The Real Holocaust: A Wholistic Analysis of the African-American Experience 1441–1994.* New York: Carlton PC, 1995.

Gilman, Sander. *The Jew's Body.* New York: Routledge, 1991.

Grosz, Elizabeth. *Space, Time, and Perversion.* New York: Routledge, 1995.

Haineault, Doris-Louise, and Jean Yves Roy. *Unconscious for Sale: Advertising Psychoanalysis and the Public.* Trans. Kimball Lockhart with Barbara Kerslake. Minneapolis: U of Minnesota P, 1993.

Hammons, David. *Rousing the Rubble.* Cambridge: MIT P, 1991.

Hays, Michael, ed. *Critical Conditions: Regarding the Historical Moment.* Minneapolis: U of Minnesota P, 1992.

Hutchinson, George. *The Harlem Renaissance in Black and White.* Cambridge: Harvard UP, 1995.

Judovitz, Dalia. *Unpacking Duchamp: Art in Transit.* Berkeley: U of California P, 1995.

Kamps, Ivo, ed. *Materialist Shakespeare: A History.* New York: Verso, 1995.

Kernahan, Mel. *White Savages in the South Seas.* New York: Verso, 1995.

Lane, Christopher. *The Ruling Passion: British Colonial Allegory and the Paradox of Homosexual Desire.* Durham: Duke UP, 1995.

Larsen, Neil. *Reading North By South: On Latin American Literature, Culture, and Politics.* Minneapolis: U of Minnesota P, 1995.

Lefebvre, Henri. *Introduction to Modernity.* Trans. John Moore. New York: Verso, 1995.

Lindenberger, Herbert. *The History in Literature: On Value, Genre, Institutions.* New York: Columbia UP, 1990.

Luhmann, Niklas. *Social Systems.* Trans. John Bednarz, Jr. with Dirk Baecker. Stanford: Stanford UP, 1995.

Lury, Celia. *Cultural Rights: Technology, Legality, and Personality.* New York: Routledge, 1993.

Mann, Paul. *The Theory-Death of the Avant-Garde.* Indianapolis: Indiana UP, 1991.

Marcus, George E., and Fred R. Myers, eds. *The Traffic in Culture: Refiguring Art and Anthropology.* Berkeley: U of California P, 1995.

Markley, Robert, ed. *Virtual Realities and Their Discontents.* Baltimore: Johns Hopkins UP, 1996.

Marshall, Donald G. *Contemporary Critical Theory: A Selective Bibliography.* New York: MLA, 1993.

Mernissi, Fatima. *The Forgotten Queens of Islam.* Trans. Mary Jo Lakeland. Minneapolis: U of Minnesota P, 1993.

Mudimbe, V. Y., ed. *The Surreptitious Speech:* Présence Africaine *and the Politics of Otherness 1947–1987.* Chicago: U of Chicago P, 1992.

Multatuli. *Max Havelaar: Or the Coffee Auctions of a Dutch Trading Company.* 1860. Trans. Roy Edwards. New York: Penguin, 1987.

Nadel, Alan. *Containment Culture: American Narratives, Postmodernism, and the Atomic Age.* Durham: Duke UP, 1995.

Nussbaum, Felicity A. *Torrid Zones: Maternity, Sexuality, and Empire in Eighteenth-Century English Narratives.* Baltimore: Johns Hopkins UP, 1995.

Pick, Daniel. *War Machine: The Rationalisation of Slaughter in the Modern Age.* New Haven: Yale UP, 1993.

Price, Richard, and Sally Price. *Equatoria.* New York: Routledge, 1992.

Ranciere, Jacques. *On the Shores of Politics.* Trans. Liz Heron. New York: Verso, 1995.

Raschke, Cark A. *Fire and Roses: Postmodernity and the Thought of the Body.* Albany: SUNY P, 1996.

Reid, Ian. *Narrative Exchange.* New York: Routledge, 1992.

Rifkin, Adrian. *Street Noises: Parisan Pleasure 1900–40.* New York: Manchester UP, 1995.

Robin, Regine. *Socialist Realism: An Impossible Aesthetic.* Trans. Catherine Porter. Stanford: Stanford UP, 1992.

Roochnik, David. *The Tragedy of Reason: Toward a Platonic Conception of Logos.* New York: Routledge,1990.

Roof, Judith, and Robyn Wiegman, eds. *Who Can Speak?: Authority and Critical Identity.* Chicago: U of Chicago P,1995

Rothenburg, Jerome, and Pierre Joris, eds. *Poems for the Millennium: The University of California Book of Modern and Postmodern Poetry.* Vol. 1. *From Fin de Siècle to Negritude.* Berkeley: U of California P, 1995.

Royle, Nicholas. *After Derrida.* New York: Manchester UP, 1995.

Rugoff, Ralph. *Circus Americanus.* New York: Verso, 1995.

Rutherford, Jonathan. *Men's Silences: Predicaments in Masculinity.* New York: Routledge, 1992.

Sassower, Raphael. *Cultural Collisions: Postmodern Technoscience.* New York: Routledge, 1995.

Savran, David. *Communists, Cowboys, and Queers: The Politics of Masculinity in the Work of Arthur Miller and Tennessee Williams.* Minneapolis: U of Minnesota P, 1992.

Schehr, Lawrence R. *Alcibiades at the Door: Gay Discourses in French Literature.* Stanford: Stanford UP, 1995.

Sedgwick, Eve Kosofsky, and Adam Frank, eds. *Shame and Its Sisters: A Silvan Tomkins Reader.* Durham: Duke UP, 1995.

Sharrad, Paul, ed. *Readings in Pacific Literature.* Wollongong: New Literatures Research Centre, 1993.

Silverman, Hugh J., ed. *Gadamer and Hermeneutics: Science, Culture, and Literature.* New York: Routledge, 1991.

Sismondo, Sergio. *Science without Myth: On Constructions, Reality, and Social Knowledge.* Albany: SUNY P, 1996.

Staiger, Janet. *Bad Women: Regulating Sexuality in Early American Cinema.* Minneapolis: U of Minnesota P, 1995.

Steiner, Wendy. *The Scandal of Pleasure.* Chicago: U of Chicago P, 1995.

Stoler, Ann Laura. *Race and the Education of Desire: Foucault's History of Sexuality and the Colonial Order of Things.* Durham: Duke UP, 1995.

Tallis, Raymond. *Not Saussure: A Critique of Post-Saussurean Literary Theory.* 2nd ed. New York: St. Martin's, 1995.

Taylor, Mark C. *NOTS.* Chicago: U of Chicago P, 1993.

Terry, Jennifer, and Jaqueline Urla, eds. *Deviant Bodies: Critical Perspectives on Difference in Science and Popular Culture.* Indianapolis: Indiana UP, 1995.

Tratner, Michael. *Modernism and Mass Politics: Joyce, Woolf, Eliot, Yeats.* Stanford: Stanford UP, 1995.

Varadharajan, Asha. *Exotic Parodies: Subjectivity in Adorno, Said, and Spivak.* Minneapolis: U of Minnesota P, 1995.

Whisnant, David E. *Rascally Signs in Sacred Places: The Politics of Culture in Nicaragua.* Chapel Hill: U of North Carolina P, 1995.

Wilentz, Gay. *Binding Cultures: Black Women Writers in Africa and the Diaspora.* Indianapolis: Indiana UP, 1992.

Zavala, Iris M. *Colonialism and Culture: Hispanic Modernisms and the Social Imaginary.* Indianapolis: Indiana UP, 1992.

Zuidervaart, Lambert. *Adorno's Aesthetic Theory: The Redemption of Illusion.* Cambridge: MIT P, 1991.

CONTRIBUTORS

Ellen Berry directs the Women's Studies Program at Bowling Green State University. She is author of *Curved Thought and Textual Wandering: Gertrude Stein's Postmodernism* (Michigan, 1992), co-editor of *Re-entering the Sign: Articulating New Russian Culture* (Michigan, 1995), and editor of *Postcommunism and the Body Politic* (NYU, 1995).

Peter Buse has just completed his doctorate on post-structuralism and theater criticism at the Centre for Critical and Cultural Theory at the University of Wales, Cardiff and will assume a lectureship in English at the University of Salford in Manchester in September. He is currently co-editing with colleague Andrew Stott a collection of essays entitled *Ghosts: Deconstruction, Psychoanalysis, History* and has published an article in *Textual Practice*.

Henry Giroux is the Waterbury Chair Professor of Secondary Education at Penn State University. He is the author of numerous books and articles. His recent books published by Routledge include *Border Crossings, Disturbing Pleasures,* and the most recent, *Fugitive Cultures: Race, Violence, and Youth.*

Anesa Miller-Pogacar is an independent scholar and translator living in Bowling Green, Ohio. She is co-editor of *Re-entering the Sign: Articulating New Russian Culture* and translator of *After the Future: The Paradoxes of Postmodernism in Contemporary Russian Culture* by Mikhail N. Epstein.

Kenneth Mostern is an assistant professor of English at the University of Tennessee. He has published or has forthcoming essays in *MELUS, International Journal of Race and Ethnic Studies,* and *Critical Mass,* and is a contributor to H. Giroux and P. McLaren, eds., *Between Borders;* P. Schmidt and A. Singh, eds., *American Ethnicity and Postcolonial Theory;* and the forthcoming *W. E. B. Du Bois Encyclopedia.* His manuscript *Autobiography and Identity Politics: The Narrative Politics of Race-ness in the Twentieth Century* will be submitted for publication this year.

Tejumola Olaniyan is an assistant professor of English at the University of Virginia. He is the author of *Scars of Conquest/Masks of Resistance: The Invention of Cultural Identities in African, African American, and Caribbean Drama* (Oxford, 1995).

Michael Quinn is a graduate student in the Communication Arts Department at the University of Wisconsin-Madison. He is writing his dissertation on the early feature film in America from 1912 to 1915.

Susan Searls is finishing her doctoral program at Penn State University. Her interests are in the history of English education, cultural studies, and critical pedagogy. She has published in *The Review of Education* and *The Review of Education/Pedagogy/Cultural Studies,* and in the forthcoming book *Measured Lies.*

Shaobo Xie teaches literary theory and English literature at the University of Calgary. He has published on Derrida and Chuang Tzu, as well as Shelley. Currently he is working on postcolonialism.

Cynthia Willett is an assistant professor of philosophy at Emory University. Her publications include articles on political ethics and desire as well as a book, *Maternal Ethics and Other Slave Moralities* (Routledge, 1995).

THE WARS WE TOOK TO VIETNAM

Cultural Conflict and Storytelling
MILTON J. BATES
"An absolutely stunning achievement
. . . . An incisively accurate analysis of
the attitudes that shaped and controlled Americans' perceptions during
the 1960s and '70s. He fuses literary
analysis with historical scholarship to
offer a comprehensive study of
American thought and writing before,
during, and after the war years."
— John Clark Pratt, author of
The Laotian Fragments
$50.00 cloth, $18.95 paper

SEDUCING THE FRENCH

The Dilemma of Americanization
RICHARD F. KUISEL
New in paper—"A subtle yet lucid
account of the Americanisation of the
French cultural and political landscape,
and of the French reaction to it."
— *The Economist*
*Winner, Chinard Prize and the New York State
Association for European Historians Prize*
$15.95 paper

MEXICO AT THE WORLD'S FAIRS

Crafting a Modern Nation
MAURICIO TENORIO-TRILLO
"This superb study . . . raises provoca-
tive questions about cultural construc-
tions of nationalism and modernity. A
fine example of interdisciplinary
thinking and writing."
— Robert W. Rydell, author of
World of Fairs
The New Historicism, $45.00 cloth, illustrated

THE SECRET MUSEUM

Pornography in Modern Culture
WALTER KENDRICK
Available again, with a new Afterword
"An engaging, readable, and deeply
perceptive analysis that details the
evolution of the *idea* of pornography
and its attendant and ever-changing
sensibilities over the last two centuries.
. . . [It] patiently attempts to supply a
cultural context for not only pornography but also the role that sexuality and
imagination themselves play in our
lives."— *Boston Phoenix*
$13.95 paper

At bookstores or order 1-800-822-6657.

UNIVERSITY OF CALIFORNIA PRESS

Where

Personal Voices on Cultural Issues

you can

Svetlana Alpers, "Museum-Going"

Margery Sabin, "Politics of Cultural Freedom"

still

Frank Kermode, "Memory and Autobiography"

Georgina Kleege, "On Reading Braille"

hear

David Bromwich, "Anti-Intellectualism"

Richard Rorty, "The Inspirational Value of Great Works of Literature"

people

Christoph Irmscher, "Rattlesnakes and the Power of Fascination"

thinking

Arts • Literature • Philosophy • Politics

for

them-

RARITAN

Edited by Richard Poirier

selves

$16/one year $26/two years
Make check payable to RARITAN, 31 Mine St., New Brunswick NJ 08903

Critical Reading from Cambridge

Art into Ideas
Essays on Conceptual Art
Robert C. Morgan

Focusing on works by a range of international artists, including
Joseph Kosuth, Hans Haacke, Sherrie Levine, and Joseph Beuys,
this text defines and elucidates the premises of conceptual art.
It examines its evolution, from its inception in the 1960s
through the 1980s.

Contemporary Artists and Their Critics

| 47367-5 | Hardback | $49.95 |
| 47922-3 | Paperback | $17.95 |

Kenneth Burke
Rhetoric, Subjectivity, Postmodernism
Robert Wess

Kenneth Burke's influence ranged across history, philosophy
and the social sciences. This text examines his influence on
contemporary theories of rhetoric and the subject, and explains
why Burke failed to complete his Motives trilogy.

Literature, Culture, Theory 18

| 41049-5 | Hardback | $54.95 |
| 42258-2 | Paperback | $18.95 |

Available in bookstores or from

CAMBRIDGE
UNIVERSITY PRESS

40 West 20th Street, N.Y., NY 10011-4211
Call toll-free 800-872-7423
MasterCard/VISA accepted.
Prices subject to change.
Web site: http://www.cup.org

TERRA NOVA

nature & *culture*

Edited by David Rothenberg, New Jersey Institute of Technology

Terra Nova: Nature & Culture is a new journal that seeks to understand the ethical, metaphysical, and aesthetic aspects of the human relationship to nature. Dissolving the borders between the academic and the readable, *Terra Nova* aims to become a journal of major cultural importance based upon the understanding that environmental issues are part of the mainstream cultural critique and commentary as well as a thriving scholarly concentration. Essays, reportage on environmental disasters and solutions, fiction, poety, art and all forms of reflection on the human relationship to nature are included.

Crossing the boundaries between disciplines, *Terra Nova* publishes contributions from a wide range of fields including philosophy, literature, history, anthropology, geography, environmental studies, psychology, politics, and the arts.

Published quarterly in winter, spring, summer, and fall. ISSN 1081-0749.
1996 Rates: $32 individual; $95 institution; $24 Student & Retired. Outside U.S.A. add $16 postage and handling. Prepayment is required. Send check drawn against a U.S. bank in U.S. funds, AMEX, MC, or VISA number to: **MIT Press Journals,** 55 Hayward Street, Cambridge, MA 02142 USA Tel: 617-253-2889 Fax: 617-577-1545 journals-orders@mit.edu

Contents appearing in Volume 1 include:
Under the Rose: Six Photograms, 1993-1995 **Amanda Means**
Will the Real Chief Seattle Please Speak Up? An Interview with **Ted Perry**
Naked on Mount Sinai **Michael Tobias**
Epiphany **Sandra Lopez** and **Terry Tempest Williams**
The Postmodern Challenge to Environmentalism **Michael Zimmerman**
The Loneliest Road in America **David Robertson**

Browse through MIT Press Journals online catalog at http://www.mitpress.mit.edu